The Articulate Mammal
An Introduction to
Psycholinguistics

I find my position as an articulate mammal
bewildering and awesome
Would to God I were a tender apple blawssom
Ogden Nash

The Articulate Mammal

An Introduction to
Psycholinguistics

Jean Aitchison

78-   39535

UNIVERSE BOOKS, NEW YORK

Published in the United States of America in 1977
by Universe Books
381 Park Avenue South, New York, N.Y. 10016

© Jean Aitchison 1976

Library of Congress Catalog Card Number: 76–42061

ISBN 0–87663–268–1

Printed in Great Britain

Contents

Preface

Three years ago, I gave an evening course entitled 'Psycholinguistics'. I was quite amazed at the response. A large, eager and intelligent group of people arrived, many of them with a serious reason for wanting to know about the subject. There were speech therapists, infant school teachers, an advertising executive, a librarian, an educational psychologist – to name just a few of those whose jobs I noted. There were also parents interested in understanding how children acquire language, and one student who wanted to know how she might help a relative who had lost her language as a result of a stroke. In addition, there were a number of men and women who said they 'just wanted to find out more about language'.

The Articulate Mammal was written for the members of that class, and for others like them: people like me who would like to know why we talk, how we acquire language, and what happens when we produce or comprehend sentences. The book is also intended for students at universities, polytechnics and colleges of education who need an introduction to the subject. It cannot, of course, provide all the answers. But I have tried to set out clearly and briefly what seem to me to have been the major topics of interest in psycholinguistics in recent years, together with an assessment of the 'state of play' in the field at the moment. I hope it will be useful.

I am extremely grateful to a number of scholars who made helpful comments on the manuscript. In particular, and in alphabetical order, Michael Banks of The London School of Economics, David Bennett of The School of Oriental and African Studies, Paul Fletcher of Reading University, Jerry Fodor of the Massachusetts Institute of Technology, Phil Johnson-Laird of The University of Sussex, Geoffrey Sampson of Lancaster University, and Deirdre Wilson of University College, London.

The book would probably have been better if I had taken more notice of their comments – but as the suggested improvements were often contradictory, it was difficult to decide whose opinion to accept. In cases of doubt, I preferred my own, so I am wholly responsible for any errors or over-simplifications that the text may still contain.

My thanks also go to Irene Fekete, the evening course student (and Hutchinson executive) who persuaded me to write this book.

Let me add a brief note on style. In English, the so-called 'unmarked' or 'neutral between sexes' pronoun is *he*. Had I used this all the way through *The Articulate Mammal*, it might have given the misleading impression that only male mammals are articulate. I have therefore tried to use an equal number of *he*'s and *she*'s in passages where a 'neutral between sexes' pronoun is required, and because the book is meant for reading, not sporadic consultation, it does not contain an index.

Jean Aitchison

Introduction

Psycholinguistics is sometimes defined as the study of language and the mind. As the name suggests, it is a subject which links psychology and linguistics. The common aim of all who call themselves psycholinguists is to find out about the structures and processes which underlie a human's ability to speak and understand language. Psycholinguists are not necessarily interested in language interaction between people. They are trying above all to probe into what is happening within the individual.

Both psychologists and linguists are involved in studying psycholinguistics. Both types of people can be classified as social scientists, so in one way their approach is similar. All social scientists work by forming and testing hypotheses. For example, a psycholinguist might hypothesize that the speech of someone who is suffering from a progressive disease of the nervous system will disintegrate in a certain order, perhaps suggesting that the constructions the patient learned most recently will be the first to disappear. He will then test his hypothesis against data collected from the speech of someone who is brain-damaged. This is where psychologists and linguists differ. Psychologists test their hypotheses mainly by means of carefully controlled experiments. Linguists, on the other hand, test their hypotheses mainly by checking them against spontaneous utterances. They feel that the rigidity of experimental situations sometimes falsifies the results. Neither way is right or wrong. Provided that each side is sympathetic to and interested in the work of the other, it can be a great advantage to have two approaches to the subject. And when the results of linguists and psychologists coincide, this is a sure sign of progress.

Most introductory books published so far have been written by psychologists. This is an attempt to provide an introduction to the subject from the linguist's point of view – although inevitably and rightly it includes accounts of work done by psychologists. This book does not presuppose any knowledge of linguistics – though for those who become interested in the subject, a number of elementary books are suggested on p. 240.

Psycholinguistics is in many ways like the proverbial hydra – a monster with an endless number of heads. There seems no limit to the aspects of the subject which could be explored. This is a rather unsatisfactory state of affairs. As one researcher expressed it: 'When faced with the inevitable question, "What do psycholinguists do?" it is somehow quite unsatisfactory to have to reply, "Everything".' (Maclay, 1973: 574). In this situation, it is necessary to specialize fairly rigidly. And amidst the vast array of possible topics, *three* seem to be of particular interest at the present time:

1. *The question of innateness*. Is language wholly learned, or are human beings pre-programmed with linguistic knowledge? If so, what kind of knowledge?

2. *The link between language knowledge and language usage*. Linguists claim to be describing a person's internal representation of language (his language *knowledge*), rather than how he actually *uses* the language. How then does usage link up with knowledge? If we put this another way, we can say that anybody who has learned a language can do three things:

1. Understand sentences or 'decode' 2. Produce sentences or 'encode'	LANGUAGE USAGE
3. Store linguistic knowledge	LANGUAGE KNOWLEDGE

'Pure' linguists claim to be interested in (3) rather than (1) or (2). What psycholinguists need to know is this: is it correct to assume that the type of grammar proposed by linguists really reflects a person's internalized knowledge of his language? And how is that knowledge actually *used* when a person encodes or decodes?

3. *Producing and comprehending speech*. Assuming that language usage does differ from language knowledge, what actually happens when a person encodes or decodes?

These are the three questions which this book examines. It does so by considering four types of evidence:

(a) animal communication

(b) child language
(c) the language of normal adults
(d) the speech of dysphasics (people with speech disturbances).

As the diagram below shows, these are not watertight compartments. Each type of evidence is connected to the next by an intermediate link. Animal communication is linked to child language

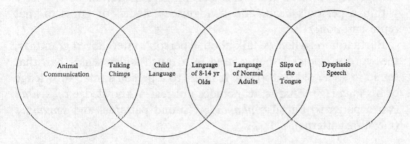

by the 'talking chimps' – apes who are being taught a language system. The link between child and adult language is seen in the speech of eight- to fourteen-year-olds. The language of normal adults is linked to those with speech disturbances by 'slips of the tongue' which occur in the speech of all normal people, yet show certain similarities with the speech of dysphasics.

Before moving on to the first topic, the question of innateness, we must make a few comments about the use of the word *grammar*.

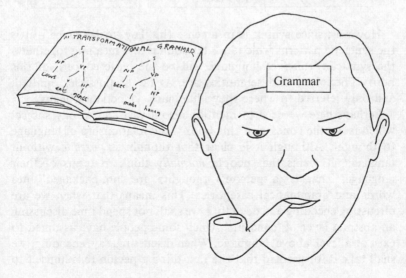

We assume that, in order to speak, every person who knows a language has the grammar of his language internalized in his head. The linguist who is writing a grammar is making a hypothesis about this internalized system. He is in effect saying, 'My guess as to the knowledge stored in the head of someone who knows a language is as follows . . .'. For this reason, the word *grammar* is used interchangeably to mean both the internal representation of language within a person's head, and a linguist's 'model' or guess of that representation.

Furthermore, when we talk about a person's internalized grammar, the word *grammar* is being used in a much wider sense than that found in some old textbooks. It refers to a person's total knowledge of his language. That is, it includes not just a knowledge of *syntax* (word patterns) but also *phonology* (sound patterns) and *semantics* (meaning patterns).

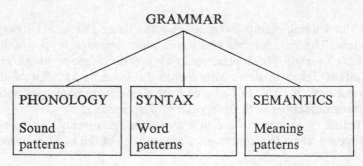

However, since syntax is in a sense the 'key' to language – it is the syntactic patterns which link the sounds and meaning together – the syntactic 'rules' of language will be the basic concern of this book. Phonology and semantics are, as far as possible, omitted, and only referred to where they illuminate syntactic problems.

Perhaps here we need to mention also a vast and woolly subject which is *not* the concern of this book – the relationship of language to thought. Although it is clear that thought is *possible* without language, it seems that people *normally* think in terms of their language. That is, a person's thoughts are 'pre-packaged' into words and grammatical categories. This means that when we are discussing encoding and decoding, we shall not spend time discussing an abstract layer of 'concepts' which some people have assumed to exist at a level 'above' language. When discussing, say, encoding, we shall take it for granted that the first thing a person tells himself to do is, 'Select the relevant words and syntax' rather than 'Package together concepts and see if they can be translated into language'. In other words, if it is necessary to take sides in the controversy as to which comes first, language or thought, we are more on the side of the nineteenth-century poet Shelley, who said 'He gave men speech, and speech created thought' than that of the eighteenth-century lexicographer Samuel Johnson, who claimed that 'Language is the dress of thought'.

1 The Great Automatic Grammatizator

Need anything be innate?

He reached up and pulled a switch on the panel.
Immediately the room was filled with a loud humming noise,
and a crackling of electric sparks . . . sheets of quarto paper
began sliding out from a slot to the right of the control
panel. . . . They grabbed the sheets and began to read. The
first one they picked up started as follows: 'Aifkjmbsaoegwez
tpplnvoqudskigt, fuhpekanvbertyuiolkjhgfdsazxcvbnm,
peruitrehdjkgmvnb, wmsuy . . .'. They looked at the others.
The style was roughly similar in all of them. Mr Bohlen
began to shout. The younger man tried to calm him down.
  'It's all right, sir. Really it is. We've got a connection
wrong somewhere, that's all. You must remember,
Mr Bohlen, there's over a million feet of wiring in this room.'
  'It'll never work,' Mr Bohlen said.

Roald Dahl
The Great Automatic Grammatizator

Every normal human being can talk. So the average person tends
to think that there is little or nothing mysterious about language.
As Chomsky has pointed out, 'We lose sight of the need for explanation when phenomena are too familiar and "obvious". We tend
too easily to assume that explanations must be transparent and
close to the surface. . . . As native speakers, we have a vast amount
of data available to us. For just this reason it is easy to fall into
the trap of believing that there is nothing to be explained. Nothing
could be further from the truth . . .' (Chomsky, 1972a: 25–6).
  But the mysterious nature of human language becomes more
apparent when one realizes that no one has yet managed to simulate
the language ability of a human being. Computers can play chess,
sort bank statements, and even talk about limited topics such as
cubes, squares and cones. But we are far from producing a 'great
automatic grammatizator' which could unaided hold conversations

on any topic. Why is this? Perhaps we should think about language more carefully.

Nature or nurture?

When people start thinking about language, the first question which often occurs to them is this: is language *natural* to man? – in the same way that grunting is natural to pigs, and barking comes naturally to dogs. Or is it just something we happen to have *learned*? – in the same way that dogs may learn to beg, or elephants may learn to waltz, or humans may learn to play the guitar.

Clearly, in one sense, the child 'learns' whatever language he is exposed to, be it Chinese, Nootka or English. So no one would deny that 'learning' is very important. But the crucial question is whether children are born with 'blank sheets' in their head as far as language is concerned – or whether humans are 'programmed' with an outline knowledge of the structure of languages in general.

This question of whether language is partly due to *nature* or wholly due to learning or *nurture* is often referred to as the *nature-nurture* controversy, and has been discussed for centuries. For example, it was the topic of one of Plato's dialogues, the *Cratylus*. Controversies which have been going on for literally ages tend to behave in a characteristic fashion. They lie dormant for a while, then break out fiercely. This particular issue resurfaced in linguistics in 1959 when the linguist Noam Chomsky wrote a devastating and witty review of *Verbal Behavior*, a book by the Harvard psychologist B. F. Skinner (Chomsky, 1959; Skinner, 1957). This book claimed to 'explain' language as a set of habits gradually built up over the years. According to Skinner, no complicated innate or mental mechanisms are needed. All that is necessary is the systematic observation of the events in the external world which prompt the speaker to utter sounds.

Skinner's claim to understand language was based on his work with rats and pigeons. He had proved that, given time, rats and pigeons could be trained to perform an amazing variety of seemingly complex tasks, provided two basic principles were followed. Firstly, the tasks must be broken down into a number of carefully graduated steps. Secondly, the animals must be repeatedly rewarded.

In a typical experiment, a rat is put in a box containing a bar. If it presses the bar, it is rewarded with a pellet of food. Nothing forces it to press the bar. The first time it possibly does so accidentally.

When the rat finds that food arrives, it presses the bar again. Eventually it learns that if it is hungry, it can obtain food by pressing the bar. Then the task is made more difficult. The rat only gets rewarded if it presses the bar while a light is flashing. At first the rat is puzzled. Eventually it learns the trick. Then the task is made more difficult again. This time the rat only receives food if it presses the bar a certain number of times. After initial confusion, it learns to do this also. And so on, and so on.

This type of 'trial-and-error' learning is called *operant conditioning* by Skinner, which can be translated as 'training by means of voluntary responses' (the word 'operant' means a voluntary response rather than an automatic one). Skinner suggests that it is by means of this mechanism that the vast majority of human learning takes place, including language learning:

'The basic processes and relations which give verbal behaviour its special characteristics are now fairly well understood. Much of the experimental work responsible for this advance has been carried out on other species, but the results have proved to be surprisingly free of species restrictions. Recent work has shown that the methods can be extended to human behaviour without serious modification' (Skinner, 1957: 3).

All one needs to do in order to understand language, he says, is to identify the 'controlling variables', which will enable us to predict specific utterances. For example, in the same way as it is possible to say that a rat's bar-pressing behaviour is partly 'under the control' of a flashing light, so a feeling of hunger might 'control' or predict a human utterance such as 'Please pass the bread and butter'. Or the presence of a beautiful painting might call forth the exclamation, 'Oh how beautiful'. Or a bad smell might cause one to exclaim 'O what a terrible smell'. A French notice, such as *'Ne touchez pas'*, might result in one saying, 'That means "Don't touch"'. And if a child said 'Hickory Dickory Dock', you are likely to continue 'The mouse ran up the clock'. In theory, Skinner sees no difficulty in linking up any particular set of words which a human might wish to produce with an identifiable external happening.

In practice, the matter is far from simple, as Chomsky points out. Chomsky makes two major criticisms of Skinner's work. Firstly, the behaviour of rats in boxes is irrelevant to human language. Secondly, Skinner fundamentally misunderstands the nature of language.

The irrelevance of rats

Chomsky points out that the simple and well-defined sequence of events observed in the boxes of rats is just not applicable to language. And the terminology used in the rat experiments cannot be re-applied to human language without becoming hopelessly vague.

For example, how do you know that someone is likely to say 'Oh what a beautiful picture' when he sees a beautiful painting? Someone might say instead, 'It clashes with the wallpaper', 'It's hanging too low', 'It's hideous'. Skinner would say that instead of the utterance being 'controlled' by the beauty of the picture, it was 'controlled' by its clash with the wallpaper, its hanging too low, its hideousness. But this reduces the idea of 'control' to being meaningless, because you have to wait until you hear the utterance before you know what controlled it. This is quite unlike the predictable behaviour of rats, which could be relied upon to respond to certain stimuli such as a flashing light with a fixed response.

Another problem is that the rats were repeatedly rewarded. It is quite clear that children do not receive pellets of food when they make a correct utterance. However, the idea of reward or *reinforcement* (since it reinforces the behaviour that is being learned) can in humans be naturally extended to approval or disapproval. One might suppose that a parent smiles and says 'Yes dear, that's right' when a child makes a correct utterance. Even if this were so, what happens to this idea of approval when there is nobody around, since children are frequently observed to talk to themselves? Skinner suggests that in these cases children automatically 'reinforce' *themselves* because they know they are producing sounds which they have heard in the speech of others. Similarly, Skinner assumes that someone like a poet who is uttering words to himself in an empty room will be 'reinforced' by the knowledge that others will be influenced by his work in the future. So reinforcement seems a very woolly notion, since an actual reward need not exist, it need only be imagined or hoped for. Such a notion is certainly not comparable to the food pellets given to rats when they make a correct response.

More recent studies by Roger Brown and his associates provide even more problems for Skinner's notion of reinforcement (Brown, Cazden, Bellugi, 1968). After observing mother–child interactions they have pointed out that parents tend to approve statements which are *true* rather than those which are grammatically correct. So a child who said 'Teddy sock on' and showed his mother a teddy bear wearing a sock would probably meet with approval. But if the child said the grammatically correct utterance 'Look, Teddy is wearing a sock', and showed his mother a bear *without* a sock, he would meet with disapproval. In other words, if approval and disapproval worked in the way Skinner suggests, you would expect children to grow up telling the truth, but speaking ungrammatically. In fact the opposite seems to happen.

Another example of a problem which crops up in trying to match rat and human behaviour is that of defining the notion of *response strength*. When a rat has learned to respond to a particular external happening, the extent to which it has learned the lesson can be measured in terms of the speed, force, and number of times which it presses the bar. Skinner suggests that similar measures of response strength might be found in some human responses. For example, a person who is shown a prized work of art might, much to the gratification of the owner, instantly exclaim 'Beautiful!' in a loud voice. Chomsky points out: 'It does not appear totally obvious that in this case the way to impress the owner is to shriek "Beautiful" in a loud, high-pitched voice, repeatedly, and with no delay (high response strength). It may be equally effective to look at the picture silently (long delay), and then to murmur "Beautiful" in a soft, low-pitched voice (by definition, very low response strength)' (Chomsky, 1959: 35).

Chomsky used these and similar arguments to show the irrelevance of Skinner's experiments to the problem of understanding language. Perhaps 'irrelevance' is too strong a word, since there are areas of language where habit forming works. For example, some people invariably say 'Damn' if they drop a raw egg, or 'Good night' when they are going to bed, or 'London Transport gets worse every day' when standing at a bus-stop. And there is one sad character in a Beatles song who only ever says 'Good morning'.

> I've got nothing to say but it's OK,
> Good morning, good morning, good morning.

But apart from trivial exceptions such as these, language is infinitely more complex and less predictable than Skinner's theory would suggest.

The nature of language

What is there about language that makes it so special? There are a large number of human activities such as learning to drive or learning to knit which seem to be learnt in the same way as bar pressing by rats. Why not language also?

Chomsky pointed out some of the special properties of language in his review of Skinner's book, where he suggested that Skinner was not in a position to talk about the causation of verbal behaviour, since he knew little about the character of such behaviour. 'There is little point in speculating about the process of acquisition without a much better understanding of what is acquired' (Chomsky, 1959: 55).

Chomsky has since discussed the nature of language in a number of places (e.g. Chomsky, 1972, 1972a). One point which he stresses is that language makes use of *structure-dependent operations*. By this he means that the composition and production of utterances is not merely a question of stringing together sequences of words. Every sentence has an inaudible internal structure which must be understood by the hearer.

In order to see more clearly what is meant by a *structure-dependent* operation, it is useful to look at *structure-independent* operations. Suppose a Martian had landed on earth, and was trying to learn English. He might hear the sentence:

AUNT JEMIMA HAS DROPPED HER FALSE TEETH DOWN THE DRAIN,

as well as the related question:

HAS AUNT JEMIMA DROPPED HER FALSE TEETH DOWN THE DRAIN?

If he was an intelligent Martian, he would immediately start trying to guess the rules for the formation of questions in English. His first guess might be that English has a rule which says, 'In order to form a question, scan the sentence for the word *has* and bring it to the front.' Superficially, this strategy might occasionally work. For example, a sentence such as:

PETRONELLA HAS HURT HERSELF

would quite correctly become,

HAS PETRONELLA HURT HERSELF?

But it is clearly a wrong strategy, because it would also mean that the Martian would turn a statement such as:

THE MAN WHO HAS RUN AWAY SHOUTING WAS ATTACKED BY A WASP

into

*HAS THE MAN WHO RUN AWAY SHOUTING WAS ATTACKED BY A WASP?

which is not English. (An asterisk denotes an impossible sentence.)

Looking at the Aunt Jemima sentence again, the Martian might make a second guess, 'In order to form a question, bring the third word to the front.' Once again, this might superficially appear to work because a sentence such as:

THE ALLIGATOR HAS ESCAPED

would correctly become,

HAS THE ALLIGATOR ESCAPED?

But it is obviously accidental that this type of rule gets the right result, because it also produces a number of non-sentences.

SLUGS ARE SLIMY

would become,

*SLIMY SLUGS ARE?

and

MARY HAS SWALLOWED A SAFETY PIN

turns into,

*SWALLOWED MARY HAS A SAFETY PIN?

The Martian went wrong in his guesses because he was trying out structure-independent operations – manoeuvres which relied solely on mechanical counting or simple recognition procedures without looking at the *internal* structure of the sentences concerned. In order to grasp the principles of question formation, the Martian must first realize that

AUNT JEMIMA, THE MAN WHO HAS RUN AWAY SHOUTING, SLUGS, MARY

each behaves as a unit of structure. The number of words within each unit is irrelevant, so no amount of counting will produce the right result for question formation. In these sentences (though not in all English sentences) the solution is to take the word which follows the first unit and bring it to the front:

AUNT JEMIMA	HAS	DROPPED HER FALSE TEETH DOWN THE DRAIN
THE MAN WHO HAS RUN AWAY SHOUTING	WAS	ATTACKED BY A WASP
SLUGS	ARE	SLIMY
MARY	HAS	SWALLOWED A SAFETY PIN

This may seem an obvious solution to people who already know English – but it is not at all clear *why* language should behave in this way. As Chomsky points out: 'The result is . . . surprising from a certain point of view. Notice that the structure-dependent operation has no advantages from the point of view of communicative efficiency or "simplicity". If we were, let us say, designing a language for formal manipulations by a computer, we would certainly prefer structure-independent operations. These are far simpler to carry out, since it is only necessary to scan the words of the sentence, paying no attention to the structure which they enter, structures that are not marked physically in the sentence at all' (Chomsky, 1972: 30).

Yet, amazingly, all children learning language seem to know automatically that language involves structure-dependent operations. On the face of it, one might expect them to go through a prolonged phase of testing out Martian-like solutions – but they do not. This type of phenomenon leads Chomsky to suggest that humans may have an innate knowledge of the properties of language: 'Given such facts, it is natural to postulate that the idea of "structure-dependent operations" is part of the innate schematism applied by the mind to the data of experience' (Chomsky, 1972: 30).

The structure-dependent nature of the operations used in language is all the more remarkable because there are often no overt clues to the structure. Experiments carried out by psycholinguists have made it quite clear that listeners do not rely on *acoustic* clues for interpreting the main structural divisions. For example, Garrett, Bever and Fodor (1966) constructed two sentences which each contained the words:

GEORGE DROVE FURIOUSLY TO THE STATION:
1. IN ORDER TO CATCH HIS TRAIN GEORGE DROVE FURIOUSLY TO THE STATION
2. THE REPORTERS ASSIGNED TO GEORGE DROVE FURIOUSLY TO THE STATION.

In the first sentence, it is GEORGE who is driving furiously. In the second, it is the REPORTERS. In order to understand the sentence, the listener must (mentally) put the structural break in the correct place:

IN ORDER TO CATCH HIS TRAIN   GEORGE DROVE FURIOUS-
LY TO THE STATION.

THE REPORTERS ASSIGNED TO GEORGE   DROVE FURIOUSLY TO
THE STATION.

Just to check that the listeners were *not* using acoustic clues, the experimenters recorded both these sentences on to tapes. Then they cut the words GEORGE DROVE FURIOUSLY TO THE STATION off each tape, and spliced them to the *other* sentence:

IN ORDER TO CATCH HIS TRAIN   GEORGE DROVE FURIOUSLY TO THE
STATION.

THE REPORTERS ASSIGNED TO   GEORGE DROVE FURIOUSLY TO THE
STATION.

They then played the newly spliced tapes to students – but into one ear only. In the other ear the students heard a click, which was placed in the middle of a word, e.g. GEÒRGE. The students were then asked whereabouts in the sentence the click had occurred. The interesting result was that in their reports students tended to move the location of the click in the direction of the structural break:

IN ORDER TO CATCH HIS TRAIN GEORGE DROVE FURIOUSLY TO THE
STATION.

THE REPORTERS ASSIGNED TO GEORGE DROVE FURIOUSLY TO THE
STATION.

This indicates clearly that listeners impose a structure on what they hear for which there is often *no* physical evidence.

Another point which has been made by Chomsky (1959) and a number of other writers (e.g. Bever, Fodor and Weksel, 1965) is that simple slot-filling operations are inadequate as explanations of language. It has sometimes been suggested that anyone learning language allocates to each sentence a number of 'slots' and then fits units of structure into each hole:

e.g.

1	2	3
BEES	LOVE	HONEY
I	WANT	MY TEA
MY BROTHER	HAS HIT	ME

No one would deny the existence of such substitutions and their value in language learning. But the problem is that there is a lot more going on besides, which cannot be accounted for by the 'slot' idea: 'It is evident that more is involved in sentence structure than insertion of lexical items in grammatical frames' (Chomsky, 1959: 54). For example, look at the following sentences:

PERFORMING FLEAS	CAN BE	AMUSING
PLAYING TIDDLYWINKS	CAN BE	AMUSING

Other words which fit into the centre slot differ: *are* fits in with the first sentence but not the second, whereas *is* fits in with the second but not the first:

PERFORMING FLEAS	ARE	AMUSING
*PERFORMING FLEAS	IS	AMUSING
*PLAYING TIDDLYWINKS	ARE	AMUSING
PLAYING TIDDLYWINKS	IS	AMUSING

If slot-filling was the sole principle on which language worked, one would not expect this result. Slot-filling explanations cannot tell us how the listener knows, in the sentences where the centre slot is filled by *can be*, that it is the fleas who are performing, but that it is not the tiddlywinks who are playing. But examples of 'constructional homonymity' (as Chomsky calls such superficially similar utterances) are by no means rare.

Even more inexplicable from a slot-filling point of view are sentences which can be interpreted in two different ways:

CLEANING LADIES CAN BE DELIGHTFUL:
1. LADIES WHO CLEAN CAN BE DELIGHTFUL.
2. TO CLEAN LADIES CAN BE DELIGHTFUL.

THE MISSIONARY WAS READY TO EAT:
1. THE MISSIONARY WAS ABOUT TO EAT.
2. THE MISSIONARY WAS ABOUT TO BE EATEN.

Sentences such as these indicate that merely filling a grammatical frame may be only part of what is happening when we speak.

It would be possible to proliferate examples of slot-filling problems. But two interesting ones to which much attention has been paid are those involving *reflexive* and *imperative* sentences in English (Postal, 1964).

On the basis of slot-filling one might expect all four sentences below to occur:

*I	HAVE HURT	ME
YOU	HAVE HURT	ME
I	HAVE HURT	YOU
*YOU	HAVE HURT	YOU

But the asterisked sentences are ungrammatical. Why? It seems that English speakers have an internalized rule which states that *if* there is identity between the subject and object of a sentence, then the second of the two identical nouns becomes reflexive:

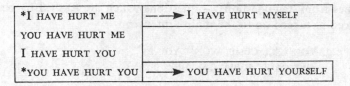

This type of example has led Chomsky to suggest that language is organized on two levels: a *surface* level (e.g. I HAVE HURT MYSELF) and an (abstract) *deep* level where such facts as subject and object identity are obvious:

e.g. *Deep level*   *Surface level*

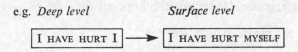

This explanation becomes more convincing when imperative sentences are considered:

e.g. SING!
    BE QUIET!

These do not normally have surface subjects, but they can have objects:

e.g. HELP HIM!
WASH YOURSELF!

If a reflexive object is found, it is always YOURSELF. Sentences such as:

*WASH MYSELF
*DON'T HURT HIMSELF

never occur. But since reflexives only occur if the subject and object are identical, then presumably speakers must somehow 'know' that sentences such as WASH YOURSELF have an identical subject and object. But on the surface there is no sign of a subject. So this subject perhaps exists at a 'deeper' level, but is then erased or 'deleted'.

Deep level	*Intermediate level*	*Surface level*
YOU WASH YOU →	YOU WASH YOURSELF →	WASH YOURSELF

Further support for the existence of a 'deep' YOU in imperatives comes from 'tag-questions' – questions which are formed by being tacked or tagged on to the main sentence:

e.g. YOU WILL COME, WON'T YOU?
BILL CAN'T SWIM, CAN HE?

The pronoun in the tag is always 'copied' from the subject of the main sentence:

YOU   WILL COME, WON'T . . . .

However, tags are also found with imperatives:

e.g. SIT DOWN, WON'T YOU

In this case the tag pronoun appears to have been copied from an invisible subject, one which perhaps exists at some deeper level, but does not appear on the surface:

Deep Level	*Intermediate Level*	*Surface Level*
YOU WILL SIT DOWN →	YOU WILL SIT DOWN, WON'T YOU →	SIT DOWN, WON'T YOU

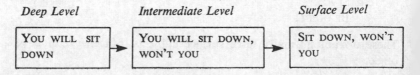

Chomsky's arguments that a 'deeper' level of syntax underlies the surface level are persuasive – but not necessarily right. Other explanations are possible. The important point to note is that the type of phenomenon found in reflexives and imperatives can *not* be explained by means of the bar-pressing antics of rats, nor by means of simple slot-filling operations. Some more complex mechanism is involved.

So far, then, language can be said to be structure-dependent – and the type of structure-dependent operations involved seem to be complex.

Another fundamental aspect of language which is stressed repeatedly by Chomsky is its *creativity*. By this, Chomsky seems to mean two things. Firstly, and primarily he means the fact that humans have the ability to understand and produce novel utterances. Even quite strange sentences, which are unlikely to have been uttered before, cause no problems for speakers and hearers:

THE ELEPHANT DRANK SEVENTEEN BOTTLES OF SHAMPOO, THEN SKIPPED DRUNKENLY ROUND THE ROOM.
THE AARDVARK CLEANED HIS TEETH WITH A PURPLE TOOTHBRUSH.

This means that it is quite impossible to assume that a man gradually accumulates strings of utterances throughout his life and stores them ready for use on an appropriate occasion. Note also that, as well as producing new grammatical sequences, anyone who has mastered a language is automatically able to discard deviant utterances which he may never have met before. Sequences such as:

*HE WILL HAD BEEN SINGING

or:

*GIRAFFE UNDER IN WALKS GORILLA THE

will be rejected instantaneously.

Chomsky also uses 'creativity' in a second, subsidiary sense to mean that utterances are not controlled by external happenings. The appearance of a daffodil does not force a human to shriek 'Daffodil'. He can say whatever he likes: 'What a lovely colour', 'It's spring, I must remember to clean my car', or 'Why do flowers always give me hay fever?'.

Most humans are so used to these properties of language that they no longer seem odd – but they have not yet been fully explained.

Chomsky speaks of 'this still mysterious ability' when referring to the creative nature of man's speech: 'Having mastered a language, one is able to understand an indefinite number of expressions that are new to one's experience, that bear no simple physical resemblance and are in no simple way analogous to the expressions that constitute one's linguistic experience; and one is able with greater or less facility to produce such expressions on an appropriate occasion, despite their novelty and independently of detachable stimulus configurations, and to be understood by others who share this still mysterious ability. The normal use of language is, in this sense, a creative activity. This creative aspect of normal language is one fundamental factor that distinguishes human language from any known system of animal communication' (Chomsky, 1972a:100).

Chomsky stresses that the creative aspect of language is *normal*. Man produces novel utterances all the time, and anybody who does not is likely to be brain damaged: 'It is important to bear in mind that the creation of linguistic expressions that are novel but appropriate is the normal mode of language use. If some individual were to restrict himself largely to a definite set of linguistic patterns, to a set of habitual responses to stimulus configurations . . . we would regard him as mentally defective, as being less human than animal. He would immediately be set apart from normal humans by his inability to understand normal discourse, or to take part in it in the normal way – the normal way being innovative, free from control by external stimuli, and appropriate to a new and ever-changing situation' (Chomsky, 1972a:100).

It becomes clear that there is much more to language than merely stringing together words. In order to speak, a human possesses a highly complex internalized set of rules which enables him to utter any of (and only) the permissible sequences of English – though he is unlikely to have any conscious knowledge of the rules. The rules are both complex and stringent, as Mr Knipe discovered (a character in a short story by Roald Dahl): 'Then suddenly he was struck by a powerful but simple little truth, and it was this: that English grammar is governed by rules that are almost mathematical in their strictness! . . . Therefore, it stands to reason that an engine built along the lines of the electric computer could be adjusted to arrange words in their right order according to the rules of grammar. . . . There was no stopping Knipe now. He went to work immediately. After fifteen days of continuous labour, Knipe had finished building his "Great Automatic Grammatizator".'

But Mr Knipe is a character in a science-fiction story. As already noted, in real life no linguist, no computer expert has yet managed to build an 'automatic grammatizator' – a device which will account for all and only the permissible sequences of English.

Yet children do it all the time: in a remarkably short period, they acquire a complex set of internalized rules. And children have considerably less data to work from than the linguists who have failed to produce 'automatic grammatizators'. They are often restricted to hearing their parents and relatives talking – and, according to Chomsky, this speech is likely to be full of unfinished sentences, mistakes and slips of the tongue. Furthermore, according to him, the acquisition of one's native language seems to be largely independent of intelligence. The language ability of dim children is not noticeably inferior to that of bright children – yet in most other areas of human activity – such as roller-skating or playing the piano – the gap between different children is enormous.

Although Chomsky is now generally thought to exaggerate the rapidity of acquisition, the sub-standard nature of the data, and perhaps even the uniformity of ability, the great mystery remains: how do children construct 'automatic grammatizators' for themselves?

At the moment, no theory of learning put forward by psychologists can account for the acquisition of language. So two possibilities exist:

Possibility I

Psychologists who have been working on problems of learning have not yet produced a theory sufficiently advanced to account for language.

Possibility II

Human infants 'know' in advance what languages are like. This is the possibility preferred by Chomsky: 'The child must acquire a generative grammar of his language on the basis of a fairly restricted amount of evidence. To account for this achievement, we must postulate a sufficiently rich internal structure – a sufficiently restricted theory of universal grammar that constitutes his contribution to language acquisition' (Chomsky, 1967:437).

It may not be necessary to choose between these possibilities –

recent research indicates that the answer exists somewhere between the two.

However, the possibility that a certain amount of language is innate, that children are 'pre-programmed' to speak is a serious and interesting one. It would explain such puzzling factors as structure-dependence, creativity, and rapidity of acquisition in a natural way. Note that there is some ambiguity in the word 'innate'. It is here used simply to mean 'genetically programmed'. It does not literally mean that children are born with language in their heads ready to be spoken. It merely means that a 'blueprint' is there, which is not necessarily brought into use until the behaviour is 'triggered' by other aspects of the environment and the child's development.

The next three chapters will explore the question of innateness more thoroughly.

2 Animals That Try to Talk

Is language restricted to humans?

An ant who can speak
French, Javanese and Greek
    Doesn't exist.
    Why ever not?

Robert Desnos

Judging by newspapers and popular books, there appear to be a vast number of animals which 'talk' – talking budgerigars, talking dolphins – even a talking fish:

> Anne, Anne, come quick as you can
> There's a fish that talks in the frying pan.

(Walter de la Mare)

Clearly, the word 'talk' can be used in two totally different senses. On the one hand, it can mean simply 'to utter words', as in 'Archibald's got a talking parrot which says *Damn* if you poke it'. On the other hand, it can mean 'to use language in a meaningful way'. We already know that animals such as budgerigars can 'talk' in the first sense of the word. Psycholinguists would like to find out whether animals can 'talk' in the second sense also. They are interested in this problem because they want to know the answer to the following question: are we the only species which possesses language? If so, are we the only species capable of acquiring it?

These are the topics examined in this chapter. First of all animal communication systems are compared with human language to see if animals can be said to 'talk' in any real sense. Secondly, various attempts to teach language to animals are considered. The overall purpose behind such inquiries is to find out whether humans alone have the power of speech. Are we biologically singled out as 'articulate mammals' or not?

Of course, if we discover that animals *do* talk, then we shall not have learned anything useful, just as the fact that we can do the breast stroke does not tell us anything about a frog's innate swimming ability. Or, as Fodor, Bever and Garrett acidly note, 'The fact that a dog can be trained to walk on its hind legs does not prejudice the claim that bipedal gait is genetically coded in humans. The fact that we can learn to whistle like a lark does not prejudice the species-specificity of birdsong' (Fodor, Bever and Garrett, 1974:451). If, on the other hand, we find that animals do *not* talk, this will provide some support for the claim that language is 'innate' in humans.

Do animals talk naturally?

Our first task is to find out whether any animals naturally have a true 'language'. In order to answer this question, we must compare human language with animal communication. But such a comparison presents a number of perhaps unsolvable problems. Two in particular need to be discussed before we can start to give a coherent reply to the query, 'Do animals talk naturally?'

The first problem we must consider is this: are we comparing systems which differ quantitatively or qualitatively? On the one hand, human language may have gradually evolved from a more primitive animal means of communication in a continuous line of growth – a viewpoint sometimes known as a 'continuity' theory. On the other hand, human language may be something quite different from our basic animal heritage, and superimposed on it. This is a 'discontinuity' theory.

Supporters of continuity theories suggest that language grew out of a primate call system, like the ones used by apes today. They assume that humans started out with a simple set of cries in which each one meant something different, such as, 'Danger!' or 'Follow me!' or 'Don't touch that female, she is mine!' These cries gradually became more elaborate, and eventually evolved into language. A possible intermediate stage is seen in the cries of the vervet monkey. This monkey has several alarm calls which distinguish between different types of danger (Struhsaker, 1967). The *chutter* announces that a puff adder or cobra is around. The *rraup* gives warning of an eagle. A *chirp* is used for lions and leopards. A less panic-stricken utterance, the *uh!*, signals the presence of a spotted hyena or Masai tribesman. According to some, it is a very short step from an alarm call warning of a poisonous snake to using the *chutter* as a 'word' symbolizing a poisonous snake.

But another interpretation of these signals is possible. The monkeys could merely be distinguishing between the *intensity* of different types of danger. They may be more frightened of puff adders than eagles – or vice versa. This is a plausible explanation, since the monkeys sometimes give a *chirp* (used for lions) when they see an eagle. So it is likely that eagles and lions represent the same degree of danger – unless you conclude that monkeys cannot tell the difference between them. This suggests that a discontinuity theory may be better than a continuity one.

Proponents of discontinuity theories claim that man still retains his basic set of animal cries, which exist alongside language. Yelps of pain, shrieks of fear, and the different types of crying observed in babies may be closely related to the call systems of monkeys. If this view is correct, then it is fairly difficult to compare human and animal means of communication. It may be like comparing two things as different as the Chinese language and a set of traffic lights. But at the moment the question is an open one. We do not yet know whether the continuity or the discontinuity theorists are correct. But we must keep both possibilities in mind when discussing the main topic of this chapter.

The second major problem we face is that it is not always easy to decide what counts as communication in animals. As one researcher notes, 'Students of animal behaviour have often noted the extreme difficulty of restricting the notion of communication to anything less than every potential interaction between an organism and its environment' (Marshall, 1970:231). So that, at the very least, sticklebacks mating, cats spitting, and rabbits thumping their back legs must be taken into consideration – and it isn't at all clear where to stop. It is sometimes suggested that this problem could be solved by concentrating on examples where the animal is *intentionally* trying to convey information. But such distinctions are difficult to draw, both in humans and animals. If a woman repeatedly flutters her eyelashes when an attractive man walks into the room, is this an unconscious response? Or is she doing it intentionally in order to attract his attention? In the sea, so-called 'snapping shrimps' can produce loud cracks (which are capable of upsetting naval sonar devices) by closing their claws sharply. But no one has yet discovered the significance of the snaps. They may be informative – but they may not. There is no way yet in which we can be sure about making the right decision when it comes to interpreting such a phenomenon.

Having outlined these fundamental problems – which show that any conclusions we draw are only tentative – we can now return to our main theme: a comparison of human language and animal communication. How should we set about this?

A useful first step might be to attempt to define 'language'. This is not as easy as it sounds. Most of the definitions found in elementary textbooks are too wide. For example: 'The faculty of language consists in man's ability to make noises with the vocal organs and marks on paper or some other material, by means of which groups of people "speaking the same language" are able to interact and co-operate as a group' (Robins, 1971:12). This definition, if one ignores the word 'man' and the phrase involving 'marks on paper', might equally well apply to a pack of wolves howling in chorus.

Perhaps the most promising approach is that suggested by the linguist Charles Hockett. In a series of articles stretching over ten years he has attempted to itemize out the various 'design features' which characterize language. For example: *'Interchangeability*: Adult members of any speech community are interchangeably transmitters and receivers of linguistic signals'; *'Complete Feedback*: The transmitter of a linguistic signal himself receives the message' (Hockett, 1963:9). Of course, such an approach is not perfect. A list of features may even be misleading, since it represents a random set of observations which do not cohere in any obvious way. To use this list to define language is like trying to define a man by noting that he has two arms, two legs, a head, a belly button, he bleeds if you scratch him, and shrieks if you tread on his toe. But in spite of this, a definition of language based on design features or 'essential characteristics' seems to be the most useful proposed so far.

But how many characteristics should be considered? Two? Ten? A hundred? The number of design features Hockett considers important has changed over the years. The longest list contains sixteen (Hockett, 1963), though perhaps most people would consider that eight features capture the essential nature of language: *use of the vocal-auditory channel, arbitrariness, semanticity, cultural transmission, duality, displacement, structure-dependence* and *creativity*.

Let us discuss each of these features in turn, and see whether it is present in animal communication. If any animal naturally possesses *all* the design features of human language, then clearly that animal can talk.

The use of the *vocal-auditory channel* is perhaps the most obvious characteristic of language. Sounds are made with the vocal organs, and a hearing mechanism receives them – a phenomenon which is neither rare nor particularly surprising. The use of sound is wide-spread as a means of animal communication. One obvious advantage is that messages can be sent or received in the dark or in a dense forest. Not all sound signals are vocal – woodpeckers tap on wood, and rattlesnakes have a rattle apparatus on their tail. But vocal-auditory signals are common and are used by birds, cows, apes and foxes, to name just a few. The advantages of this method of produc-ing the sound are that it leaves the body free to carry on other activi-ties at the same time, and also requires relatively little physical energy. But this design feature is clearly neither unique to humans, nor all-important, since language can be transferred without loss to visual symbols (as in deaf-and-dumb language, or writing) and to tactile symbols (as in Braille). Patients who have had their vocal cords removed, and communicate mainly by writing, have not lost their language ability. It follows that this characteristic is of little use in an attempt to distinguish animal from human communication. So let us proceed to the second feature, arbitrariness.

Arbitrariness means that human languages use neutral symbols. There is no connection between the word 'dog' and the four-legged animal it symbolizes. It can equally be called UN CHIEN (French), EIN HUND (German), or CANIS (Latin). GÜL (Turkish) and RHODON (Greek) are equally satisfactory names for a 'rose'. As Juliet notes:

> What's in a name? that which we call a rose
> By any other name would smell as sweet.

> (Shakespeare)

Onomatopoeic words such as CUCKOO, POP, BANG, SLURP and SQUISH are exceptions to this. But there are relatively few of these in any language. On the other hand, it is normal for animals to have a strong link between the message they are sending and the signal they use to convey it. A crab which wishes to convey extreme aggression will extend a large claw. A less angry crab will merely raise a leg: 'Extending a major chaliped is more effective than raising a single ambulatory leg in causing the second crab to retreat or duck back into its shell' (Marshall, 1970). However, arbitrary symbols are not unique to man. Gulls, for example, sometimes indicate aggression by turning away from their opponent and uprooting beakfuls of grass. So we are forced to conclude that arbitrariness cannot be regarded as a critical distinction between human and animal communication.

Semanticity, the third suggested test for language ability, is the use of symbols to 'mean' or refer to objects and actions. To a human, a CHAIR 'means' a four- legged contraption you can sit on. Humans can generalize by applying this name to all types of chairs, not just one in particular. Furthermore, semanticity applies to actions as well as objects. For example, to JUMP 'means' the act of leaping in the air. Some writers have claimed that semanticity is exclusively human. Animals may only be able to communicate about a total situation. A hen who utters 'danger' cries when a fox is nearby is possibly conveying the message 'Beware! beware! there is terrible danger about!' rather than using the sound to 'mean' FOX. But, as was shown by the call of the vervet monkey who might or might not mean 'snake' when he *chutters*, it is difficult to be certain. We must remain agnostic about whether this feature is present in animal communication.

Cultural transmission or *tradition* indicates that human beings hand their languages down from one generation to another. The role played by teaching in animal communication is unclear and varies from animal to animal – and even within species. Among birds it is claimed that the song-thrush's song is largely innate, but can be slightly modified by learning, whereas the skylark's song is almost wholly learned. Birds such as the chaffinch are particularly interesting: the basic pattern of the song seems to be innate, but all the finer detail and much of the pitch and rhythm have to be acquired by learning (Thorpe, 1961, 1963). However, although the distinction between man and animals is not clear-cut as regards this feature, it seems that a far greater proportion of communication is genetically inbuilt in animals than in man. If a child is brought up in isolation, away from human beings, he does not acquire language. In contrast, birds reared in isolation sing songs that are sometimes recognizable (though almost always abnormal).

The fifth property, *duality* or *double-articulation*, means that language is organized into two 'layers': the basic sound units of speech, such as P, I, G, are normally meaningless by themselves. They only become meaningful when combined into sequences such as P—I—G PIG. This property is sometimes claimed to be unique to humans. But this is not so. Duality is also present in bird song, where each individual note is itself meaningless – it is the combination of notes which convey meaningful messages. So once again we have not found a critical difference between animals and humans in the use of this feature.

A more important characteristic of language is *displacement*, the ability to refer to things far removed in time and place. Humans frequently say things such as 'My Aunt Matilda, who lives in Australia, cracked her knee-cap last week'. It may be impossible for an animal to convey a similar item of information. However, as in the case of other design features, it is sometimes difficult to decide whether displacement is present in an animal's communication system. A bird frequently continues to give alarm cries long after the disappearance of a cat which was stalking it. Is this displacement or not? The answer is unclear. Definite examples of displacement are hard to find. But it is undoubtedly found in bee communication (von Frisch, 1950, 1954, 1967). When a worker bee finds a source of nectar she returns to the hive to perform a complex dance which informs the other bees of its location. She does a 'round dance', which involves turning round in circles if the nectar is close to the hive, and a 'waggle dance' in which she wiggles her tail from side to side if it is far away. The other bees work out the distance by noting the tempo of her waggles, and discover what kind of flower to look for by smelling its scent on her body. After the dance, they unerringly fly to the right place, even if it is several miles away, with a hill intervening.

This is an unusual ability – but even this degree of displacement is considerably less than that found in human speech. The bee cannot inform other bees about anything further removed than the nectar patch she has just visited. She cannot say 'The day before yesterday we visited a lovely clump of flowers, let's go and see if they are still there' – she can only say, 'Come to the nectar I have just visited'. Nor can she communicate about anything further away in place. She could not say 'I wonder whether there's good nectar in Siberia'. So displacement in bee communication is strictly limited to the number of miles a bee can easily fly, and the time it takes to do this. At last, it seems we may have found a feature which seems to be of importance in human language, and only partially present in non-human communication.

The seventh feature, *structure-dependence*, was discussed in Chapter 1. Humans do not just apply simple recognition or counting techniques when they speak to one another. They automatically recognize the patterned nature of language, and manipulate 'structured chunks'. For example, they understand that a group of words can sometimes be the structural equivalent of one:

SHE	
THE OLD LADY WHO WAS WEARING A WHITE BONNET	GAVE THE DONKEY A CARROT

and they can rearrange these chunks according to strict rules:

A CARROT	WAS GIVEN TO THE DONKEY	BY THE OLD LADY WHO WAS WEARING A WHITE BONNET

As far as we know, animals do not use structure-dependent operations. We do not know enough about the communication of all animals to be sure, but no definite example has yet been found.

Finally, there is one feature that seems to be of overwhelming importance, and unique to humans – the ability to produce and understand an indefinite number of novel utterances. This property of language has several different names. Chomsky calls it *creativity* (Chapter 1), others call it *openness* or *productivity*. A human can talk about anything he likes – even a platypus falling backwards downstairs – without causing any linguistic problems to himself or the hearer. He can say *what* he wants *when* he wants. If it thunders, he does not automatically utter a set phrase, such as 'It's thundering, run for cover'. He can say 'Isn't the lightning pretty?' or 'Better get the dog in' or 'Thunder is two dragons colliding in tin tubs, according to a Chinese legend'.

In contrast, most animals have a fixed number of signals which convey a set number of messages, sent in clearly definable circumstances. A North American cicada can give four signals only. It emits a 'disturbance squawk' when it is seized, picked up or eaten. A 'congregation call' seems to mean 'Let's all get together and sing in chorus!' A preliminary courtship call (an invitation?) is uttered when a female is several inches away. An advanced courtship call (a buzz of triumph?) occurs when the female is almost within grasp (Alexander and Moore, quoted in McNeill, 1966). Even the impressive vervet monkey has only thirty-six distinct vocal sounds in its repertoire. And as this total includes sneezing and vomiting, the actual number used for communication is several fewer. Within this range, choice is limited, since circumstances generally dictate which call to use. An infant separated from its mother gives the lost *rrah* cry. A female who wishes to deter an amorous male gives the 'anti-copulatory squeal-scream' (Struhsaker, 1967).

But perhaps it is unfair to concentrate on cicadas and monkeys. Compared with these, bees and dolphins have extremely sophisticated communication systems. Yet researchers have reluctantly concluded that even bees and dolphins seem unable to say anything new. The bees were investigated by the famous 'bee-man', Karl von Frisch (1954). He noted that worker bees normally give information about the *horizontal* distance and direction of a source of nectar. If bee communication is in any sense 'open', then a worker bee should be able to inform the other bees about *vertical* distance and direction if necessary. He tested this idea by placing a hive of bees at the foot of a radio beacon, and a supply of sugar water at the top. But the bees who were shown the sugar water were unable to tell the other bees where to find it. They duly performed a 'round dance', indicating that a source of nectar was in the vicinity of the hive – and then for several hours their comrades flew in all directions *except* upwards, looking for the honey source. Eventually, they gave up the search. As von Frisch noted, 'The bees have no word for "up" in their language. There are no flowers in the clouds' (von Frisch, 1954:139). Failure to communicate this extra item of information means that bee communication cannot be regarded as 'open-ended' in the same way that human language is open-ended.

The dolphin experiments carried out by Dr Jarvis Bastian were considerably more exciting – though in the long run equally disappointing. Bastian tried to teach a male dolphin Buzz and a female dolphin Doris to communicate across an opaque barrier.

First of all, while they were still together, Bastian taught the dolphins to press paddles when they saw a light. If the light was kept steady, they had to press the right paddle first. If it flashed, the left-hand one. When they did this correctly they were rewarded with fish.

As soon as they had learned this manoeuvre, he separated them. They could now hear one another, but they could not see one another. The paddles and light were set up in the same way, except that the light which indicated which paddle to press first was seen only by Doris. But in order to get fish both dolphins had to press the levers in the correct order. Doris had to *tell* Buzz which this was, as only she could see the light. Amazingly, the dolphins 'demonstrated essentially perfect success over thousands of trials at this task' (Evans and Bastian, 1969:432). It seemed that dolphins could *talk*! Doris was conveying novel information through an opaque barrier!

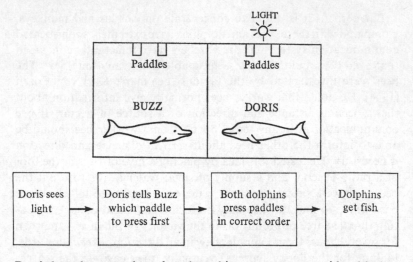

But it later became clear that the achievement was considerably less clever. Even while the dolphins were together Doris had become accustomed to making certain sounds when the light was flashing and different sounds when it was continuous. When the dolphins were separated she continued the habit. And Buzz had, of course, already learnt which sound of Doris's to associate with which light. Doris was therefore not 'talking creatively'.

So not even dolphins have a 'creative' communication system, it seems – though it is always possible that more is known about 'delphinese' than has been made public. The high intelligence of dolphins has obvious implications for naval warfare, and so has attracted the attention of military authorities, with the result that much research is shrouded in official secrecy. But on the whole it seems unlikely that there exist hidden tanks of 'talking dolphins' (as was suggested in a recent film). Most researchers would agree with the comment of the psychologist John Morton: 'On the question as to whether dolphins have a language, I would like to comment parenthetically from the evidence I have seen, if they do have a language they are going to extraordinary lengths to conceal the fact from us' (Morton, 1971:83).

It seems, then, that animals cannot send truly novel messages, and that Ogden Nash encapsulates a modicum of truth in his comment:

> The song of canaries
> Never varies.

And so does Alice in her complaint about kittens:

It is a very inconvenient habit of kittens that, whatever you say to them, they always purr. If they would only purr for 'yes' and mew for 'no', or any rule of that sort, so that one could keep up a conversation! But how *can* you talk with a person if they *always* say the same thing?

(Lewis Carroll)

It is now possible to answer the question, can animals talk? If, in order to qualify as 'talkers' they have to utilize all the design characteristics of human language 'naturally', the answer is clearly 'no'. Some animals possess some of the features. Bird song has duality, and bee dancing has some degree of displacement. But, as far as we know, no animal communication system has duality *and* displacement. No animal system can be proved to have semanticity or to use structure-dependent operations. Above all, no animal can communicate creatively with another animal.

But although animals do not 'naturally' talk, this does not mean that they are *incapable* of talking. Perhaps they have just never had the chance to learn language. The next section examines the results obtained with animals which have had this opportunity.

Teaching animals to talk: Washoe and Sarah

In discussing attempts to teach language to animals it is important (as we have already noted) to distinguish mimicry from 'true' language. Parrots and mynah birds can imitate humans with un-canny accuracy. But it is unlikely that they ever understand what people are saying. There are reports of a grey parrot which could say 'Good morning' and 'Good evening' at the right times, and 'Goodbye' when guests left (Brown, 1958). But most talking birds are merely 'parrotting' back what they hear. For example, a budgerigar I knew heard a puppy being trained with words such as 'Sit!' 'Naughty boy!' and used to shriek 'Sit!' 'Naughty boy!' whenever anyone went near its cage, whether or not the dog was present.

Although psychologists have spent considerable time experi-menting with mynah birds, it is perhaps not surprising that the results have been disappointing. Apes seem more promising candidates. Over the past forty years several attempts have been made to teach human language to chimpanzees.

The first experiment was a failure. An animal named Gua was acquired by Professor and Mrs Kellogg in 1931, when she was seven months old (Brown, 1958; Kellogg, 1933). She was brought up as if she was a human baby, and was fed with a spoon, bathed, pinned up in nappies, and continuously exposed to speech. Although she eventually managed to understand the meaning of over seventy single words, she never spoke. Gua showed clearly that it is *not* just lack of opportunity which prevents a chimp from learning language. The Kelloggs' son Donald, who was brought up alongside Gua, and was approximately the same age, grew up speaking normally.

A second chimp acquired by Keith and Cathy Hayes in 1947 also proved disappointing (Brown, 1958; Hayes, 1951). Viki was given intensive coaching in English. She eventually learnt four words: PAPA, MAMA, CUP, UP. But these were very unclearly articulated, and remained the sum total of Viki's utterances after three years of hard training.

It is now clear why these attempts failed. Chimps are not physiologically capable of uttering human sounds. More recent experiments have avoided this trap and used sign language, the manipulation of tokens, or button pressing. Let us consider some of this later research.

At the moment, teaching language to chimpanzees seems to be a popular pastime among American psychologists – there has been a minor population explosion of 'talking chimps' recently. We shall confine our discussion to Washoe (Gardner and Gardner, 1969; Gardner and Allen, 1971) and Sarah (Premack, 1970, 1971, 1972). These are the two chimps who, so far, seem to have acquired most 'language', and whose achievements have been most widely reported.

Washoe's exact age is unknown. She is a female chimp acquired by Professor and Mrs Gardner in 1966, when she was thought to be approximately a year old. She has been taught to use American deaf-and-dumb sign language (ASL). In this system signs stand for words. For example, Washoe's word for 'sweet' is made by putting her finger on the top of her tongue, while wagging the tongue. Her word for 'funny' is signalled by pressing the tip of her finger on to her nose, and uttering a snort.

Washoe acquired her language in a fairly 'natural' way. The Gardners kept her continuously surrounded by humans who communicated with her and each other by means of signs. They hoped that some of all this would 'rub off' on her. Sometimes they asked her to imitate them, or tried to correct her. But there were no rigorous training schedules.

Even so, teaching a wild chimpanzee can be quite a problem:

'Washoe can become completely diverted from her original object, she may ask for something entirely different, run away, go into a tantrum, or even bite her tutor' (Gardner and Gardner, 1969:666). But her progress was impressive and, at least in the early stages, her language development was not unlike that of a human child.

First, she acquired a number of single words, e.g. COME, GIMME, HURRY, SWEET, TICKLE – which amounted to thirty-four after twenty-one months, but later crept up to well over one hundred. The number is accurate because a rota of students and researchers made sure that Washoe, who lived in a caravan in the Gardners' garden, was never alone when she was awake. And a sign was assumed to be acquired only after Washoe had used it spontaneously and appropriately on consecutive days.

Washoe's speech clearly had 'semanticity'. She had no difficulty in understanding that a sign 'means' a certain object or action, as was shown by her acquisition of the word for 'toothbrush' (index finger rubbed against teeth). She was forced, at first against her will, to have her teeth brushed after every meal. Consequently, she had seen the sign for 'toothbrush' on numerous occasions, though she had never used it herself. One day, when she was visiting the Gardner's home, she found a mug of toothbrushes in the bathroom. Spontaneously, she made the sign for 'toothbrush'. She was not asking for a toothbrush, as they were within reach. Nor was she asking to have her teeth brushed, a procedure she hated. She appeared simply to be 'naming' the object. Similarly, Washoe made the sign for 'flower' (holding the fingertips of one hand together and touching the nostrils with them) when she was walking towards a flower garden, and another time when she was shown a picture of flowers.

Washoe could also generalize from one situation to another, as was clear from her use of the sign meaning 'more'. Like all chimps, she loved being tickled, and she would pester any companion to continue tickling her by using the 'more' sign. At first, the sign was specific to the tickling situation. Later, she used it to request continuation of another favourite activity – being pushed across the floor in a laundry basket. Eventually, she extended the 'more' sign to feeding and other activities. Similarly the word for 'key' referred originally only to the key used to unlock the doors and cupboards in Washoe's caravan. Later she used the sign spontaneously to refer to a wide variety of keys, including car ignition keys. Her 'speech' also incorporated a limited amount of displacement, since she could ask for absent objects and people.

But most impressive of all was Washoe's creativity – her apparently spontaneous use of combinations of signs. She produced two- and three-word sequences of her own invention, such as GIMME TICKLE 'Come and tickle me', GO SWEET 'Take me to the raspberry bushes', OPEN FOOD DRINK 'Open the fridge', LISTEN EAT 'Listen to the dinner gong', HURRY GIMME TOOTHBRUSH, and ROGER WASHOE TICKLE. Washoe's signs were not just accidental juxtapositions. During a sequence of signs Washoe kept her hands up in the 'signing area'. After each sequence she let them drop. This is comparable to the use of intonation by humans to signal that words are meant to be joined together in a construction. Does this mean that Washoe can actually 'talk'? At least superficially, her sequences seem parallel to the utterances of a human child. Washoe's requests for MORE SWEET, MORE TICKLE seem similar to requests for MORE MILK or MORE SWING recorded from children. But there is one important difference. Children normally preserve a fixed word order. English children put the subject or agent of a sentence before the action word, as in MUMMY COME, EVE READ, ADAM PUT, CAR GONE. But Washoe did not always seem to care in what order she gave her signs. She was as likely to say SWEET GO as GO SWEET to mean 'Take me to the raspberry bushes'.

There are a number of possible explanations. Firstly, the over-eagerness of the researchers who worked with Washoe. They were so anxious to encourage her that they rushed to gratify every whim. Since SWEET GO and GO SWEET have only one possible interpretation – Washoe wants some raspberries – they immediately understood and took her there. The idea that word ordering was necessary may never have occurred to her. Perhaps if she had ever experienced difficulty in making herself understood she might have been more careful about structuring her sequences.

Another possibility is that it may be easier to utter vocal sounds in sequence than it is to maintain a fixed order with signs. Preliminary studies suggest that deaf adults are inconsistent in their ordering of sign language (Schlesinger, 1971a).

A third possibility is that the fluctuating order in Washoe's signing was merely a temporary intermediate stage which occurred before Washoe eventually learnt to keep to a fixed sequence. This is the point of view supported by the Gardners in a recent television programme. They claim that Washoe settled down to a standard sign order which was based on the order of adult English (since, of course, Washoe's companions had used an English word order when they used sign language with her). For example, when shown a doll inside a mug, she spontaneously signed, BABY—IN—MY—DRINK.

Yet another possible explanation of Washoe's unreliable sign order is that she did not, and cannot, understand the essentially patterned nature of language. In this case, she certainly did not understand or use structure-dependent operations – one of the key tests for determining whether she can 'talk'. But it is difficult to be sure. And we may never know for certain as she is no longer in the situation where she is continually surrounded by humans whose main task is to hold conversations with her. She grew so large and potentially dangerous that the Gardners were obliged to send her to live at a primate station. However, though her period of intensive exposure to sign language is over, research assistants still come to talk to her. She is continuing to acquire 'signs', and is still showing quite striking evidence of creativity. A recent addition to her repertoire is the sequence WATER-BIRD to mean 'duck' – a spontaneous creation which occurred when she saw a duck. A further (as yet unfulfilled) hope is that she will teach her sign language to the other chimps around her. However, on her present showing, we have to conclude that although Washoe's speech is creative, and shows semanticity and displacement, it has not been proved to be structure-dependent.

Let us now consider Sarah. Sarah began her training in 1966, under Dr David Premack at the University of California, Santa Barbara. Unlike Washoe, whose life was one continuous game, Sarah is being strictly trained by methods not unlike those used by Skinner with his rats. She lives in a cage, and is being taught to manipulate plastic tokens on a magnetic board. Each token represents a word. A mauve triangle means 'apple', and a red square means 'banana'. A black T-shaped token denotes the colour 'yellow', and a pale blue star means 'insert'. Sarah now understands over one hundred words, including complicated ideas such as 'colour of', 'same', 'different', and 'if . . . then'. For example, if she is given a choice of an apple or banana, and told IF APPLE, THEN CHOCOLATE, she can correctly take the apple in order to get a reward of chocolate, her favourite food. Note, however, that the fact that Sarah can understand the logical notion IF . . . THEN does not prove that she has language. The relationship of language to logic is still very unclear.

But Sarah's communication is rather odd. She does not hold conversations, as Washoe did. She sits in her cage and is tested at intervals by her trainers. Most of the tests are comprehension ones. She can obey orders such as SARAH INSERT APPLE DISH. And when told to put GREEN ON RED she can place the symbol for green on top of the red one. If she is asked QUERY CUP EQUAL SPOON ('Is the cup the same thing as a spoon?') she can respond appropriately with the token for NO. Whenever she gets a response right, she is rewarded, usually with chocolate. She has been trained to use a fixed word order – she does not get her chocolate if she gets the order wrong.

Some people have suggested that Sarah does not really understand what she is doing. They suggest that she may be responding to cues in the questioner's behaviour. Animals, like people, frequently guess from the look on someone's face what answer they are required to give. It is difficult to be sure how much Sarah actually comprehends. But her achievements seem too complex to be completely explained away by the 'behavioural cue' theory.

Sarah does not initiate 'speech', and since her responses to new sequences are so carefully drilled, it is difficult to decide whether she uses her token system creatively. However, the crucial question with regard to Sarah is this: can she carry out operations which are *structure-dependent*? She certainly understands and carries out simple 'slot-filling' exercises:

1	2	3	4
SARAH	INSERT	APPLE	PAIL
SARAH	INSERT	BANANA	DISH
SARAH	INSERT	APPLE	RED DISH
SARAH	INSERT	BANANA	GREEN DISH

She can respond appropriately to all of these commands. And she understands that more than one word can fit into one slot, e.g. RED DISH is equivalent to PAIL or DISH by itself. In other words, she may understand the notion of *hierarchical structure* – the idea that a group of words is structurally substitutable for a single word.

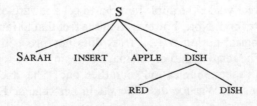

But humans can do more than this. They can alter the order around without losing track of the basic structure, for example:

> IS IT THE RED DISH INTO WHICH THE APPLE WAS INSERTED BY SARAH?

and they can also omit or 'delete' items without getting confused:

> SING! 'You sing'
> MARY AND JOHN WENT FISHING 'Mary went fishing and John went fishing'

Sarah has not been trained to cope with any alterations in word order. The questions she is presented with are formed by putting the token for 'query' in front of a sentence, e.g.

> QUERY RED COLOUR OF APPLE 'Are apples red?'

But she *is* able to delete items. With difficulty and accompanied by 'emotional outbursts' she succeeded in correctly carrying out the instructions:

SARAH INSERT APPLE RED DISH BANANA GREEN DISH

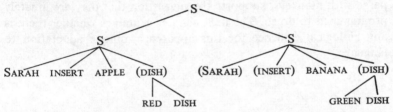

This appears to involve an understanding both of hierarchical structure and of deletion. But it is difficult to be sure of what is happening. Since Sarah is only asked to do one type of task in each session, she may develop non-linguistic strategies to deal with each test. And considering her extreme love of chocolate, it does seem slightly odd that her correct response average is as low as 70 or 80 per cent. Perhaps we cannot assess Sarah's achievements accurately until she learns to initiate conversations – which at the moment she shows no signs of doing.

The results of the Washoe and Sarah experiments are not clear cut. It is difficult to make an accurate assessment of their achievements. On the one hand, it is obvious that the systems they are learning are less complicated than human language. This is proved by the fact that severely mentally handicapped children who are unable to acquire normal language are being taught Sarah's token system with considerable success. On the other hand, between them the two chimps seem to show a possible grasp of some basic design characteristics of language hitherto thought to be 'human' only. Washoe's 'speech' shows semanticity, displacement and creativity; Sarah's also shows semanticity and may involve structure-dependent operations. This suggests that it may now be necessary for Chomsky to revise his opinion that 'acquisition of even the barest rudiments of language is quite beyond the capacities of an otherwise intelligent ape' (Chomsky, 1972a:66).

But although intelligent animals seem *capable* of learning language in a rudimentary fashion, they do not seem *predisposed* to learn it. The situation is parallel to that found among birds (Thorpe, 1963). Some birds are able to learn the songs of a different species. But they find the task a difficult one. When the birds are removed from the alien species, and placed among their own kind, they learn their normal song with extreme rapidity. They seem to have an innate predisposition towards one kind of song rather than another.

The apparent ease with which humans acquire language, compared with monkeys, supports the suggestion that they are innately programmed to do so. The next chapter examines whether there is any biological evidence for this apparently unique adaptation to language.

3 Grandmama's Teeth

Is there biological evidence for innate language capacity?

'O grandmama, what big teeth you have!' said Little Red
   Riding Hood.
'All the better to *eat* you with, my dear,' replied the wolf.

If an animal is innately programmed for some type of behaviour, then
there are likely to be biological clues. It is no accident that fish have
bodies which are streamlined and smooth, with fins and a powerful
tail. Their bodies are structurally adapted for moving fast through
the water. The same is true of whales and dolphins, even though
they evolved quite separately from fish. Similarly, if you found a
dead bird or mosquito, you could guess by looking at its wings that
flying was its normal mode of transport.

However, we must not be over-optimistic. Biological clues are
not essential. The extent to which they are found varies from animal
to animal and from activity to activity. For example, it is impossible
to guess from their bodies that birds make nests, and, sometimes,
animals behave in a way quite contrary to what might be expected
from their physical form: ghost spiders have tremendously long legs,
yet they weave webs out of very short strands. To a human observer,
their legs seem a great hindrance as they spin and move about the
web. On the other hand, the orb spider, who has short legs, makes
its web out of very long cables, and seems to put a disproportionate
amount of effort into walking from one side of the web to another
(Duncan, quoted in Lenneberg, 1967:75). In addition, there are
often inexplicable divergences between species which do not correlate
with any obvious differences in behaviour. The visible sections of the
ear differ in chimps, baboons and men – but there is no discernible
reason behind this. However, such unpredictability is not universal,
and need not discourage us from looking for biological clues connected with speech – though we must realize that we are unlikely to
find the equivalent of a large box labelled 'language'.

Changes in the form of the body or *structural* changes are the most direct indications of innate programming. But we must also take into consideration *physiological* adaptations – change in the bodily functions such as rate of heart-beat, and breathing. The first part of this chapter looks at parts of the human body where adaptations related to language are likely to be found. The organs used to produce and plan it are examined – the mouth, vocal cords, lungs and the brain.

The second part of the chapter is slightly different. It considers aspects of language where complex neuromuscular sequencing is involved. It becomes clear that the co-ordination required is perhaps impossible without biological adaptations.

Mouth, lungs and grey matter

If we look at the organs used in speech, humans seem to be somewhere in the middle between the obvious structural adaptation of birds to flying, and the apparent lack of correlation between birds and nest-building. That is, the human brain and vocal tract have a number of slightly unusual features. By themselves, these features are not sufficient to indicate that people can talk. But if we first assume that all humans speak a language, then a number of puzzling biological facts fall into place. They can be viewed as *partial* adaptations of the body to the production of language (Lenneberg, 1967; Liebermann, 1972).

For example, human teeth are unusual compared with those of other animals. They are even in height, and form an unbroken barrier. They are upright, not slanting outwards, and the top and bottom set meet. Such regularity is surprising – it is certainly not needed for *eating*. Yet evenly spaced, equal-sized teeth which touch one another are essential for the articulation of a number of sounds, s, f, and y, for example, as well as sh (as in *shut*), th (as in *thin*) and several others. Human lips have muscles which are considerably more developed, and show more intricate interlacing than those in the lips of other primates. The mouth is relatively small, and can be opened and shut rapidly. This makes it simple to pronounce sounds such as *p* and *b*, which require a total stoppage of the airstream with the lips, followed by a sudden release of pressure as the mouth is opened. The human tongue is thick, muscular, and mobile, as opposed to the long thin tongues of monkeys. The advantage of a thick tongue is that the size of the mouth cavity can be varied, allowing a range of vowels to be pronounced.

It seems, then, that man is naturally geared to produce a number of different sounds rapidly and in a controlled manner. His mouth possesses features which either differ from, or appear to be missing in the great apes. In all one cannot help agreeing with the comment of a nineteenth-century writer: 'What a curious thing speech is! The tongue is so serviceable a member (taking all sorts of shapes just as it is wanted) – the teeth, the lips, the roof of the mouth, all ready to help; and so heap up the sound of the voice into the solid bits which we call consonants, and make room for the curiously shaped breathings which we call words!' (Oliver Wendell Holmes, quoted in Critchley, 1970).

Another important difference between man and monkeys concerns the larynx, commonly known as the 'voice box' or 'vocal cords'. Strangely, it is simpler in structure than that of other primates. But this is an advantage. Air can move freely past and then out through the nose and mouth without being hindered by other appendages. Biologically, streamlining and simplification are often indications of specialization for a given purpose. For example, hooved animals have a reduced number of toes, and fish do not have limbs. So the streamlining of the human larynx may be a sign of adaptation to speech. But man pays a price for his specialized larynx. A monkey can seal its mouth off from its windpipe and breathe while it is eating. Man cannot do this, and food can get lodged in his windpipe, causing him to choke to death (Lieberman, 1972).

We now come to the lungs. Although there is no apparent peculiarity in the structure of man's lungs, his breathing seems to be remarkably adapted to speech. In most animals the respiratory system is a very finely balanced mechanism. A human submerged under water for more than two minutes will possibly drown. Anyone who pants rapidly and continuously for any length of time faints, and sometimes dies. Yet during speech the breathing rhythm is altered quite noticeably without apparent discomfort to the speaker. The number of breaths per minute is reduced. Breathing-in is considerably accelerated, breathing-out is slowed down. Yet people frequently talk for an hour or more with no ill-effects. A child learning to play the flute or trumpet has to be carefully instructed in breathing techniques – but no one has to instruct a two-year-old in the breathing adaptations required for talking. It is impossible to tell which came first – speech or breathing adaptations. As Lenneberg inquires (1967:81), do donkeys say *hee-haw* on inspired and expired air so efficiently because of the way their breathing mechanisms were organized, or did the *hee-haw* come first? The answer is irrelevant. All that matters to us is that any child born in the twentieth century has a breathing mechanism apparently 'biologically organized' for speech.

It seems, then, that there are clear indications in the mouth, larynx and lungs that man speaks 'naturally'. However, let us now consider the human brain. To what extent is this programmed for speech? The answer is unclear. Man's brain is very different in appearance from that of other animals. It is heavier, with more surface folding of the *cortex*, the outer layer of 'grey matter' which surrounds the inner core of nerve fibres. Of course, size alone is not particularly important. Elephants and whales have bigger brains than humans, but they do not talk. But elephants and whales also have bigger bodies, so some people have suggested that it is the brain– body ratio which matters. At first sight, this seems a promising approach. It appears quite reasonable to suggest that a high brain– body ratio means high intelligence, which in turn might be a prerequisite for language – especially when we find that the brain of an adult human is more than 2 per cent of his total weight, while that of an adult chimp is less than 1 per cent. But we soon realize that such ratios can be very misleading. Some animals are designed to carry around large reserves of energy which make their bodies enormously heavy. Camels, for example, are not necessarily stupider than horses just because they have huge humps.

But even apart from problems such as this, brain–body ratio cannot be a decisive factor as far as language is concerned, since it is possible to find young chimpanzees and human children who have similar brain–body ratios – yet the child can talk and the chimp cannot. Even more convincing is a comparison between a three-year-old chimp and a twelve-year-old nanocephalic dwarf – a human who because of a genetic defect grows to a height of around 760 mm (or two foot six inches). Although the chimp and the dwarf have exactly the same brain and body weights (and so, of course, the same brain–body ratio), 'the dwarfs speak, in a somewhat limited fashion, but the chimps do not.

	Brain (kg)	Body (kg)	Ratio
Human, age 13½	1.35	45	1 : 34
Human dwarf, age 12	0.4	13.5	1 : 34
Chimp, age 3	0.4	13.5	1 : 34

(Lenneberg, 1967: 70)

These figures show conclusively that the difference between human and chimp brains is a *qualitative*, not a *quantitative* one.

Superficially, the brains of a chimp and a human have certain similarities. As in a number of animals, the human brain is divided into a lower section, the *brain stem*, and a higher section, the *cerebrum*. The brain stem keeps the body alive by controlling breathing, heart beats and so on. A cat with the upper section of its brain removed but with the brain stem intact could still swallow milk, purr, and pull its paw away from a thorn when pricked. The higher section, the cerebrum, is not essential for life. Its purpose seems to be to integrate an animal with its environment. This is the part of the brain where language is likely to be organized.

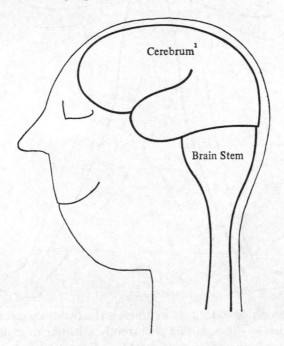

The cerebrum is divided into two halves, the *cerebral hemispheres*, which are linked to one another by a series of bridges. The left hemisphere controls the right side of the body, and the right hemisphere the left side.

[1] The cerebrum actually occupies a slightly larger area than that shown in the diagram.

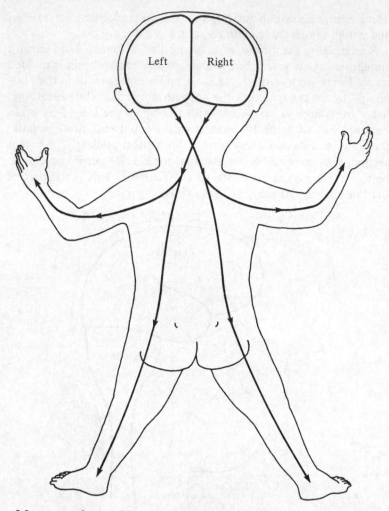

Many people consider that in animals the two hemispheres function identically – though this is currently a matter of controversy.
But in humans there is a considerable difference between the two.
This was first discovered over a hundred years ago. A Frenchman,
Marc Dax, read a paper at Montpelier in 1836, pointing out that
paralysis of the right side of the body was often associated with
loss of speech, while patients whose left side was paralysed could
usually talk normally. This suggested that the left hemisphere
controlled not only the right side of the body, but *speech* also. Dax's
hypothesis turned out to be correct. Speech in the majority of

humans is the concern of the *left*, not the right hemisphere. But it was a long time before this was reliably confirmed. Until relatively recently, statistics could only be drawn up by chance observations, when researchers managed to note cases of people in whom loss of speech was associated with right side paralysis. But in the twentieth century more sophisticated methods have been adopted. One is the 'sodium amytal' test developed by Wada in the 1940s. In this test the patient is asked to count out loud while a barbiturate (sodium amytal) is injected into an artery carrying blood to one side of the brain. If this is the hemisphere used in speech, the patient loses all track of his counting and experiences severe language difficulties for several minutes. If it is not, the patient can resume normal counting almost immediately after the injection. Although this test is effective, it also carries an element of risk. So it is only used when brain surgery is advisable (as in severe epilepsy) and the surgeon wishes to know whether he is likely to disturb vital speech areas. If so, he is unlikely to operate.

The simplest and most recently developed method for discovering which hemisphere controls speech is the use of dichotic listening tests (Kimura, 1967). The subject wears headphones, and is played two different words simultaneously, one into each ear. For example, he might hear *six* in one ear, and *two* in the other. Most people can report the word played to the right ear (which is directly linked to the left hemisphere) more accurately than the word played to the left ear (linked to the right hemisphere). It is clear that this is not

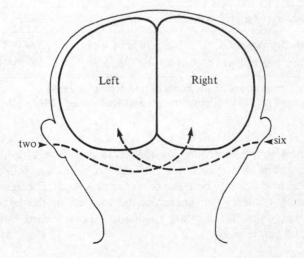

simply due to an overall preference for sounds heard in the right ear, because for non-linguistic sounds the left ear is better. If, simultaneously, different tunes are played into each ear, subjects will identify the tune played into the left ear better than the one played into the right ear. We conclude that the left hemisphere is better at processing linguistic signals – and so is normally the dominant one for speech.

The results of the observations and tests described above are surprisingly consistent. The majority of normal human beings – perhaps as many as 90 per cent – have speech located primarily in the left hemisphere. This cannot be due to chance.

A further interesting and related discovery is that the location of speech centres in the left hemisphere seems to be linked to right-handedness. That is, most people are right-handed, and most people's speech is controlled by the left hemisphere. In the nineteenth century it was commonly assumed that left-handers must have speech located in the right hemisphere, and this seemed to be confirmed by a report in 1868 by the influential neurologist John Hughlings Jackson that he had discovered loss of speech in a left-hander who had sustained injury to the right side of the brain. But this viewpoint turns out to be false. Surprisingly, most left-handers also have language controlled predominantly by the left hemisphere, though the picture is not completely straightforward. Of the relatively few people who do have their speech centres located in the right hemisphere, more are left-handed than right-handed.

Location of speech centres	R-handers	L-handers
Left hemisphere	90% or more	70–90%
Right hemisphere	10% or less	10–30%

(figures averaged from Penfield and Roberts, 1959; Zangwill, 1973; Milner, Branch and Rasmussen, 1964)

These figures indicate two things: firstly, it is normal for speech and handedness to be controlled by the same hemisphere (and it has been suggested that speech and writing problems are found more frequently in children where the two are not linked). Secondly, there is a strong tendency for speech to be located in the left hemisphere even when this appears to disrupt the standard linking of speech and handedness.

More recent work has been directed at finding out if *all* speech processing must be located in one hemisphere or whether subsidiary linguistic abilities remain in the non-dominant hemisphere. One group of researchers at Montreal, Canada, claim to have found ten patients who had speech abilities in both halves of the brain. The sodium amytal test disturbed speech whichever side of the brain it was injected. Interestingly enough, all these patients were either left-handed or ambidextrous (Milner, Branch and Rasmussen, 1964).

Further experiments of this type have been carried out on 'split brain' patients (Gazzaniga, 1970). In cases of severe epilepsy it is sometimes necessary to sever the major links between the two hemispheres. This means that a patient has virtually two separate brains, each coping with one half of the body independently. A patient's language can be tested by dealing with each hemisphere separately. An object shown to the *left* visual field is relayed only to the *right* (non-language hemisphere). Yet sometimes the patient is able to name such an object. This indicates that the right hemisphere *may* be able to cope with simple naming problems – but it seems unable to cope with syntax. However, the results of these experiments are disputed. Some people have suggested that the information is being transferred from one hemisphere to the other by a 'back route' after the major links have been severed.

This lateralization or localization of language in one half of the brain, then, is a definite, biological characteristic of the human race. In connection with this, Zangwill (1973:210) notes: 'There must be some special property of the human nervous system that predisposes man to acquire speech . . . I venture to suggest, very tentatively, that this property may lie in a certain asymmetry in the function of the two halves – or hemispheres – of the human brain.'

But children are not born with this brain asymmetry. Before the age of two, both hemispheres function identically. From two onwards, one hemisphere becomes progressively dominant. If an infant is involved in an accident which damages the left hemisphere, his speech will possibly develop normally. The brain seems to have the ability to relocate speech in the undamaged hemisphere at a young age. But as the child gets older, the likelihood of permanent speech impairment is stronger, and from adolescence onward, serious damage to the left hemisphere almost certainly causes speech problems for life (Lenneberg, 1967:146). So lateralization seems to occur gradually between the ages of two and fourteen – and, as we shall see in Chapter 4, is possibly linked to a 'critical period' for language acquisition.

Although most neurologists agree that language is mainly restricted to one hemisphere, further localization of speech is still the centre of a raging controversy. The basic difficulty is that all the evidence available is derived from brain-damaged patients. And injured brains may not be representative of normal ones. After a stroke or other injury the damage is rarely localized. A wound usually creates a blockage, causing a shortage of blood in the area beyond it, and a build-up of pressure behind it. So detailed correlations of wounds with speech defects cannot often be made, especially as a wound in one place may trigger off severe speech problems in one person, but only marginally affect the speech of another. This suggests to some neurologists that speech can be 're-located' away from the damaged area – it has (controversially) been suggested that there are 'reserve' speech areas which are kept for use in emergencies. This creates an extremely complex picture – like a ghost, speech drifts away to another area just as you think you have located it. But these problems have not deterred neurologists – and some progress has been made.

There are two main methods of investigation – observation and experiment. Observation depends on unfortunate accidents and post-mortems. A man called Phineas Gage had an accident in 1847 in which a four-foot iron bar became embedded in the front left-hand section of his head. The bar remained there until his death, twenty years later, and bar and skull are now preserved in a museum at the Harvard Medical School. Although Gage's personality changed for the worse – he became unreliable and unpredictable – his language was unaffected. This suggests that the front part of the brain is not involved in language. Conversely, a French surgeon named Broca noted at a post-mortem in 1861 that two patients who had had severe speech defects (one could only say *tan* and *sacré nom de Dieu*) had significant damage to an area just in front of, and slightly above, the left ear – which suggests that this area, now named 'Broca's area', is important for speech.

The experimental method was pioneered by two Canadian surgeons, Penfield and Roberts (1959). They were primarily concerned with removing abnormally functioning cells from the brains of epileptics. But before doing this they had to check that they were not destroying cells involved in speech. So, with the patients fully conscious, they carefully opened the skull, and applied a minute electric current to different parts of the exposed brain. Electrical stimulation of this type normally causes temporary interference. So if the area which controls leg movement is stimulated, the patient is unable to move his leg. If the area controlling speech production is involved, the patient is briefly unable to speak.

There are obvious disadvantages in this method. Only the surface of the brain was examined, and no attempt was made to probe what was happening at a deeper level. The brain is not normally exposed to air or electric shocks, so the results may be quite unrepresentative. But in spite of the problems involved, certain outline facts have become clear.

First of all, it is possible to distinguish the area of the brain which is involved in the actual articulation of speech. The so-called 'primary somatic motor area' controls all voluntary bodily movements and is situated just in front of a deep crack or 'fissure' running down from the top of the brain. The control for different parts of the body works upside down: control of the feet and legs is near the top of the head, and control of the face and mouth is further down.

The bodily control system in animals works in much the same way – but there is one major difference. In humans, a dispropor-

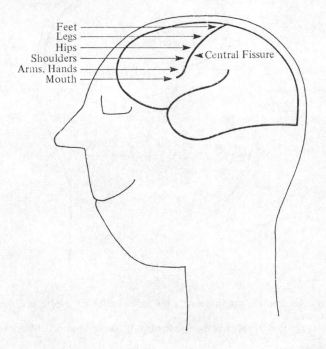

tionate amount of space is allotted to the area controlling the hands and mouth.

But the sections of the brain involved in the actual articulation of speech seem to be quite distinct from those involved in its planning and comprehension. Where are these planning and comprehension areas? This is where experts disagree, often fundamentally. Nevertheless, perhaps the majority of neurologists agree that some areas of the brain are statistically likely to be involved in speech planning and comprehension. Two areas seem to be particularly relevant: the neighbourhood of *Broca's area* (in front of and just above the left ear), and the region around and under the left ear, which is sometimes called *Wernicke's area* after the neurologist who first suggested this area was important for speech (in 1874). Damage to Wernicke's area often destroys speech comprehension, and damage to Broca's frequently hinders speech production – though this is something of an over-simplification, since serious damage to either area usually harms all aspects of speech – and in occasional cases, it does not lead to serious speech disturbances at all.

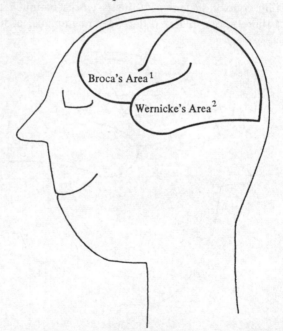

[1] Broca's Area covers approximately the space under the *s* of *Broca's* and the *A* of *Area*.
[2] Wernicke's Area is roughly the space directly above the word *Wernicke's*.

In addition to these areas there are likely to be deeper interconnections about which little is known. Some neurologists have suggested that the interconnections are as important as the areas themselves, and claim that major speech defects occur when these connections are severed (Geschwind, 1972; Penfield and Roberts, 1959).

A further highly complex and as yet unsolved problem is the relationship between language and intelligence. There is undoubtedly a level of intelligence below which language is unable to develop (Lenneberg, 1967) – though this seems to be very low. This finding indicates that Chomsky may be exaggerating when he claims that language develops independently of intelligence. But certain aspects of intelligence, in particular spatio-temporal intelligence (intelligence involving judgements of time and space), are largely independent of language. Patients with major speech problems due to severe left hemisphere damage can still solve spatio-temporal puzzles – though to a lesser level of skill than previously (Zangwill, 1964). In all, the whole question is a tricky one on which further work needs to be done.

Another unsolved problem is that of heredity. Can language defects be handed down from generation to generation? At the moment, the evidence is fragmentary (Lenneberg, 1967:248). Perhaps the likeliest candidate at the moment is dyslexia or 'word blindness' which does seem to run in families. But, again, more research needs to be done on this topic.

In conclusion, then, the lungs, teeth, lips and vocal cords have evolved in such a way as to facilitate speech. More importantly, man's brain seems to be pre-programmed for language. Lateralization – the localization of language to one half of the brain – is a natural phenomenon, occurring between the age of two and adolescence. Further localization within this hemisphere is a matter of controversy, although the sections of the brain known as Broca's area and Wernicke's area seem more likely to be involved than other areas.

But whatever the outcome of the various arguments connected with speech and the brain, it is clear that the human brain 'is 'wired' for language in a way that the brains of chimps and grasshoppers are not.

Patting one's head and rubbing the stomach

Another type of biological adaptation which is not so immediately obvious – but which is on second sight quite amazing – is the 'multiplicity of integrative processes' (Lashley, 1951) which are taking place in speech production and comprehension.

In some areas of activity it is extremely difficult to do more than one thing at once. As schoolchildren discover, it is extraordinarily difficult to pat one's head and rub one's stomach at the same time. If you also try to swing your tongue from side to side, and cross and uncross your legs, as well as patting your head and rubbing your stomach, the whole exercise becomes impossible. The occasional juggler might be able to balance a beer bottle on his nose, twizzle a hoop on his ankle and keep seven plates aloft with his hands – but he is likely to have spent a lifetime practising such antics. And the exceptional nature of these activities is shown by the fact that he can earn vast sums of money displaying his skills.

Yet speech depends on the simultaneous integration of a remarkable number of processes, and in many respects what is going on is considerably more complex than the juggler's manoeuvres with his beer bottle, plates and hoop.

In speech, three processes, at the very least, are taking place simultaneously: firstly, sounds are actually being uttered; secondly, phrases are being activated in their phonetic form ready for use; thirdly, the rest of the sentence is being planned. And each of these processes is possibly more complicated than appears at first sight. The complexities involved in actually pronouncing words are not immediately apparent. One might assume that in uttering a word such' as GEESE one first utters a G-sound, then an EE-sound, then an S-sound in that order. But the process is considerably more involved.

Firstly, the G-sound in GEESE differs quite considerably from the G in GOOSE. This is because of the difference in the following vowel. The speaker appears to anticipate (subconsciously) the EE or OO and alter the G accordingly. Secondly, the vowel in GEESE is shorter than in a word such as GEEZER. The speaker is anticipating the voiceless hissing sound of S in GOOSE rather than the voiced, buzzing sound of Z in GEEZER, since in English (and some other languages) vowels are shortened before voiceless sounds (sounds which do not involve vibration of the vocal cords).

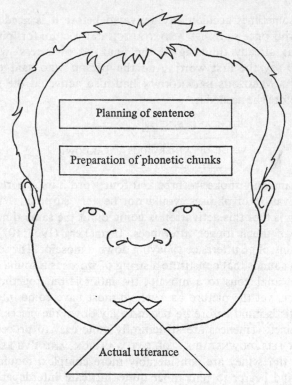

Therefore a speaker does not just utter a sequence of separate elements:

    1   2   3
    G . EE . SE

Instead he executes a series of overlapping actions in which the preceding sound is significantly influenced by the sound which follows it:

    G . . .
        EE . . .
            SE . . .

Such overlapping requires considerable neuro-muscular co-ordination, particularly as the rate of speech is often quite fast. A normal person often utters over 200 syllables a minute. Meanwhile, simultaneously with actually uttering the sounds a speaker is activating phrases of two or three words in advance in their phonetic form. This is shown by slips of the tongue, in which a sound several words away is sometimes accidentally activated before it is needed. The linguist who once said PISS AND STRETCH in a lecture for 'pitch and stress' was already thinking of the final –SS of 'stress' when he started to say the first word. And the person who said ON THE NERVE OF A VERGEOUS BREAKDOWN had also activated the syllable 'nerve' before she needed it.

If humans only spoke in three and four word bursts, perhaps the prior activation of phrases would not be very surprising. What *is* surprising is that this activation is going on at the same time as the planning of much longer utterances. Lenneberg (1967:107) likens the planning of an utterance to laying down a mosaic: 'The sequence of speech sounds that constitute a string of words is a sound pattern somewhat analagous to a mosaic; the latter is put together stone after stone, yet the picture as a whole must have come into being in the artist's mind before he began to lay down the pieces.'

Sometimes, sentences are structurally quite easy to process as in THE BABY FELL DOWNSTAIRS, THE CAT WAS SICK, AND I'VE RESIGNED. At other times they are considerably more complex, requiring the speaker and hearer to remember quite intricate interdependencies between clauses. Take the sentence IF EITHER THE BABY FALLS DOWNSTAIRS OR THE CAT IS SICK, THEN I SHALL EITHER RESIGN OR GO MAD. Here, IF requires a dependent THEN, EITHER requires a partner OR. In addition, FALLS must have the right ending to go with BABY, and IS must 'agree' with CAT – otherwise we would get *IF EITHER THE BABY FALL DOWNSTAIRS OR THE CAT ARE SICK . . . This whole sentence with its 'mirror-image' properties must have been planned considerably in advance.

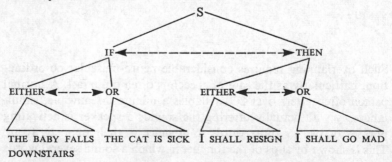

These examples show that in most human utterances, the amount of simultaneous planning and activity is so great that it seems likely that humans are specially constructed to deal with this type of co-ordination. But what type of mechanism is involved? In particular, how do humans manage to keep utterances in the right order, and not utter them in an incoherent jumble, as they think of them? How do most people manage to say RABBIT quite coherently, instead of BARIT or TIRAB – examples of misordering found in the speech of brain-damaged patients?

Lenneberg (1967) suggests that correct sequencing is based on an underlying rhythmic principle. Everybody knows that poetry is much easier to remember than prose because of the underlying 'pulse' which keeps going like the ticking of a clock:

> I WANDERED LONELY AS A CLOUD
> (ti-tum-ti-tum-ti-tum-ti-tum)
> THAT FLOATS ON HIGH O'ER VALES AND HILLS.
> (ti-tum-ti-tum-ti-tum-ti-tum)
> (Wordsworth)

There may be some underlying biological 'beat' which enables humans to organize language into a temporal sequence. Breakdown of this beat might also account for the uncontrollable acceleration of speech found in some illnesses such as Parkinson's disease. Lenneberg suggests that one-sixth of a second may be a basic time unit in speech production. He bases his proposals on a number of highly technical experiments, and partly on the fact that around six syllables per second seems to be the normal rate of uttering syllables. These conclusions, however, are still speculative and may have to be amended.

But the overall picture is clear. Humans are physically adapted to language in a way in which snails, apes and sheep are not. Their vocal organs, lungs and brains are 'pre-set' to cope with the intricacies of speech in much the same way that monkeys are pre-set to climb trees, or bats to squeak. The next chapter gives further evidence of this biological programming by showing that language follows an inner 'time-clock' as it emerges and develops.

4 Predestinate Grooves

Is there a pre-ordained language 'programme'?

There once was a man who said, 'Damn!'
It is born in upon me I am
An engine that moves
In predestinate grooves,
I'm not even a bus, I'm a tram.

Maurice Evan Hare

Language emerges at about the same time in children all over the world. 'Why do children normally begin to speak between their eighteenth and twenty-eighth month?' asks one researcher. 'Surely it is not because all mothers on earth initiate language training at that time. There is, in fact, no evidence that any conscious and systematic teaching of language takes place, just as there is no special training for stance or gait' (Lenneberg, 1967:125).

This regularity of onset suggests that language may be set in motion by a biological time-clock, similar to the one which causes kittens to open their eyes when they are a few days old, chrysalises to change into butterflies after several weeks, and humans to become sexually mature at around thirteen years of age. However, until relatively recently, few people had considered language within the framework of biological maturation. But in 1967 E. H. Lenneberg, a biologist at the Harvard Medical School, published an important book, entitled *The Biological Foundation of Language*. Much of what is said in this chapter is based on his pioneering work.

The characteristics of biologically triggered behaviour

Behaviour which is triggered off biologically has a number of special characteristics. In the following pages we shall list these features, and see to what extent they are present in language. If it can be shown that speech, like sexual activities and the ability to walk, falls into the category of biologically scheduled behaviour, then we shall be rather clearer about what is meant by the claim that language is 'innate'.

Biologically scheduled behaviour has one predominant characteristic: it occurs sooner or later in every ordinary member of a species, providing that he is brought up in normal circumstances.

Exactly how many further 'hallmarks' of biologically controlled behaviour we should itemize is not clear. Lenneberg lists four. The six listed below were obtained mainly be subdividing Lenneberg's four:

1. The behaviour emerges before it is needed.
2. Its appearance is not the result of a conscious decision.
3. Its emergence is not triggered by external events.
4. There is likely to be a 'critical period' for the acquisition of the behaviour.
5. Direct teaching and intensive practice have relatively little effect.
6. There is a regular sequence of 'milestones' as the behaviour develops, and these can usually be correlated with age and other aspects of development.

Let us discuss these features in turn. Some of them seem fairly obvious. It hardly seems necessary to set about testing the first one, that 'the behaviour emerges before it is needed'. Language develops long before children *need* to communicate. Their parents still feed them, clothe them, and look after them. Without some type of inborn mechanism, language would develop only when parents left children to fend for themselves. It would emerge at different times in different cultures, and this would lead to vastly different levels of language skills. Although children differ enormously in their ability to knit or play the violin, their language proficiency varies to a much lesser extent.

Again, little explanation is needed for the second characteristic of biologically triggered behaviour: 'It's appearance is not the result of a conscious decision'. Clearly, a child does not suddenly think to himself, 'Tomorrow I am going to start to learn to talk'. Children acquire language without making any conscious decision about it. This is quite unlike a decision to learn to jump a four-foot height, or hit a tennis ball, when a child sets himself a target, then organizes strenuous practice sessions as he strives towards his goal.

The first part of feature (3) also seems straightforward: 'The emergence of the behaviour is not triggered by external events'. Children start to talk even when their surroundings remain unchanged Most of them live in the same house, eat the same food, have the same parents, and follow the same routine. No specific event or feature in the child's surroundings suddenly sets him off talking. However, we must here digress briefly in order to point out an aspect of biologically scheduled behaviour that is sometimes misunderstood: although no external event *causes* the behaviour, the surrounding environment must be sufficiently 'rich' for it to develop adequately. Biologically programmed behaviour does not develop properly in impoverished or unnatural surroundings. We have the apparent paradox that some types of 'natural' behaviour require careful 'nurturing'. Just as Chris and Susie, two gorillas reared away from other gorillas in Sacramento Zoo, are unable to mate satisfactorily (according to a recent item in the *Evening Standard*) – so an impoverished linguistic environment is likely to retard language acquisition. Children brought up in institutions, for example, tend to be backward in speech development. Lenneberg notes that a child raised in an orphanage will begin to talk at the same time as other non-institutionalized children. But his speech will gradually lag behind the norm, being less intelligible, and showing less variety of construction. A less obvious example of linguistic impoverishment has been suggested by Basil Bernstein, a sociologist at London University's Institute of Education. He claims (somewhat controversially) that children from working-class families are often language deprived (e.g. Bernstein, 1972). They may be unable to learn language adequately because they do not have sufficient data at their disposal. He claims that such families use informal and elliptical speech, in contrast to the more formal and explicit language of middle-class households. For example, working class 'Op it' may correspond to middle class, 'Go outside and play, and stop worrying me, I'm busy.' As one (subsequently well-educated) working-class man described it, 'In a working-class family the words may be limited in number . . . there is a perpetual exchange of pebbled phrases: "Ah well, some folk are like that; she's nowt but mutton dressed as lamb." For most of what is said is not said by words but by tone of voice, by silences, by look, gesture and most keenly by touching.' The same man describes the cultural shock of school, where he was faced with 'an unending rush of words, multitudinous, fresh, and ordered in different ways' (Brian Jackson in the *Daily Telegraph* colour supplement). Children seem to need this 'unending rush of words', and those who are deprived of it may lag back in their development. Luckily, the problem is usually only temporary. Language impoverished children tend to catch up quickly once their verbal environment is enriched: the biological factor takes over as soon as the environment enables it to do so.

Rather more discussion is needed to jusify the existence in language of a fourth characteristic of biologically controlled behaviour: 'There is likely to be a critical period for the acquisition of the behaviour.' It is clear that there is a biologically scheduled starting point for language acquisition, but far less clear that there is a biologically scheduled finishing point.

We know for certain that language cannot emerge before it is programmed to emerge. Nobody has ever taught a young baby to talk – though it seems that there is nothing much wrong with the vocal cords of a new-born infant, and from five or six months onwards it can 'babble' a number of the sounds needed in speech. Yet children utter few words before their first birthday, and they do not normally combine words before the age of eighteen months. It is clear that they have to wait for some biological trigger. The 'trigger' appears to be connected with brain growth. Two-word utterances, which are usually regarded as the beginning of 'true-language', begin just as a massive spurt in brain growth slows down. Children do not manufacture any new brain cells after birth. They are born with millions, perhaps billions. At first the cells are not all interconnected, and the brain is relatively light (about 300 g). From birth to around two years, many more cells interconnect, and brain weight increases rapidly. By the age of two, it weighs nearly 1000 g (Lenneberg, 1967).

It is not nearly so easy to tell when a child has finished acquiring a language. Nevertheless, there are a number of indications that, after the onset of adolescence, humans can acquire a new language only after a considerable struggle.

First of all, almost everybody can remember how difficult it was to learn French at school. Even the best pupils had a slightly odd accent, and made numerous grammatical mistakes. The difficulty was not that one was learning a second language, since children who are brought up speaking French and English as equal 'mother tongues' do not experience similar problems. Nor is there much difficulty for children who emigrate to France around the age of five or six, when they already speak fluent English. Moreover, the failure to learn perfect French cannot be due simply to lack of exposure to the language. There are numerous people who have emigrated to France as adults, and converse only in French – yet they never acquire a mastery of the new language equivalent to that of their native tongue. It seems that the brain loses its 'plasticity' for language learning after a certain age.

However, evidence concerning difficulties with French at school is mainly anecdotal. Perhaps the most impressive evidence for the existence of a critical period comes from comparing the case histories of two socially isolated children, Isabelle and Genie. Both these children were cut off from language until long after the time they would have acquired it, had they been brought up in normal circumstances.

Isabelle was the illegitimate child of a deaf mute. She had no speech, and made only a croaking sound when she was found in Ohio in the 1930s at the age of six and a half. Mother and child had spent most of the time alone in a darkened room. But once found, Isabelle's progress was remarkable: 'Isabelle passed through the usual stages of linguistic development at a greatly accelerated rate. She covered in two years the learning that ordinarily occupies six years. By the age of eight and one half Isabelle was not easily distinguishable from ordinary children of her age' (Brown, 1958: 192).

Genie, however, was not so lucky. She was not found until she was nearly fourteen. Born in April 1957, she had lived most of her life in bizarre and inhuman conditions. 'From the age of twenty months, Genie had been confined to a small room. . . . She was physically punished by her father if she made any sounds. Most of the time she was kept harnessed into an infant's potty chair; otherwise she was confined in an home-made sleeping bag in an infant's crib covered with wire mesh' (Curtis *et al.*, 1974:529). When found, she was totally without language. She began acquiring speech well after the onset of adolescence – after the apparent 'critical period'. Although she is learning to speak, she is progressing much more slowly than normal children. For example, ordinary children go through a stage in which they utter two words at a time (WANT MILK, WHERE TEDDY?), which normally lasts a matter of weeks. Genie's two-word stage lasted for more than five months. Again, ordinary children briefly pass through a phase in which they form negative sentences by putting the word NO in front of the rest of the utterance, as in NO MUMMY GO, NO WANT APPLE. The most recent progress report of Genie notes that she has been using this primitive form of negation for a year and a half. The only aspect of speech in which Genie outstrips ordinary children is her ability to learn vocabulary. She knows many more words than normal children at a comparable stage of grammatical development. However, the ability to memorize lists of items is not evidence of language capacity – even the chimps Washoe and Sarah found this relatively easy. It is the rules of grammar which are the important part, and this is what Genie finds difficult. Her slow progress compared with that of Isabelle seems to provide clear evidence in favour of there being a 'cut-off' point for language acquisition.

Further evidence in favour of a critical period is provided by mentally handicapped children, such as 'mongols' (Down's syndrome cases). These follow the same general path of development as normal children, but much more slowly. (Lenneberg, 1967). They never catch up because their ability to learn language slows down dramatically at puberty (though a few researchers have disputed this claim).

The recovery possibilities of brain-damaged patients provide further support and in addition, indicate that the critical period coincides with the period of lateralization – the gradual specialization of language to one side of the brain. As noted in the last chapter, this process occurs between the ages of two and fourteen. If a child under the age of two sustains severe damage to the left (language) hemisphere of the brain, his speech will develop normally – though it will be controlled by the right hemisphere. But as the child gets older, the likelihood of left hemisphere damage causing permanent impairment gets progressively greater. In an adolescent or adult, such damage usually results in lifelong speech disturbance. When lateralization is complete, the brain seems to have lost a natural 'bent' for learning languages.

We have now considered several pieces of indirect evidence for the existence of a 'critical period'. They all suggest (though do not conclusively prove) that toddler time to adolescence is a time set aside by nature for the acquisition of language. Lenneberg notes: 'Between the ages of two and three years language emerges by an interaction of maturation and self-programmed learning. Between the ages of three and the early teens the possibility for primary language acquisition continues to be good; the individual appears to be most sensitive to stimuli at this time and to preserve some innate flexibility for the organization of brain functions to carry out the complex integration of sub-processes necessary for the smooth elaboration of speech and language. After puberty, the ability for self-organization and adjustment to the physiological demands of verbal behaviour quickly declines. The brain behaves as if it had become set in its ways and primary, basic skills not acquired by that time usually remain deficient for life' (Lenneberg,

1967:158). A similar critical period is found for the acquisition of their song by some species of birds. A chaffinch's song, for example, becomes fixed and unalterable when it is around fifteen months old. If the chaffinch has not been exposed to chaffinch song before that time, it never learns to sing normally (Thorpe, 1972).

Let us now turn to the fifth characteristic of biologically triggered behaviour, 'Direct teaching and intensive practice have relatively little effect.' In activities such as typing or playing tennis, a person's achievement is often directly related to the amount of teaching he receives and the hours of practice he puts in. Even people who are not 'naturally' superb athletes can sometimes win tennis tournaments through sheer hard work and good coaching. But the same is not true of language, where direct teaching seems to be a failure. Let us consider the evidence for this.

When one says that 'direct teaching is failure', people smile and say, 'Of course – whoever tries to *teach* a child to speak?' Yet many parents, often without realizing it, try to persuade their children to imitate them. They do this in two ways: firstly, by means of overt correction, secondly, by means of unconscious 'expansions'.

The pointlessness of overt correction has been noted by numerous researchers. One psychologist attempted over a period of several weeks to persuade his daughter to say OTHER + noun instead of OTHER ONE + noun. The interchanges went somewhat as follows:

Child: WANT OTHER ONE SPOON, DADDY.
Father: YOU MEAN, YOU WANT THE OTHER SPOON.
Child: YES, I WANT OTHER ONE SPOON, PLEASE DADDY.
Father: CAN YOU SAY 'THE OTHER SPOON'?
Child: OTHER . . . ONE . . . SPOON.
Father: SAY 'OTHER'.
Child: OTHER.
Father: 'SPOON.'
Child: SPOON.
Father: 'OTHER SPOON.'
Child: OTHER . . . SPOON. NOW GIVE ME OTHER ONE SPOON?

(Braine, 1971:161)

Another researcher tried vainly to coax a child into saying the past tense form HELD:

Child: MY TEACHER HOLDED THE BABY RABBITS AND WE PATTED THEM.

Adult: DID YOU SAY YOUR TEACHER HELD THE BABY RABBITS?
Child: YES.
Adult: WHAT DID YOU SAY SHE DID?
Child: SHE HOLDED THE BABY RABBITS AND WE PATTED THEM.
Adult: DID YOU SAY SHE HELD THEM TIGHTLY?
Child: NO, SHE HOLDED THEM LOOSELY.

(Cazden, 1972:92)

So forcing children to imitate is a dismal failure. Children cannot be trained like parrots. Equally unsuccessful is the second type of coaching often unconsciously adopted by parents – the use of 'expansions'. When talking to a child an adult continuously 'expands' the youngster's utterances. If the child says, THERE GO ONE, a mother is likely to expand this to 'Yes, there goes one.' MOMMY EGGNOG becomes 'Mommy had her eggnog', and THROW DADDY is expanded to 'Throw it to Daddy'. Children are exposed to an enormous number of these expansions. They account for perhaps a third of parental responses. Roger Brown notes: 'The mothers of Adam and Eve responded to the speech of their children with expansions about 30 per cent of the time. We did it ourselves when we talked with the children. Indeed, we found it very difficult to withold expansions. A reduced or incomplete English sentence seems to constrain the English-speaking adult to expand it into the nearest properly formed complete sentence' (Brown and Bellugi, 1964:144). At first researchers were uncertain about the role of expansions. Then Courtney Cazden carried out an ingenious experiment using two groups of children, all under three and a half (Cazden, 1972). She exposed one group to intensive and deliberate expansions, and the other group to well-formed sentences which were *not* expansions. For example, if a child said, DOG BARK, an expanding adult would say, 'Yes, the dog is barking.' An adult who replied with a non-expanded sentence might say 'Yes, he's trying to frighten the cat' or 'Yes, but he won't bite', or 'Yes, tell him to be quiet'. After three months the rate of progress of each group was measured. Amazingly, the expansion group were *less advanced* than the other group, both in average length of utterance and grammatical complexity.

Several explanations of this unexpected result have been put forward. Perhaps adults misinterpret the child's intended meaning when they expand. Erroneous expansions could hinder his learning. Several 'wrong' expansions have been noted. For example:

Child: WHAT TIME IT IS?
Adult: UH HUH, IT TELLS WHAT TIME IT IS.

Alternatively, a certain degree of novelty may be needed in order to capture a child's attention, since he may not listen to apparent repetitions of his own utterances. Or it may be that expansions over-restrict the data the child hears. His speech may be impoverished because of an insufficiently rich verbal environment. As we noted earlier, the child *needs* copious and varied samples of speech.

The last two explanations seem to be supported by a Russian experiment (Pines, 1969:165). One group of infants was shown a doll, and three phrases were repeatedly uttered, 'Here is a doll . . . Take the doll . . . Give me the doll.' Another group of infants was shown the doll, but instead, *thirty* different phrases were uttered, such as 'Rock the doll . . . Look for the doll.' The total number of words heard by both groups was the same, only the composition differed. Then the experimenters showed the children a selection of toys, and asked them to pick out the dolls. To their surprise, the children in the second group, the ones who had heard a richer variety of speech, were considerably better at this task.

This suggests that parents who consciously try to 'coach' their children by simplifying and repeating may be actually *interfering* with their progress. It does not pay to talk to children as if one was telling a foreign tourist how to get to the zoo. Language that is impoverished is harder to learn, not simpler. Children appear to be naturally 'set' to extract a grammar for themselves, provided they have sufficient data at their disposal. Direct teaching is irrelevant, and those who get on best are those who are exposed to a rich variety of language – in other words, those whose parents talk to them in a normal way.

But what does 'talk in a normal way' mean? Before we go on to discuss the role of practice, this is perhaps the best place to clear up a misunderstanding which seems to have originated with Chomsky. He claims that what children hear 'consists to a large extent of utterances that break rules, since a good deal of normal speech consists of false starts, disconnected phrases and other deviations' (Chomsky, 1967:441). Certainly, children are likely to hear *some* deviant sentences. But recent research indicates that the speech children are exposed to is not particularly sub-standard. Adults tend to speak in shorter sentences and make fewer mistakes when they address children. There is a considerable difference between the way a mother talks to another adult, and the way she talks to her child. One researcher recorded a mother talking to an adult friend. Her sentences were on average fourteen to fifteen words long, and she used several polysyllabic medical terms:

'I was on a inhalation series routine. We wen' aroun' from ward to ward. People are, y'know, that get all this mucus in their chest, and it's very important to breathe properly an' to be able to cough this mucus up and out an' through your chest, y'know as soon as possible. And we couldn't sterilize the instruments 'cause they were plastic.'

But when she spoke to her child the same mother used five- or six-word sentences. The words were shorter, and referred to things the child could see or do:

COME LOOK AT MOMMA'S COLORIN' BOOK.
YOU WANNA SEE MY COLORING BOOK?
LOOK AT MY COLORING BOOK.
LOOKIT, THAT'S AN INDIAN, HUH?
IS THAT AN INDIAN?
CAN YOU SAY INDIAN?
TALK TO ME.
(Drach, quoted in Ervin-Tripp, 1971)

It seems that parents automatically simplify both the content and syntax when they talk to children. This is not particularly surprising – after all, we do not address bus conductors and boy friends in the same way. The use of language appropriate to the circumstances is a normal part of a human's language ability.

Let us now return to the question of practice. What is being claimed here is that practice alone cannot account for language acquisition. Children do not learn language simply by repetition and imitation. Two types of evidence support this view.

The first concerns the development of 'inflections' or word endings. English has a number of very common verbs which have an 'irregular' past tense form (e.g. CAME, SAW, WENT,) as opposed to the 'regular' forms such as LOVED, WORKED, PLAYED. It also has a number of irregular plurals such as FEET and MICE, as well as the far more numerous plurals ending in -s such as CATS, GIRAFFES and PYTHONS. Quite early on, children learn correct past tense and plural forms for common words such as CAME, SAW and FEET. Later, they abandon these correct forms and replace them with overgeneralized 'regular' forms such as COMED, SEED and FOOTS (Ervin, 1964). The significance of this apparent regression is immense. It means that language acquisition cannot possibly be a straightforward case of 'practice makes perfect' or of simple imitation. If it were, children would never replace common forms such as CAME and SAW, which they hear and use all the time, with odd forms such as COMED, SEED and FOOTS which they are unlikely to have come across.

The second type of practice which turns out to be unimportant for language acquisition is spontaneous imitation. Just as adults subconsciously imitate and expand their children's utterances, so children appear to imitate and 'reduce' sentences uttered by their parents. If an adult says 'I shall take an umbrella', a child is likely to say TAKE 'RELLA. Or 'Put the strap under her chin' is likely to be repeated and reduced to STRAP CHIN. At first sight, it looks as if this might be an important mechanism in the development of language. But Susan Ervin of the University of California at Berkeley came to the opposite conclusion when she recorded the spontaneous utterances of a small group of toddlers (Ervin, 1964). To her surprise she found that when a child spontaneously imitates an adult, her imitations are not any more advanced than her normal speech. She shortens the adult utterance to fit in with her current average length of sentence and includes the same number of endings and 'little' words as in her non-imitated utterances. Not a single child produced imitations which were more advanced. And one child, Holly, actually produced imitations that were less complex than her spontaneous sentences! Susan Ervin notes: 'There is not a shred of evidence supporting a view that progress toward adult norms of grammar arises merely from practice in overt imitation of adult sentences' (Ervin, 1964:172).

We may conclude, then, that mere practice – in the sense of direct repetition and imitation – does not affect the acquisition of language in a significant way. However, we must be careful that such a statement does not lead to misunderstandings. What is being said is that practice alone cannot account for language acquisition: children do not learn merely by constant repetition of items. In another sense, they do need to 'practice' talking but even this requirement is not as extensive as might be expected. They can learn a surprising amount by just listening. It has been shown that the amount of talking a child needs to do in order to learn language varies considerably. Some children seem to speak very little. Others are constantly chattering, and playing with words. One researcher wrote a whole book on the pre-sleep monologues of her first child

Anthony, who murmured paradigms to himself as he prepared for sleep:

GO FOR GLASSES
GO FOR THEM
GO TO THE TOP
GO THROW
GO FOR BLOUSE
PANTS
GO FOR SHOES.
    (Weir, 1962)

To her disappointment, her second child David, was nowhere near as talkative although he eventually learned to speak just as well. These repetitious murmurs do not seem to be essential for all children.

So far, then, we have considered five of the six characteristics of biologically triggered behaviour which we listed at the beginning of this chapter. All these features seem to be present in language. We now come to the sixth and final feature, 'There is a regular sequence of "milestones" as the behaviour develops, and these can usually be correlated with age and other aspects of development.' We shall deal with this in a section by itself.

The pre-ordained programme

All children seem to pass through a series of more or less fixed 'stages' as they acquire language. The age at which different children reach each stage or 'milestone' varies considerably, but the relative chronology remains the same. The milestones are always reached in the same order, though they may be nearer together for some children and farther apart for others.

Consequently, we can divide language development up into a number of approximate phases. The diagram overleaf is highly oversimplified. The stages overlap, and the ages given are only a very rough guide – but it does give some idea of a child's likely progress.

In order to illustrate this progression we shall describe the successive phases which a typical (and non-existent) English child is likely to go through as she learns to speak. Let us call this child *Barbara* – a name derived from the Greek word for 'foreigner' and meaning literally 'someone who says bar-bar, who talks gibberish'.

Language Stage	Beginning Age
CRYING	Birth
COOING	6 weeks
BABBLING	6 months
INTONATION PATTERNS	8 months
1-WORD UTTERANCES	1 year
2-WORD UTTERANCES	18 months
WORD INFLECTIONS	2 years
QUESTIONS, NEGATIVES	2¼ years
RARE OR COMPLEX CONSTRUCTIONS	5 years
MATURE SPEECH	10 years

Barbara's first recognizable vocal activity was *crying*. During the first four weeks of her life, she was truly:

> An infant crying in the night:
> An infant crying for the light:
> And with no language but a cry.
>
> (Tennyson)

A number of different types of cry could be detected. She cried with hunger when she wanted to be fed. She cried with pain, when she had a tummy ache, and she cried with pleasure when she was fed, comfortable and lying in her mother's arms. However, strictly speaking, it is perhaps inaccurate to speak of crying as a 'language phase', because crying seems to be instinctive communication and may be more like an animal call system than a true language. This seems to be confirmed by recent work which suggests that the different 'messages' contained in the crying of babies may be universal, since English parents could identify the 'messages' of Italian and Spanish babies as easily as those of English babies (Ricks, reported in Cromer, 1974). So although crying may help to strengthen the lungs and vocal cords (both of which are needed for speech), crying itself perhaps should not be regarded as part of true language development.

Barbara then passed through two reasonably distinct pre-language phases, a *cooing* phase and a *babbling* phase. Early researchers confused these stages and sometimes likened them to birdsong. The nineteenth-century scholar Taine noted of his daughter: 'She takes delight in her twitter like a bird, she seems to smile with joy over it, but as yet it is only the twittering of a bird, for she attaches no meaning to the sounds she utters' (Taine, 1877, cited in Bar-Adon and Leopold, 1971:21).

The first of these two phases, *cooing*, began when Barbara was approximately six weeks old. To a casual observer, she sounded as if she was saying, GOO GOO. But cooing is difficult to describe. Some textbooks call it 'gurgling' or 'mewing'. The sound is superficially vowel-like, but the tracings produced on a sound spectogram show that it is quite unlike the vowels produced by adults. Cooing seems to be universal. It may be the vocal equivalent of arm and leg waving. That is, just as babies automatically strengthen their muscles by kicking their legs and moving their arms about, so cooing may help them to gain control over their vocal apparatus.

Gradually, consonant type sounds become interspersed in the cooing. By around six months, Barbara had reached the *babbling* stage. She gave the impression of uttering consonants and vowels together, at first as single syllables – but later strung together. The consonants were often made with the lips, or the teeth, so that the sequences sounded like MAMA, DIDIDI, or PAPAPA. On hearing these sounds, Barbara's parents confidently but wrongly assumed that she was addressing them. Such wishful thinking accounts for the fact that MAMA, PAPA and DADA are found as nursery words for mother and father all over the world (Jakobson, 1962). Barbara soon learned that a cry of MAMA meant immediate attention – though she often used it to mean, 'I am hungry' rather than to refer to a parent. This phenomenon has been noted by numerous researchers. Charles Darwin, for example, remarked that at the age of one year his son 'made the great step forward of inventing a word for food, namely, *mum* but what led him to it I did not discover' (Darwin, 1877, cited in Bar-Adon and Leopold, 1971:28). Another investigator observed that his child called MAMA as a request for a piece of bread being buttered by himself, the father.

Throughout the babbling period Barbara seemed to enjoy experimenting with her mouth and tongue. She not only babbled, she blew bubbles, gurgled and spluttered. Superficially, she appeared to be uttering an enormous variety of exotic sounds. At one time, researchers wrongly assumed that children are naturally capable of producing every possible speech sound. A Canadian psychologist once commented: 'During this period that peculiarly charming infantile babble begins which, though only an "awkward twittering", yet contains in rudimentary form nearly all the sounds which afterwards by combination, yield the potent instrument of speech. A wonderful variety of sounds, some of which afterwards give the child difficulty when he tries to produce them, are now produced automatically, by purely impulsive exercise of the vocal muscles' (Tracy, 1909, cited in Bar-Adon and Leopold, 1971:32). More recent investigators have noted that the variety of sounds used in babbling is not particularly great. But because the child does not yet have complete control over his vocal organs, the noises are often unlike adult sounds, and seem exotic to an untrained observer. In general, babbling seems to be a period when a child experiments and gradually gains muscular control over his vocal organs. Many people claim that babbling is universal. But there are a few puzzling records of children who did not babble, which provide problems for this point of view. All we can say at the moment is that babbling is sufficiently widespread to be regarded as a normal stage of development.

Some investigators have tried to compare babbling babies who have been exposed to different languages. Preliminary reports suggest that Chinese babbles are distinguishable from American, Russian and Arabic ones (Weir, 1966). Because Chinese is a language which distinguishes words by means of a change in 'tone' or 'pitch', Chinese babies tend to produce monosyllabic utterances with much tonal variation. American babies produce polysyllabic babbles with intonation spread over the whole sequence. The non-tone babies sound superficially similar – though American mothers could often pick out the American baby, Russians the Russian baby, and Arabs the Arab baby. But the mothers could not distinguish between the babies babbling the other two languages. This research supports the notion of a 'babbling drift', in which a child's babbling gradually moves in the direction of the sounds he hears around him. In this respect babbling is clearly distinct from crying, which has no discernable relationship with any one language.

A question which perhaps should be asked at this stage is the following: how much can children actually distinguish of their parents speech? It is sometimes assumed that babies hear merely a general mish-mash of sound, and only gradually notice the difference between say P and B. However, recent research indicates that infants are capable of discriminating a lot more than we realize. Eimas and his colleagues (1971), for example, have shown that babies between one and four months old *can* distinguish between P and B. They started by playing a repeated B sound to selected infants. Then they switched to P. A clear change in the babies' sucking behaviour showed that they had noticed the alteration. So even though infants may not listen carefully to everything their parents say, they may well be *capable* of hearing it clearly from a very young age. These results of Eimas are still regarded as controversial – but several other researchers have come to the conclusion that a child's perception may be much sharper than had previously been supposed (e.g. Smith, 1973; Drachmann, 1973).

Simultaneously with babbling, and from around eight or nine months, Barbara began to imitate *intonation patterns*. These made her output sound so like speech that her mother sometimes said, 'I'm sure she's talking, I just can't catch what she's saying.' An eighteenth-century German researcher observed of this stage: 'He attempted also to imitate conversations, to which end he produced a profusion of incomprehensible sounds' (Tiedemann, 1782, cited in Bar-Adon and Leopold, 1971:15). English mothers have noted that their children often use a 'question' intonation, with a rise in tone at the end of the sentence. This may be due to a normal parent's tendency to bend over the child, asking, 'What are you trying to say then?' 'Do you want some milk?' 'Do you know who this is?' and so on.

Somewhere between one year and eighteen months Barbara began to utter *single words*. She continued to babble as well, though her babbling gradually diminished as true language developed. The number of single words acquired at around this time varies from child to child. Some have only four or five, others have almost fifty. As an average child Barbara acquired around fifteen. Many of them were names of people and things, such as UF, (woof) 'dog', DABA 'grandma', DA 'doll'. Then as she neared her second birthday, she reached the more impressive *two-word stage*.

From the time Barbara started to put words together she seemed to be in a state of 'language readiness', and mopped up language like a sponge. The most noticeable feature of this process was a dramatic increase in her vocabulary. By the time she was two and a half years old, she knew several hundred words. Meanwhile, there was a gradual but steady increase in her average or mean length of utterance – usually abbreviated to MLU. MLU is calculated in terms of grammatical items or 'morphemes': plural -s and past tense -D, for example, each count as one item and so do ordinary words such as MUMMY and BATH. Compound words such as BIRTHDAY and QUACK-QUACK also count as a single item (Brown, 1973:54).

Most (but not all) researchers accept this as a useful gauge of progress – though the child with the longest utterances does not necessarily have the most grammatically advanced, or even the most grammatically correct utterances.

The fact that a steady increase in MLU occurs from the age of around two onwards has been shown by Roger Brown of Harvard University, who carried out a detailed study of the speech development of three unacquainted children, Adam, Eve and Sarah – though he found that the chronological age at which different children reached an MLU stage differed considerably (Brown, Cazden and Bellugi, 1968; Brown, 1973). A comparison of Adam and Eve showed that Eve outstripped Adam by far. Eve's MLU was two items at around twenty months, three at twenty-two months and four at twenty-eight months. Adam was over twenty-six months old before he achieved an MLU of two items. He was nearly three years old before his MLU reached three items and three and a half before it reached four items – a whole year behind Eve.

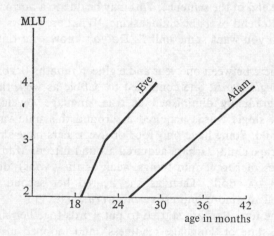

If we assume that Barbara is not as advanced as Eve, but ahead of Adam, she possibly had an MLU of two items a little before her second birthday, an MLU of three items at two and a half, and four items around her third birthday.

In the early part of the two-word stage, when she was around two years old, Barbara's speech was 'telegraphic'. She sounded as if she was sending urgent telegrams to her mother: WANT MILK, WHERE DUCK? As in a real telegram, she tended to preserve the nouns and verbs in the correct order, but omitted the 'little' words such as THE, A, MY, HIS, AND. She also left out word endings, such as the plural -S or past tense -D, as in TWO SHOE and MILK SPILL.

Then, gradually, the 'little' words and *inflections* were added. 'All these, like an intricate sort of ivy, begin to grow up between and upon the major construction blocks, the nouns and verbs' (Brown, 1973:249).

In this aspect of language, Barbara is following exactly the same path of development as the Harvard child Adam, but at a slightly earlier age (Brown, 1973:271). Between the ages of two and three and a half, Barbara acquired the following grammatical forms:

Age 2	Progressive –ING	I SINGING
	Plural –S	BLUE SHOES
	Copula AM, IS, ARE	HE IS ASLEEP
	Articles A, THE	HE IS A DOCTOR
Age 3	3rd person singular –S	HE WANTS AN APPLE
	Past tense –D	I HELPED MUMMY
	Full progressive AM, IS, ARE + –ING	I AM SINGING
	Shortened copula	HE'S A DOCTOR
	Shortened progressive	I'M SINGING

The actual age at which Barbara acquired each form is not significant because it varies widely from child to child. What is important and interesting is the order in which each form appeared. The sequence seems to be almost identical among all English-speaking children. Roger Brown notes that in the unacquainted Harvard children, the developmental order of these grammatical forms was 'amazingly consistent'. There were one or two minor variations: Sarah, for example, acquired the progressive -ING after the plural, whereas Adam and Eve acquired it before. But in all the children, both the progressive -ING and the plural -S occurred before the past tense, the third person singular -S, and the copula AM, IS, ARE.

Perhaps even more surprising, is the fact that in all the Harvard children the copula AM, IS, ARE as in I AM A DOCTOR developed before AM, IS, ARE when it was part of the progressive construction, e.g. I AM SINGING. And the shortened copula as in HE'S A BEAR came before the shortened progressive, e.g. HE'S WALKING. This is really quite an astonishing discovery. Although we might expect children to go through similar general lines of development, there seems to be no obvious reason why a variety of English children should correspond so closely in their acquisition of specific items. Possible reasons for this phenomenon will be discussed in Chapter 7.

A similar consistency of order is found in the acquisition of more complicated constructions, such as *questions* and *negatives*. For example, in the acquisition of WH-questions (questions beginning with WHAT, WHY, WHERE, WHO, etc), we can safely assume that Barbara, like Adam, Eve and Sarah, went through three intermediate stages before she acquired them perfectly (Klima and Bellugi, 1966). First of all, soon after her second birthday, she placed the WH- word in front of the rest of the sentence:

WHAT	MUMMY DOING?
WHY	YOU SINGING?
WHERE	DADDY GO?

A second stage occurred three or four months later when she added an auxiliary verb such as CAN or WILL to the main verb:

WHERE	YOU	WILL GO?
WHY	KITTY	CAN'T SEE?
WHY	YOU	DON'T KNOW?

Finally, before she was three, she realized that the subject noun must change places with the auxiliary and produced correct sentences such as:

WHERE	WILL YOU	GO?
WHY	CAN'T KITTY	SEE?
WHY	DON'T YOU	KNOW?

Once again, the rather surprising finding that all English children follow the same pattern will be discussed later. As already noted, the actual *age* at which each stage is reached is irrelevant. It is the order which matters.

By the age of three and a half, Barbara, like most children, was able to form most grammatical constructions – and her speech was reasonably intelligible to strangers. Her constructions were, however, less varied than those of an adult. For example, she tended not to use the 'full' passive such as THE MAN WAS HIT BY A BUS. But she was able to converse quite adequately on most topics.

By five, she gave the superficial impression of having acquired language more or less perfectly. But this was an illusion. Language acquisition was still continuing, though more slowly. The grammar of a child of five differs to a perhaps surprising degree from adult grammar. But the five-year-old is not usually aware of his shortcomings. In comprehension tests, children readily assign interpretations to the structures presented to them – but they are often the wrong ones. 'They do not, as they see it, fail to understand our sentences. They understand them, but they understand them wrongly' (Carole Chomsky, 1969:2). To demonstrate this point, the researcher (Chomsky's wife) showed a group of five- to eight-year-olds a blindfolded doll, and said: 'Is this doll hard to see or easy to see?' All the five- and six-year-olds said, HARD TO SEE, and so did some of the seven- and eight-year-olds. The response of six-year-old Lisa was typical:

Chomsky: IS THIS DOLL EASY TO SEE OR HARD TO SEE?
Lisa: HARD TO SEE.
Chomsky: WILL YOU MAKE HER EASY TO SEE?
Lisa: IF I CAN GET THIS UNTIED.
Chomsky: WILL YOU EXPLAIN WHY SHE WAS HARD TO SEE?
Lisa: (to doll) BECAUSE YOU HAD A BLINDFOLD OVER YOUR EYES.

Some psychologists have criticized this particular test. A child sometimes believes, ostrich-fashion, that if his own eyes are covered, others will not be able to see him. And he may be partly switching to the doll's viewpoint when he says a blindfolded doll is hard to see. But a re-run of this experiment using wolf and duck puppets, and sentences such as

THE WOLF IS HARD TO BITE.
THE DUCK IS ANXIOUS TO BITE.

confirmed the original results (Cromer, 1970). Children of five and six just do not realize that pairs of sentences such as THE RABBIT IS NICE TO EAT and THE RABBIT IS EAGER TO EAT have completely different underlying meanings.

But the discrepancies gradually disappeared over the next four or five years. By the age of ten, Barbara exhibited a command of the structure of her language comparable to that of an adult. At the age of puberty, her language development was essentially complete.

She would continue to add individual vocabulary items all her life, but her grammatical rules were unlikely to change except in trivial respects. The 'critical period' set by nature for the acquisition of language was over.

We must now briefly consider how closely the language milestones we have been discussing are linked to physical and cognitive development. Clearly, there is no essential correlation between langauge and motor development, since there are numerous examples of children who learn to talk, but never walk, and vice versa. However, researchers are agreed that in normal children the two often go together. Language milestones are often loosely linked to physical milestones. For example, the gradual change of cooing to babbling occurs around the time an infant begins to sit up. A child utters single words just before he starts to walk. Grammar becomes complex as hand and finger co-ordination develops.

The language milestones also seem to be linked to cognitive development, though experts disagree over the tightness of the link. In one rather obvious sense, language follows cognitive development: 'If a child is able to use the word *dog* to refer to dogs, it follows that he must have the concept of "dog" ... it is tautological that linguistic development presupposes cognitive development in the uninteresting sense that one cannot express a concept that one doesn't have' (Fodor, Bever and Garrett, 1974:463).

But beyond this there have been some attempts to establish a much closer link between the two. In particular, some psychologists have argued that the different stages of cognitive growth proposed by the Genevan psychologist Jean Piaget are important for language acquisition. For example, it has been suggested that the development of comparative constructions (e.g. I AM BIGGER THAN YOU) does not occur until a child has reached a stage at which she can recognize that a pint of milk remains the same whether it is poured into a long thin container or a short fat one (Sinclair-de-Zwart, 1969). At the moment, this claim is unproven. All we can safely say is that there is a tendency for cognitive development and language acquisition to keep in step with one another. We do not yet know whether the connection is essential. Clearly, this is an interesting field in which more work needs to be done.

Let us now summarize our conclusions. In this chapter we have shown that language seems to have all the characteristics of biologically programmed behaviour. It emerges before it is needed, and its emergence cannot be accounted for either by an external event, or by a sudden decision taken by the child. There is a 'critical period' set aside by nature for its acquisition, and direct teaching and intensive practice have relatively little effect. Language acquisition follows a regular sequence of milestones in its development, which can be loosely correlated with other aspects of the child's development. In other words, there is an internal mechanism both to trigger it off and to regulate it.

However, it would be wrong to think of language as something which is governed *only* by internal mechanisms. These mechanisms require external stimulation in order to work properly. The child needs a rich verbal environment during the critical acquisition period.

This suggests that the so-called nature–nurture controversy mentioned in Chapter 1 may be misconceived. Both sides are right: nature triggers off the behaviour, and lays down the framework, but careful nurture is needed for it to reach its full potential. The dividing line between 'natural' and 'nurtured' behaviour is by no means as clear-cut as was once thought. In other words, language is 'natural' behaviour – but it still has to be carefully 'nurtured' in order to reach its full potential.

But, although we have now shed considerable light on the problem of innateness, we have not yet begun to answer the crucial question, exactly *what* is innate? We noted in Chapter 1 that Chomsky argued in favour of postulating a 'rich internal structure'. What in his opinion does this structure consist of? This is the topic considered in the next chapter.

5 The Blueprint In The Brain

What grammatical information might conceivably be innate?

There are very deep and restrictive principles that determine the nature of human language and are rooted in the specific character of the human mind.

Chomsky
Language and Mind

It is relatively easy to show that humans are innately predisposed to acquire language. The hard part is finding out exactly *what* is innate. People have indulged in speculation about this for centuries. Over two thousand years ago the Egyptian king Psammetichus had a theory that if a child was isolated from human speech, the first word he spontaneously uttered would come from the world's oldest inhabitants. Naturally he hoped this would be Egyptian. He gave instructions for two new-born children to be brought up in total isolation. When eventually the children uttered the word BEKOS, Psammetichus discovered to his dismay that this was the Phrygian word for 'bread'. He reluctantly concluded that the Phrygians were more ancient than the Egyptians.

Nobody takes Psammetichus's theory seriously today – especially as the few reliable accounts we have of children brought up without human contact indicate that they were totally without speech when they were found. The famous French boy Victor of Aveyron, who was discovered naked rooting for acorns in the Caune woods in 1797, did not speak Phrygian or any other language. He merely grunted like an animal.

Although the speculations of Psammetichus can safely be ignored, the ideas of Noam Chomsky on the topic of innateness must be taken seriously. As we have already noted, he claims that for language acquisition to be possible, a child must be endowed with a 'rich internal structure', and the biological evidence examined in the last two chapters is consistent with his claim. But what exactly does

Chomsky regard as innate? In his words, 'What are the initial assumptions concerning the nature of language that the child brings to language learning, and how detailed and specific is the innate schema?' (Chomsky, 1965:27).

In this chapter we will outline the ideas put forward by Chomsky in his linguistic classic *Aspects of the Theory of Syntax*, published in 1965.

Chomsky's ideas on innateness

Chomsky does not regard his proposals on the matter of innateness as definitive. He considers that he can, at the moment, make only outline suggestions. 'For the present we cannot come at all close to making a hypothesis that is rich, detailed and specific enough to account for the fact of language acquisition' (1965:27). Nevertheless, Chomsky's ideas are specific enough to be interesting – even if they are, in his own judgement, incomplete.

Chomsky starts out with the basic assumption that anybody who acquires a language is not just learning an accumulation of random utterances but a set of 'rules' or underlying principles for forming speech patterns: 'The person who has acquired knowledge of a language has internalized a system of rules that relate sound and meaning in a particular way' (Chomsky, 1972a:26). It is these 'rules' which enable a speaker to produce an indefinite number of novel utterances, rather than straight repetitions of old ones. As we saw in Chapter 1, an essential characteristic of language is its 'creativity' – people do not just run through a repertoire of stereotyped phrases when they speak. Instead, they are continually producing novel utterances such as 'My baby swallowed four ladybirds', or 'Serendipity upsets me'. But where do the rules come from? How do speakers discover them? Somehow, children have to construct their own set of rules from the jumble of speech they hear going on around them. This is a formidable task. Chomsky points out that children are to some extent in the same situation as a linguist faced with an unknown language. Both child and linguist are surrounded by a superficially unintelligible confusion of sound which they must somehow sort out.

So let us first consider how a *linguist* deals with this unknown language situation. She possibly starts by finding simple sound sequences which refer to single objects, such as TREE, NOSE, CONGER EEL. But this stage is not particularly interesting from a syntactic point of view. Learning off lists of vocabulary items is a relatively simple task, as is clear from the ease with which the chimps Sarah and Washoe managed to do this. In addition, Genie, the Californian teenager who is learning language after the 'critical period', finds the acquisition of vocabulary easy – it is the grammatical rules which are slowing her down. For a linguist working on an exotic language, the interesting stage is likely to come when she starts to notice recurring syntactic patterns among the data. As soon as she has found some, she begins to make guesses or *hypotheses* concerning the principles which underlie the patterns. For example, suppose she repeatedly finds the utterances WOKKI SNIZZIT, WOKKI UGGIT and WOKKI SNIFFIT. She might hazard, as a first guess that the sequence WOKKI always has to be followed by a sequence which ends in -IT. But if, later, she finds utterances such as LIKKIT WOKKI and UKKING WOKKI, she would have to abandon her original, over-simple theory, and form a new, more complex hypothesis to account for the fresh data. She continues this process of forming hypotheses, testing them, then abandoning them when they prove inadequate until, ideally, she has compiled a set of rules which can account for all the possible sequences of the language she is studying.

A child, according to Chomsky, is constructing an internalized grammar in the same way. He looks for regularities in the speech he hears going on around him, then makes guesses as to the rules which underlie the patterns. His first guess will be a simple one. His second amended hypothesis will be more complex, his third, more elaborate still. Gradually his mental grammar will become more sophisticated. Eventually his internalized rules will cover all the possible utterances of his language. Fodor (1966:109) describes the situation clearly: 'Like the scientist, the child finds himself with a finite body of observations, some of which are almost certain to be unsystematic. His problem is to discover regularities in these data that, at the very least, can be relied upon to hold however much additional data is added. Characteristically the extrapolation takes the form of the construction of a theory that simultaneously marks the systematic similarities among the data at various levels of abstraction, permits the rejection of some of the observational data as unsystematic, and automatically provides a general charac-terization of the possible future observations.'

If this hypothesis-testing view of language acquisition is correct, a child must be endowed with an innate *hypothesis-making device* which enables him, like a miniature scientist, to construct increasingly complex hypotheses:

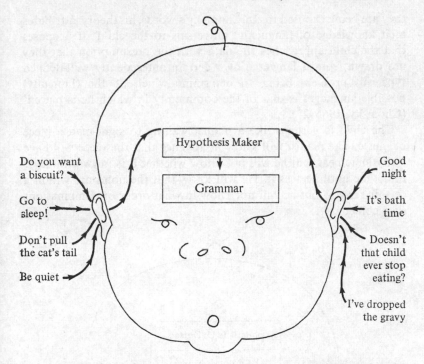

Do you want a biscuit?

Go to sleep!

Don't pull the cat's tail

Be quiet

Hypothesis Maker

Grammar

Good night

It's bath time

Doesn't that child ever stop eating?

I've dropped the gravy

However, there are a number of differences between a linguist working on an unknown language, and a child acquiring language for the first time. The linguist has considerably more help at his disposal. He can say to a native speaker of the language he is working on, 'Does LEGLESS DADDY-LONG-LEGS make sense?' 'Is ATE UP IT grammatical?' 'Is PLAYING CARDS ambiguous?' and so on. The child cannot do this. Yet the amazing fact remains: it is the child who acquires the complete grammar. No linguist has ever written a perfect grammar of any language. This suggests that by itself, an internal hypothesis-making device is not sufficient to account for the acquisition of language. The child must have rather more information at his disposal. It cannot be information about any particular language because babies learn all languages with equal ease. A Chinese baby brought up in England will learn English as easily as an English baby in China will learn Chinese. The wired-in knowledge must therefore, says Chomsky, consist of *language universals*. Children learn language so fast and so efficiently because they 'know' in outline what languages look like. They know what is, and what is not, a possible language. All they have to discover is *which* language they are being exposed to. In Chomsky's words, his theory 'attributes tacit knowledge of [linguistic] universals to the child. It proposes that the child approaches the data with the presumption that they are drawn from a language of a certain antecedently well-defined type, his problem being to determine which of the (humanly) possible languages is that of the community in which he is placed' (Chomsky, 1965:27).

The child is perhaps like a pianist waiting to sight-read a piece of music. The pianist will know in advance that the piece will have a rhythmic beat, but he will not know whether it is in two, three or four time until he sees it. He will know that the notes are within a certain range – but he will not know in what order or combinations they come.

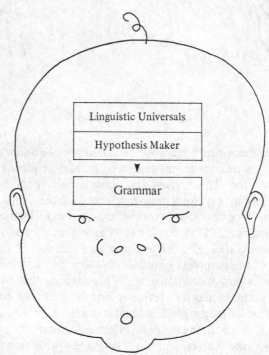

But it is not very satisfactory to speak airily of 'innate linguistic universals'. What *are* these shadowy phenomena?

Language universals, Chomsky suggests (1965), are of two basic types, *substantive* and *formal*. Substantive universals represent the fundamental 'building blocks' of language, the substance out of which it is made, while formal universals are concerned with the form or shape of a grammar. An analogy might make this distinction clearer. If, hypothetically, Eskimos were born with an innate knowledge of igloo-building they would have *two* kinds of knowledge. On the one hand they would know in advance that the *substance* out of which igloos are made is ice and snow, just as thrushes automatically know that their nests are made of twigs, not bricks or worms or glass. On the other hand, their innate knowledge of igloo-building would include the information that igloos are round in *shape*, not square or diamond-shaped or sausage-like, just as thrushes instinctively build round nests, not ones shaped like bathtubs.

To return to the substantive universals of human language, a child might know instinctively the possible set of sounds to be found in speech. He would automatically reject sneezes, belches, hand-clapping and foot-stamping as possible sounds, but accept B, O, G, L, and so on. He would dismiss PGPGPG as a possible word, but accept POG, PIG, PEG or PAG.

But the idea of *substantive* universals is not particularly new. For a long time linguists have assumed that all languages have nouns, verbs and sentences, even though the exact definition of these terms is in dispute. And for a long time linguists have been trying to identify a 'universal phonetic alphabet' which 'defines the set of possible signals from which the signals of a particular language are drawn' (Chomsky, 1972a:121). Such a notion is not very surprising, since humans all possess similar vocal organs. More revolutionary, and therefore more interesting, are the *formal* universals proposed by Chomsky. These, we noted, are concerned with the form or shape of a grammar, including the way in which the different parts relate to one another.

According to Chomsky, children would 'know' in advance how their internalized grammar must be organized. It must have a set of *phonological* rules for characterizing sound patterns, and a set of *semantic* rules for dealing with meaning, linked by a set of *syntactic rules* dealing with word arrangement.

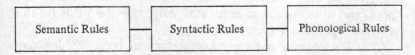

| Semantic Rules | Syntactic Rules | Phonological Rules |

Furthermore, children would instinctively realize that in its rules language makes use of *structure-dependent* operations. This, as we noted earlier (Chapters 1 and 2), involves at least two types of knowledge: firstly, an understanding of hierarchical structure – the notion that several words can fill the same slot as one:

Cows	EAT	GRASS
LARGE BROWN COWS	HAVE EATEN UP	THE GRASS

secondly, a realization that each slot functions as a unit which can be moved around:

3	2	1

THE GRASS	HAS BEEN EATEN UP	BY LARGE BROWN COWS

However, this is an over-simplification. In this case, the original sentence has *not* just been rearranged (and *been* and *by* added) because mere rearrangement (and *been* and *by* addition) would result in *THE GRASS HAVE BEEN EATEN UP BY LARGE BROWN COWS. Observations of this type have led Chomsky to an interesting and controversial conclusion. He maintains that what has been rearranged is *not* the surface sentence LARGE BROWN COWS HAVE EATEN UP THE GRASS, but a 'deeper', more abstract form of the sentence in which the subject and object are clearly distinguished but which is not yet either active or passive. It is a neutral form somewhere between the two (though it may seem to be nearer one than the other). This underlying abstract form can be 'transformed' into either the active by the application of a rule which makes the verb HAVE 'agree' with COWS, or into the passive by switching round the subject and the object, inserting *been* and *by*, followed by the application of a verb agreement transformation in which the verb HAVE is made to 'agree' with the new subject GRASS. In the diagram of these sentences facing, a simplified deep structure has been given in the form of a so-called 'tree-diagram'. Note that, somewhat counterintuitively, linguists' trees grow upside down, with their branches spreading out at the bottom. The basic NP (noun-phrase)–VP (verb-phrase) division represents the traditional 'subject' and 'predicate' distinction, e.g. BIRDS/FLY. After this the VP is (in this sentence) split into V (verb) and NP.

Chomsky assumes that every sentence has an 'inner' hidden *deep structure* and an outer manifest *surface structure*. This is a simple and elegant way of accounting for the relationship between sentence pairs such as active and passive. Other reasons behind the assumption

Deep Structure (simplified)

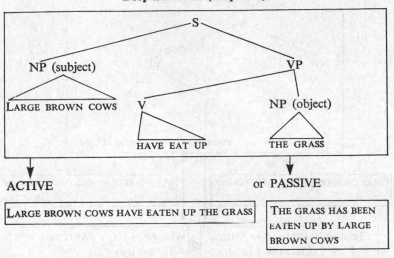

ACTIVE   or PASSIVE

LARGE BROWN COWS HAVE EATEN UP THE GRASS	THE GRASS HAS BEEN EATEN UP BY LARGE BROWN COWS

that every sentence has both an underlying and a manifest structure were mentioned in Chapter 1. (More arguments exist, but they are too technical to be included in this book.) The two levels of structure are linked by rules known as *transformations*. Chomsky notes that: 'The grammar of English will generate, for each sentence, a deep structure, and will contain rules showing how this deep structure is related to a surface structure. The rules expressing the relation of deep and surface structure are called "grammatical transformations" ' (Chomsky, 1972a: 166).

According to this view, several sentences which are quite different on the surface can be related to *one* deep structure. The four sentences:

> CHARLES CAPTURED A HEFFALUMP.
> A HEFFALUMP WAS CAPTURED BY CHARLES.
> IT WAS A HEFFALUMP WHICH CHARLES CAPTURED.
> WHAT CHARLES CAPTURED WAS A HEFFALUMP.

are all related to a similar underlying structure (see first diagram, p. 98).

Alternatively, different deep structures can undergo transformations which make them similar on the surface (see second diagram, p. 98).

Chomsky assumes that children somehow 'know' about deep structures, surface structures and transformations. They realize

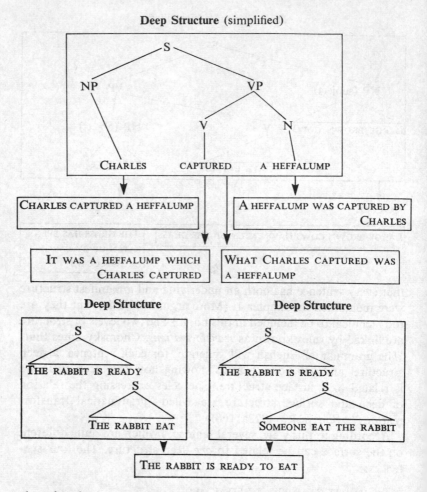

Deep Structure (simplified)

that they have to reconstruct for themselves deep structures which are *never* visible on the surface. He even makes the further controversial suggestion that deep or base structures may be the same for all languages: 'It may be that base structures can vary only very slightly from language to language' (Chomsky, 1972a:157) – though at the moment this 'universal deep structure' view is little more than speculation.

In addition, children would know that there were constraints on the ways in which deep structure can be altered by the transformational rules. Clearly, underlying structures cannot be randomly scrambled up, nor can items be haphazardly omitted or inserted.

There seem to be some rather precise conditions that govern the possibilities. Chomsky notes: 'The rules that manipulate deep structures seem to be drawn from a very narrow class of conceivable formal operations' (Chomsky, 1971:125).

For example, it seems likely that only 'meaningless' items can be inserted as extras. In English the word DO seems to be a meaningless sentence decoration or 'trapping':

Deep Structure

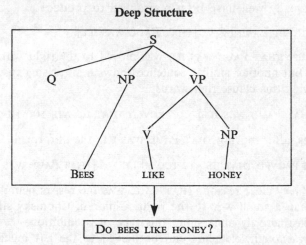

Similarly, only items which can be easily 'guessed' can be omitted:

Deep Structure

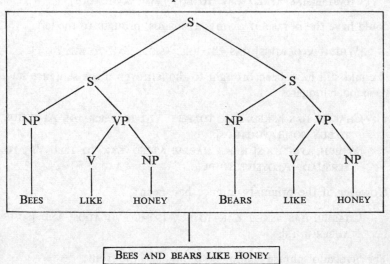

Children would be acquainted with these types of conditions without being told. In addition, they would understand some quite complex constraints on rearrangement possibilities. For example, there seems to be some type of 'natural' constraint on moving items to the right. The deep structure underlying a sentence such as:

[THAT PAUL WAS ILL]   UPSET LAVINIA

could equally well have been rearranged to produce

IT UPSET LAVINIA   [THAT PAUL WAS ILL].

The clause THAT PAUL WAS ILL was moved to the right with no ill effects. But another similar sentence shows a surprising restriction on moving this clause rightwards:

[THAT PAUL WAS ILL]   PROVED THAT HE ATE TOO MUCH

becomes, after moving THAT PAUL WAS ILL, the ill-formed

*IT PROVED THAT HE ATE TOO MUCH   [THAT PAUL WAS ILL].

For no very clear reason, THAT PAUL WAS ILL resists being moved more than a small way to the right. Children, Chomsky suggests, might instinctively understand this type of prohibition.

Oddly enough, elements can be moved to the left much more freely. A sentence such as:

CHARLIE HAS ASKED ZAK TO BUY [SOME AVOCADOS]

could have the phrase involving 'avocados' brought to the left:

[WHICH AVOCADOS] HAS CHARLIE ASKED ZAK TO BUY?

It could still have been brought to the left even if the sentence had been much longer:

CHARLIE HAS ASKED ZAK TO TELL VIC TO PERSUADE ALOYSIUS TO BUY [SOME AVOCADOS].
[WHICH AVOCADOS] HAS CHARLIE ASKED ZAK TO TELL VIC TO PERSUADE ALOYSIUS TO BUY?

However, if the original sentence had been:

CHARLIE HAS ASKED ZAK TO BUY [SOME AVOCADOS] AND [SOME AUBERGINES].

The 'avocado' phrase cannot be brought to the front:

*[WHICH AVOCADOS] HAS CHARLIE ASKED ZAK TO BUY AND [SOME AUBERGINES]?

Children may automatically know that if two things are joined together in this way, one alone cannot be separated out and brought to the front.

Another type of information which might be available to the child are some general principles of rule ordering. A sentence which has very different deep and surface structures might have a dozen or more rules to relate them. A child might 'know' in advance some principles which would shortcut the need for testing the order of application.

To summarize so far: Chomsky considers that children are endowed with an innate hypothesis-making device, which enables them to make increasingly complex theories about the rules which will account for the language they hear going on around them. In making these hypotheses, children are guided by an inbuilt knowledge of language universals. These provide a 'blueprint' for language, so that the child knows in outline what a possible language looks like. This involves, firstly, information about the 'building blocks' of language, such as the set of possible sounds. Secondly, it entails information about the way in which the components of a grammar are related to one another, and restrictions on the form of the rules. In particular, Chomsky assumes that children automatically know that language involves two levels of syntax – a deep and a surface level, linked by 'transformations'. With this help a child can speedily sift through the babble of speech he hears around him, the so-called 'primary linguistic data' and hypothesize plausible rules which will account for it.

But another problem arises. There may be *more than one* possible set of rules which will fit the data. How does a child choose between them? To take a simple, make-believe example, suppose a child had heard the following words:

MI-GOL 'cheese'	NO-POL 'octopus'
MI-KAN 'milk'	NO-BAN 'eel'
MI-GAG 'yoghurt'	NO-PAP 'crab'
NO-PAT 'butter'	NO-PIT 'shark'

He might then search for patterns underlying the use of the prefixes MI- and NO-. He would perhaps hypothesize that 'all dairy products except butter begin with MI-, and all fish begin with NO-'.

However, a simpler and better hypothesis, since it does not leave any exceptions, would be one which said 'MI- occurs if the next sound is G or K, and NO- occurs if the next sound is P or B'. But how can we be sure that the child will pick the *better* of the two possibilities? And on a larger scale how do we know that a child will not get the whole grammar wrong? Perhaps 'wrong' is too strong a word, because the innate universals already mentioned should guarantee that the child's internal grammar is to some extent 'right'. But it could still be grossly inefficient, if the child picked a number of over-complicated hypotheses to explain the data. In other words, a child is faced not only with the task of constructing rules for himself, but also of choosing between perhaps several alternative grammars. 'The problem is that of discovering which of the infinitely many grammars that satisfy universal constraints on the form and content of linguistic rules is the best one for the language from which the corpus is drawn' (Fodor, Bever and Garrett, 1974:472).

To cope with this problem, Chomsky suggests, children must in addition be equipped with an *evaluation* procedure which will allow them to choose between a number of possible grammars – that is, children must have some kind of mechanism (whose details are far from clear) which enables them to 'weigh up' one grammar against another, and discard the less efficient. At the moment this is perhaps the least satisfactory of Chomsky's proposals concerning innateness. Many psycholinguists regard it as wishful thinking. For all we know, some people *may* have grossly inefficient internal grammars.

According to Chomsky, then, these three elements – a hypothesis-making device, linguistic universals, and an evaluation procedure – constitute an innately endowed Language Acquisition Device (LAD) or Language Acquisition System (LAS), (LAD for boys and LAS for girls, as one linguist facetiously remarked). With the aid of LAD any child can learn any language with relative ease – and without such an endowment language acquisition would be impossible.

This rich innate scheme contrasts strongly with the point of view popularly held earlier in the century that children are born with 'blank sheets' as far as language is concerned. Consequently, some people consider Chomsky to be new-fangled and daring, someone who has set out to shock the world with outrageous and novel proposals. But Chomsky denies this. He points out that he is follow-ing in the footsteps of eighteenth-century 'rationalist' philosophers, who believe in the existence of 'innate ideas'. Such philosophers held that 'beyond the peripheral processing mechanisms, there are

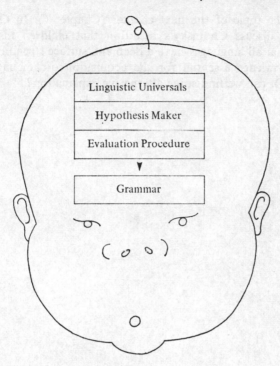

innate ideas and principles of various kinds that determine the form of the acquired knowledge in what may be a rather restricted and highly organised way' (Chomsky, 1965:48). Descartes, for example, suggested that when a child sees a triangle, the imperfect triangle before his eyes immediately reminds him of a true triangle, since we already possess within us the idea of a true triangle.

However, a discussion of philosophical predecessors is not particularly relevant. The important question is, is Chomsky right? His proposals are not necessarily an 'all-or-nothing' package deal. He may be right in some respects and wrong in others, so his suggestions can be looked at one by one. First of all, is Chomsky correct in assuming that a child acquiring a language is internalizing a set of rules? And that he is making successive hypotheses to account for the data that he hears? In other words, are children's utterances structured? Or are early attempts at talking merely clumsy efforts to copy adult speech, with words juxtaposed at random? This is the easiest of Chomsky's suggestions to test, and will be the topic of the next chapter (Chapter 6). In Chapter 7, we shall discuss Chomsky's assertion that children instinctively 'know' that all languages have a deep and surface structure. Is such prior knowledge essential for the acquisition of language, as he claims? Or can we find some alternative explanation?

6 Chattering Children

Are children following 'rules' when they learn to speak?

They can't talk straight
Any more than they can walk straight.
Their pronunciation is awful
And their grammar is flawful
> Ogden Nash
> *It must be the milk*

According to Ogden Nash, the behaviour of children and drunks is equally confusing. Linguists would perhaps agree with him. Listening to infants speaking is like being in topsy-turvy land. The problems of children faced with adult language sometimes seem trivial to a linguist who is trying to decipher infant burbles. But far worse than the problem of decipherment is the difficulty of interpreting the utterances. One writer remarked that writing about the acquisition of language 'is somewhat like the problem of reconstructing a dinosaur while the bones are still being excavated. It can happen that after you have connected what you earnestly believe are the hind legs you find that they are the jaw bones' (McNeill, 1970:vii).

Consequently, before we consider the main topic of this chapter – whether children's utterances are structured, and whether Chomsky is correct in suggesting that children are making successive hypotheses about the rules which underlie the speech they hear around them – we must outline some of the problems of interpretation which arise when linguists attempt to analyse child language. We shall do this by considering one-word utterances.

Ba, qua, ha and other one-word utterances

One-word utterances present a microcosm of the difficulties faced by linguists examining child language. Consider the following situation. Suppose a child says BA when she is in the bath, again says BA when given a mug of milk, and also says BA to the kitchen taps. How are we to interpret this? There are at least four possible explanations.

The simplest possibility is that the child is simply naming the objects to prove she knows them, but has over-generalized the word BA. That is, she has learnt the name for BA for 'bath' and has wrongly assumed that it can apply to anything which contains liquid. A typical example of this type of over-generalization was noted by one harassed mother in a letter to the London *Evening Standard*: 'My baby is Moon-struck. She saw the moon in the sky at six o'clock last week and ever since she's gaped at the sky shouting for the moon. Now she thinks anything that shines is the moon; street lamps, headlights, even the reflected light bulb in the window. All I hear is yells about the moon all day. I love my baby but I'm so ashamed. How does one get patience?'

However, this plain over-generalization interpretation may be too simple a view of what is happening when the child says BA. An alternative explanation has been proposed by the famous Russian psychologist Vygotsky (1893–1934). He suggests that when children over-generalize they do so in a quite confusing way. They appear to focus attention on one aspect of an object at a time. One much-quoted example concerns a child who uses the word QUA to refer to a duck, milk, a coin, and a teddy bear's eye (Vygotsky, 1962:70). QUA 'quack' was, originally a duck on a pond. Then the child incorporated the pond into the meaning, and by focussing attention

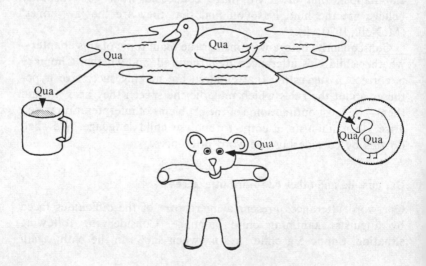

on the liquid element, QUA was generalized to milk. But the duck was not forgotten, since QUA was used to refer to a coin with an eagle on it. Then, with the coin in mind, the child applied QUA to any round coin-like object, such as a teddy bear's eye. Vygotsky calls this phenomenon a 'chain complex' because a chain of items is formed, all linked by the same name. If he is correct, then in the case of BA, we can suggest that the child originally meant 'bath'. Then, by focussing her attention on the liquid element she generalized the word to 'milk'. Meanwhile, remembering the bath taps, she used BA to mean 'kitchen taps'.

Yet even Vygotsky's 'chain complex' interpretation seems over-simple in the view of some researchers. A third, and less obvious, point of view is that of David McNeill, a psychologist at the University of Chicago. He has argued that one-word utterances show a linguistic sophistication which goes far beyond the actual sound spoken. He claims that the child is not merely involved in naming exercises, but is uttering holophrases, single words which stand for whole sentences. For example, BA might mean 'I am in my bath' or 'Mummy's fallen in the bath'. He justifies his viewpoint by claiming that misuse of words shows evidence of grammatical relationships which the child understands, but cannot yet express. For example, a one-year-old child said HA when something hot was in front of her. A month later she said HA to an empty coffee cup and a turned-off stove. Why did she do this? McNeill suggests that 'by misusing the word the child showed that "hot" was not merely the label of hot objects but was also something said of objects that could be hot. It asserted a property' (McNeill, 1970:24). He also claims that the same child understood the notion of location because she pointed to the empty top of the refrigerator, where bananas were normally kept, and said NANA. He concludes that 'there is a constant emergence of new grammatical relations, even though no utterance is ever longer than one word' (McNeill, 1970: 23). So, McNeill might perhaps suggest that BA, when applied to kitchen taps and milk, showed an understanding of location: 'There are taps like this on the bath tub', 'There is liquid like this in the bath'.

McNeill's claim that children understand a wide variety of grammatical relationships and that one-word utterances are senten-ces in embryo seems, to many researchers, over-imaginative. How-ever, his ideas encapsulate a modicum of truth – the idea that single-word utterances may be more than mere labels. This idea has been examined by Lois Bloom a researcher at Columbia University, who has put forward yet another view of one-word utterances (Bloom, 1973). After a careful analysis of the single words spoken by her daughter Allison, she suggests that there is no simple answer to the problem of interpretation because the meaning of a one-word utterance varies according to the age of the child. For example, when Allison said MUMMY at the age of sixteen months, she seemed to mean, simply, 'That's Mummy'. But at the age of nineteen months she appeared to be trying to express some kind of interaction between Mummy and the surrounding environment, as when she pointed to her mother's cup and said, MUMMY.

However, Bloom was unable to tell exactly what kind of inter-action was intended. Did Allison mean 'That's Mummy's cup', or was she saying 'Mummy's drinking from a cup too'? Because of this intrinsic ambiguity, Bloom is cautious over assigning specific meanings to BA-type words which relate either to objects, or to interaction between objects. She is more optimistic about the interpretation of words such as NO, MORE and A'GONE in which 'conceptual notions are so conveniently tied to the actual words in the child's speech' (Bloom, 1973:140). For example, Allison showed by her use of the words NO and A'GONE that she could cope with the notion of non-existence. Bloom therefore concludes (perhaps not surprisingly) that single words are grammatically fairly uninteresting. Their importance lies in the light they throw on a child's conceptual representation of experience.

This brief excursus on one-word utterances has illustrated one important point: when the data is so confusing, it is no wonder that differences of opinion abound in child language studies. All researchers, to some extent, see what they want to see. This accounts for the extraordinarily diverse viewpoints which arise over apparently simple issues.

Having pointed out the type of problem that is likely to arise, we must now return to the main topic of this chapter, which is this: is Chomsky correct in viewing children as miniature scientists who are making successive hypotheses about the rules underlying the utterances they hear? In brief, do children have their own 'grammars' which differ from those of adults? Or are they merely making imperfect attempts to copy adult speakers? We shall examine this topic by looking firstly, at children's two-word utterances. Secondly, we shall consider how they deal with more complicated aspects of language such as word endings and negation.

Two-by-two

There are basically two ways of analysing two-word utterances. We may choose either the 'Let's pretend he's talking Martian' technique or the 'Let's guess what he's trying to say' method. In the first, the linguist approaches the child's speech as he would an unknown exotic language. Having freed his mind of preconceived notions connected with his knowledge of English, he writes a grammar based entirely on the word patterns he discerns in the child's speech. In the second method, the linguist tries to provide an interpretation of what the child is saying by using his knowledge of the language and by observing the situation in which the words were uttered.

In their earliest attempts at analysing two-word utterances, linguists followed the 'Let's pretend he's talking Martian' technique. Martin Braine (1963), of the University of California at Santa Barbara, listed all the two-word utterances produced by three two-year-olds, Steven, Gregory and Andrew. The results were superficially puzzling. There were a number of inexplicable sequences such as MORE TAXI, ALLGONE SHOE, ALLGONE STICKY, NO BED, BUNNY DO, IT DOGGIE. Such utterances could not be straight imitations, as it is unlikely that any adult ever said MORE TAXI, ALLGONE SHOE, or BUNNY DO. Anyway, straight imitation would put too great a strain on the child's memory. Braine counted over 2500 different combinations uttered by one child. Are these then just accidental juxtapositions? Apparently not. To his surprise, Braine noted that the combinations did *not* seem to be random. Certain words always occurred in a fixed place, and other words never occurred alone. Andrew, Steven and Gregory all seemed to be following definite, though primitive rules when they put two words together. They had two distinct classes of word in their speech. One class contained a small number of words such as ALLGONE, MORE, THIS, NO. These words occurred frequently, never alone, and in a fixed position. They are sometimes labelled *pivots*, because the utterance appears to pivot round them. The other class contained many more words which occurred less frequently, but in any position and sometimes alone. These words often coincided with adult nouns such as MILK, SHOE, BUNNY and so on. They are sometimes called *open*-class words, since an 'open' class is a set of words which can be added to indefinitely.

For example, Steven always used WANT, GET, THERE, IT as pivots in first position, and DO as a pivot in second position. His open class words included a wide variety of names such as BABY, CAR, MAMA, DADA, BALL, DOLL, BUNNY, HORSIE. Steven seemed to have internalized a rule which said, 'A sentence consists of *either* a type 1 pivot followed by an open word ($P^1 + O$), *or* an open word followed by a type 2 pivot ($O + P^2$)':

Pivot 1	Open
WANT	BABY
GET	BALL
THERE	BOOK
IT	DADDY

Open	Pivot 2
BUNNY	DO
DADDY	

Several other researchers who independently tried the exotic language technique confirmed this phenomenon by finding other children who formed word combinations in the same way as Andrew, Steven and Gregory (Brown and Fraser, 1964; Miller and Ervin, 1964). For a time, linguists were quite excited. They thought they might have discovered a universal first grammar, a so-called *pivot grammar*. But, alas, disillusion gradually crept in. One by one, researchers noted that a number of children do not fit into this simple pattern. Although all children showed strong preferences for placing certain words in a particular position in an utterance, these preferences were not always strong enough to be regarded as 'rules'. In addition, some children used so-called pivots such as MORE, NO, by themselves, which disagreed with Braine's finding that pivot words do not occur alone. And other children confused the picture by having pivot constructions as only a small portion of their total utterances.

Perhaps the biggest difficulty for pivot grammars is the appearance of utterances such as MUMMY SOCK, DADDY CAR, KITTY BALL, which occur in the speech of many children. Here two *open* class words seem to be juxtaposed, with no pivot in sight! Braine dismissed this problem by saying that $O + O$ constructions were a second stage, which occurred only *after* the $P + O$ and $O + P$ phase. But this does not seem to be true of all children. Of course, there is nothing wrong with stating that some youngsters make sentences which can be $P + O$, $O + P$ or $O + O$. It just does not tell us very much to say that, 'As well as pivot constructions, almost any other two words can occur together.' But even if such empty statements were acceptable, it is not necessarily correct to assume that $O + O$ utterances are random juxtapositions. There may be more reason behind them than appears at first sight, and the words may be related to one another in a highly structured way. It is quite inadequate to characterize a sentence such as DADDY CAR as O+O, since such a description cannot distinguish between several possible interpretations:

1. 'Daddy is washing the car.'
2. 'That's Daddy's car.'
3. 'Daddy is under the car.'

To summarize the achievements of pivot grammars, it seems that they are not as much use as was hoped a decade ago. They only describe the rules used by a small number of children – or perhaps, more accurately, they characterize only a small portion of the output of most children. If one used pivot grammars in order to answer the question 'Are two-word utterances structured?', the answer is 'Partially – children use pivot constructions but supplement them by apparently combining open class words at random'.

Disillusioned by the pivot grammars which resulted from the 'Let's pretend he's talking Martian' technique, linguists in recent years have tended to favour the second, 'Let's guess what he's trying to say' approach. This is more time-consuming, since researchers must note not just the utterances themselves, but also the accompanying actions. Luckily, what young children say usually relates directly to what they do and see. 'If an adult or an older child mounts a bicycle, there is no need for him to inform anyone who has seen him do it that he has done it. But a young child who mounts a tricycle will often "announce" the fact: *I ride trike!*' (Bloom, 1970:9).

The linguist who has made the most careful study of two-word utterances following this method is again Lois Bloom (1970). This work preceded her work on one-word utterances, and was completed before the birth of her own daughter Allison. She kept a careful account of the actions accompanying the utterances of three children, Kathryn, Eric and Gia, and has provided convincing interpretations of what they were trying to say. For example, it is quite clear what twenty-one-month-old Kathryn meant on the two occasions when she uttered the words MOMMY SOCK. The first time, she said it as she picked up her mother's sock, indicating that she meant 'This is Mummy's sock'. The second time was when her mother was putting Kathryn's sock on Kathryn, so Kathryn was saying 'Mummy is putting on my sock for me'. Two-year-old Gia said LAMB EAR apparently meaning 'That's the lamb's ear' when her mother pointed to the ear on a toy lamb, and said, 'What's this?' She said GIRL BALL when looking at a picture of a girl bouncing a ball, and presumably meant 'The girl is bouncing a ball'. She said FLY BLANKET when a fly settled on her blanket, probably meaning 'There is a fly on my blanket'.

There is a possible objection to these interpretations. Is Bloom not reading too much into these utterances? Perhaps Gia was just saying 'That is a lamb and an ear', 'That is a girl and a ball', 'That is a fly and a blanket'. Or perhaps she was just bringing up a 'topic' of conversation, and then making a 'comment' about it: 'I'm talking about a *fly*, and it has involved itself with my *blanket*', I'm referring to a *girl* who is connected with a *ball*'. This type of suggestion was first put forward in the mid-sixties to explain two-word utterances (Gruber, 1967). How can one eliminate these possibilities? The answer is, the highly consistent word order makes it unlikely that the sequences are random juxtapositions. Whenever Gia seemed to be expressing location she put the object she was locating first, and the location second: FLY BLANKET 'The fly is on the blanket', FLY BLOCK 'The fly is on the block', BLOCK BAG 'the block is in the bag'. When she referred to subjects and objects, she put the subject first, and the object second: GIRL BALL 'The girl is bouncing the ball', GIRL FISH 'The girl is playing with a fish'. And she expressed possession by putting the possessor first, the possession second: LAMB EAR 'That's the lamb's ear'. GIA BLUEYES 'That's Gia's doll, Blueyes'. If Gia was accidentally juxtaposing the words we would expect BLANKET FLY or EAR LAMB as often as FLY BLANKET or LAMB EAR. And the possessive sentences makes it highly unlikely that Gia was using a 'topic' and 'comment' construction. It would be most odd in the case of GIA BLUEYES to interpret it as 'I am talking about myself, Gia, and what I want to comment on is that I have a doll Blueyes'.

Of course, Gia is expressing these relationships of location, possession, and subject–object in the same order as they are found in adult speech. But the important point is that she seems to realize automatically that it is necessary to express relationships consistently in a way Washoe the chimp perhaps did not. She seems to *expect* language to consist of recurring patterns, and seems naturally disposed to look for regularities or rules. But before stating conclusively that Gia's utterances are rule-governed we must consider one puzzling exception. Why did Gia say BALLOON THROW as well as THROW BALLOON when she dropped a balloon as if throwing it? Why did she say BOOK READ as well as READ BOOK when she was looking at a book? Surely this is random juxtaposition of the type we have just claimed to be non-existent? A closer look at Gia's early utterances solves the mystery. In her earliest two-word sequences, Gia *always* said BALLOON THROW and BOOK READ. She had deduced wrongly that the names of people and objects precede action words. This accounts for 'correct' utterances such as GIRL WRITE and MUMMY BACK as well as 'mistakes' such as BALLOON THROW and SLIDE GO, when she placed some keys on a slide. Soon she began to have doubts about her original rule, and experimented, using first one form, then the other. Eventually, after a period of fluctuation, the verb–object relationship was acquired permanently as the correct THROW BALLOON, READ BOOK.

In conclusion, then, our answer to the question 'Are two-word utterances structured?' must be '*Yes*'. From the moment they place two words together (and possibly even before) children seem to realize that language is *rule governed*, not just a random conglomeration of words. They express each relationship consistently, so that, for example, in the actor–action relationship, the actor comes first, the action second as in MAMA COME, KITTY PLAY, KATHY GO. The only exceptions occur when a wrong rule has been deduced, leading to fluctuation. And from the beginning children are *creative* in their speech. They use combinations of words they have not heard before.

The obvious next question is: what happens in languages which do not have fixed word order? What do children do then? The answer is not yet clear. One researcher came to the conclusion that Russian children use a fixed word order even when adults do not (Slobin, 1966). But more recent reports have been contradictory, and researchers have noted considerable individual differences in the ways in which children learn different languages (Slobin, 1973). Clearly more research needs to be done.

Perhaps here we ought to mention another controversial topic. To what extent do two-word utterances represent an inbuilt linguistic knowledge of the properties of a sentence? When a child says WANT MILK, is he showing some kind of innate understanding of a verb–object relationship? This is the view of the psychologist David Mc-Neill (whose perhaps over-imaginative proposals concerning one-word utterances have already been discussed). McNeill has suggested that a knowledge of the underlying grammatical structure of a sentence is innate (McNeill, 1966; 1970). He considers that children 'automatically' understand at least the subject–predicate relationship (e.g. MUMMY SING), the verb–object relationship (e.g. WANT MILK), and the modifier–head relationship (e.g. PRETTY SOCK). After analysing all the 'pivot' sentences he could find in the literature, he claims that almost all of them fall into expressions of these three grammatical types. His theory is therefore not so much a denial of pivot grammars, as a re-interpretation of them.

However, more recent work has shifted away from McNeill's viewpoint. As one researcher notes, the assumption that children understand grammatical relationships in a way comparable to adults is 'an act of faith based only on our knowledge of the adult language' (Bowerman, 1973:187). What may be important in these early utterances is not so much the *grammatical* relationships between the words, as the underlying meanings which they express (Slobin, 1970; Wells, 1974). It has been found that children from quite different parts of the world say much the same thing at the two-word stage (see chart opposite).

The child possibly has an understanding of the concepts expressed – location, possession, desire, and so on – before he learns how to express them linguistically. This presents linguists with a problem. What kind of grammars should they write in order to capture the child's comprehension of these concepts? Meaning and syntax seem to be inextricably tied up in a way that cannot easily be unravelled. Worse still, it is not clear to what extent a child's understanding of language is in advance of his production. His underlying grammar or linguistic 'competence' may be far ahead of his 'performance' – what he actually says.

This has given rise to much discussion. Nobody is quite sure what to do about the problem. Should grammars be based above all on 'meaning', with the concepts expressed forming the framework of the grammar? This is a viewpoint which may now be gaining acceptance. Or should we lay down syntactic categories, based on our knowledge of the adult language? If we choose the former, then we have the problem of deciding how and when a child later shifts to using a syntactic framework which does not necessarily tie in with the conceptual one. If we choose the latter, then we may be assuming a grammatical sophistication which the child does not yet possess. So far the issue is still wide open. (Brown, 1973; Bloom, 1970; Schlesinger, 1971; Bowerman, 1973; Schaerlaekens, 1973, Bloom, Lightbown and Hood, 1975). Perhaps all we can say at the moment is that it seems important for both linguists and psychologists to help one another – and for this reason this is one of the most promising areas of psycholinguistics under discussion at the current time.

	English	German	Russian	Finnish	Samoan
Locate	THERE BOOK	BUCH DA 'book there'	TOSYA TAM 'Tosya there'	TUOSSA RINA 'there Rina'	KEITH LEA 'Keith there'
Negate	NO WASH	KAFFEE NEIN 'coffee no'	VODY NET 'water no'	EI SUSI 'not wolf'	LE 'AI 'not eat'
Indicate possession	MY SHOE	MEIN BALL 'my ball'	MAMI CHASHKA 'mama's cup'	TÄTI AUTO 'aunt's car'	LOLE A'U 'candy my'
Demand, Desire	WANT GUM	BITTE APFEL 'please apple'	YESCHË MOLOKO 'more milk'		
Modify, Qualify	PRETTY DRESS	MILCH HEISS 'milk hot'	PAPA BOL'SHOY 'papa big'	TORNI ISO 'tower big'	FA'ALI'I PEPE 'headstrong baby'
Question	WHERE BALL	WO BALL 'where ball'	GDE PAPA 'where papa'	MISSÄ PALLO 'where ball'	FEA PUNAFU 'where Punafu?'
Describe Event or Situation (*actor + action*)	BAMBI GO	PUPPE KOMMT 'doll comes'	MAMA PRUA 'mama walk'	SEPPO PUTOO 'Seppo fall'	PA'U PEPE 'fall doll'

(Examples from fuller lists in Slobin 1970: 178; 1971b: 44)

So far, then, we have shown that child language is rule-governed at the two-word stage in the sense that children express relationships such as actor–action, location and possession consistently. But we have not been able to show that these are essentially and primarily syntactic relationships that are being expressed. Consequently, in order to assess Chomsky's claim that children are making successive hypotheses about the grammatical rules of their language, we must look at later aspects of language acquisition – at the development of word endings and more complex constructions such as the rules for negation in English.

The case of the wug

This is a Wug

Now there is another one.
There are two of them.
There are two ......??

'Wugs', you should say, if you understand the rules which underlie English plurals. And that is the reply given almost unanimously by a group of children who were given this test. The researcher wanted to prove that they hadn't just memorized each plural as they heard it, but had an internalized rule which could apply even to words they had never heard (Berko, 1958).

And it wasn't just wugs the children coped with correctly, so no one could argue that they misunderstood the word as 'bugs'. Another picture showed a man standing on the ceiling, with the words: 'This is a man who knows how to bing. He is binging. He did the same thing yesterday. Yesterday he —'? 'Binged' said nearly all the children tested. Admittedly, they had higher results for words they already knew. More children got the plural of GLASS right than the plural of a nonsense word TASS (TASS and GLASS rhyme in American English, having the same vowel as the word MASS). But no one can doubt that they were applying rules which they had worked out for themselves.

An even more striking example of the child's internalized rules is the development of irregular verbs such as COME and CAME, GO and WENT, BREAK and BROKE. As noted in Chapter 4, children start by acquiring the correct *irregular* forms for the past tense, CAME, WENT, BROKE. Some of these are acquired fairly early, since they are very common words (Ervin, 1964; Slobin 1971a). One might suppose that practice makes perfect and these words would remain correctly formed. But not at all. As soon as children learn the *regular* past tense for words such as HELPED, PLAYED, WALKED and WASHED, they give up using the correct irregular form, and start using the over-generalized forms COMED, GOED, BREAKED. And when they re-acquire the irregular verbs, they first produce semi-regular forms which have a normal ending, as in LOST, LEFT (Slobin, 1971a). All this indicates that children have a strong tendency to look for and apply rules, at least as far as English noun and verb endings are concerned.

But it is perhaps not surprising that children are able to generalize plurals and past tenses. After all, word endings tend to rhyme. Children are known to have a fascination for rhymes, and they frequently make up little poems such as 'I am a bug, sitting on a rug, warm and snug, with my mug'. So the extension of an -s from BUGS, MUGS and RUGS to WUGS is not particularly startling.

What further evidence of 'rules' can we find? We can note that from the moment children place three or more words together, they show an instinctive awareness of *hierarchical structure*, the realization that several words can fill the same structural 'slot' as one:

THAT	FLOWER
THAT	A BLUE FLOWER

PUT	HAT	ON
PUT	THE RED HAT	ON

They also realize that each slot functions as a whole which can be moved around in certain constructions:

WHERE	THE RED HAT?	
THE RED HAT	LOST	
PUT	THE RED HAT	ON

In other words, they understand the structure-dependent nature of linguistic operations – the facet of language found so puzzling by our mythical man from Mars in Chapter 1.

However, the sentences just quoted look like ordinary adult ones with a few words left out. This means that we need more evidence to test Chomsky's assertion that children are operating with an internalized set of 'rules' which do not correspond to the adult ones. Several researchers have hunted for this evidence, and seem to have found it. Ursula Bellugi of Harvard University notes: 'We have found several periods where the child's sentences show systematic deviations from adult language, as if they were constructed according to a different set of rules' (Bellugi, 1971:95). She and Edward Klima analysed the development of negatives and interrogatives by studying the utterances produced by the now famous Harvard trio Adam, Eve and Sarah (Klima and Bellugi, 1966). As already noted in Chapter 4, the families of these children were totally unacquainted and independent of one another, and each child heard a different set of sentences as 'input'. Nevertheless, the children passed through surprisingly similar stages in their progress towards adult constructions. Each phase was characterized by regular 'rules' and the utterances could not be regarded merely as bad imitations of adult speech. The children seemed, just as Chomsky predicts, to be devising hypotheses to account for the regularities in the speech they heard around them. The development of negative sentences, outlined below, shows this clearly.

At first, Adam, Eve and Sarah seemed to be using a primitive rule, 'Put NO or NOT in front of the whole sentence.'

Neg	Sentence
No	WANT STAND HEAD
No	FRASER DRINK ALL TEA
No	PLAY THAT

But this rule did not last long. Next came the realization that the negative goes *inside* rather than in front of the sentence. The children devised a new rule which said, 'Put the negative *after* the first noun phrase and before the rest of the sentence.'

NP	Neg	Rest of sentence
HE	NO	BITE YOU
THAT	NO	MUMMY
I	CAN'T	CATCH YOU
I	DON'T	SIT ON CROMER COFFEE

At this stage, CAN'T and DON'T seemed to be treated as alternatives to NO. The children had not yet realized that they consist of *two* elements. To them, CAN'T and DON'T were single negative units which could be substituted for NO or NOT. However, this substitution was not completely free. Just as in correct adult speech you never find CAN–ING (e.g. *I CAN SINGING) or DON'T–ING (e.g. *I DON'T SMOKING) – so the children never said *I CAN'T CATCHING YOU or *I DON'T CRYING. They had grasped the fact that CAN'T and DON'T do not occur before verbs ending in –ING.

The next stage came when the children realized that CAN'T and DON'T contained two separate elements, CAN + NOT, DO + NOT. This was guaranteed by the fact that CAN and DO began to occur in the children's speech in non-negative sentences. This led to a more sophisticated negative rule in which the negative was placed in the *third* slot in a sentence, after the noun and auxiliary or copula and before the rest of the sentence.

NP	Aux (or Cop)	Neg	Rest of the sentence
PAUL	CAN	N'T	HAVE ONE
YOU	DO	N'T	WANT SOME SUPPER
I	DID	N'T	SPILLED IT
YOU	DID	N'T	CAUGHT ME
I	AM	NOT	A DOCTOR
THAT	WAS	NOT	ME

The difference between this and the standard adult rule is that the children had not yet realized that the tense need only be included once. A final stage occurred when the children amended sentences such as YOU DIDN'T CAUGHT ME to YOU DIDN'T CATCH ME.

So, independently, Adam, Eve and Sarah each went through similar intermediate stages in their acquisition of the negative:

1. Neg + Sentence NO WANT STAND HEAD
2. NP + Neg + VP HE NO BITE YOU
3. NP + Aux + Neg + Rest of Sentence I DID N'T CAUGHT IT

Each of these can be regarded as a hypothesis to account for the rules of negation in English.

The first is a simple hypothesis. The second is slightly less simple, and the third is almost the same rule as that used by adults. Klima and Bellugi are justified in their remark that 'It has seemed to us that the language of children has its own systemacity, and that the sentences are not just an imperfect copy of those of an adult' (Klima and Bellugi, 1966:191).

So Chomsky seems to be right in regarding the child as a miniature scientist who makes successive hypotheses to account for the data. But there is one major difference. When a scientist discards a hypothesis, he abandons it totally, and works only with the new one he is testing. Children do not behave like this. The stages do not follow one another cleanly and suddenly – they overlap quite considerably. As Klima and Bellugi note: 'A characteristic of child language is the residue of elements of previous systems' (Klima and Bellugi, 1966:194). For example, beside I AM NOT A DOCTOR, IT'S NOT COLD, and THAT WAS NOT ME, the children still produced sentences such as THIS NOT ICE CREAM, I NOT CRYING, PAUL NOT TIRED.

This type of fluctuation is noticeable in all aspects of child language. For example, Roger Brown notes, in the case of word endings, that children do not 'abruptly pass from total absence to reliable presence. There is always a considerable period, varying in length, in which production-where-required is probabilistic' (Brown, 1973:257). When he analysed the speech of the child Sarah he found extraordinary swings in her use of the suffix –ING. At the age of two years she used it correctly 50 per cent of the time in sentences such as I (AM) PLAYING. But six months later this had dropped to 20 per cent. One month after this it shot up to 80 per cent, then went down again to around 45 per cent. She was over three years old before –ING occurred steadily and correctly in all her utterances.

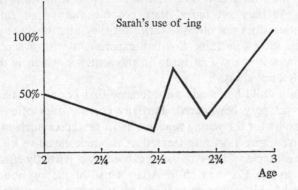

Sarah's use of -ing

And it is not only production of speech which fluctuates, but comprehension also. Richard Cromer tested children's understanding of constructions such as THE WOLF IS TASTY TO BITE, THE WOLF IS HAPPY TO BITE, THE DUCK IS HORRIBLE TO BITE. Using glove puppets of a wolf and a duck, he asked the subjects to show him who was biting whom. To his surprise he concluded that 'children may be very inconsistent in their answers from one day to the next' (Cromer, 1970:405).

What causes this baffling inconsistency? There may be more than one reason. Firstly, children make mistakes. Just as adults make grammatical errors such as DIDN'T YOU SAW BILL? instead of 'Didn't you see Bill'? or 'Didn't you say you saw Bill?' so do children. But this does not mean the utterances are random jumbles of words. The rules are there, despite lapses. A second reason for inconsistency may be selective attention. Children may choose to concentrate on one aspect of speech at a time. If Sarah is working out rules for plurals one month, she may ignore the –ING ending temporarily. As a schoolboy learning Latin said, 'If I get the verb endings right, you can't expect me to get the nouns right as well!'

However, mistakes and selective attention cannot account completely for the extreme fluctuations in Sarah's use of –ING. Linguists have realized that inconsistency is a normal transitional stage as children move from one hypothesis to the next. It seems to occur when a child has realized that his 'old' rule is wrong or partially wrong, and has formulated a new one, but remains confused as to the precise instances in which he should abandon his older primitive rule (Cromer, 1970). For example, Cromer suggests that when they hear sentences such as THE DUCK IS READY TO BITE, children start out with a rule which says 'The first noun in the sentence is doing the biting'. As they get older, they become aware that this simple assumption does not always work. But they are not quite sure why or when their rule fails. So they experiment with a second rule, 'Sometimes it is the first noun in the sentence which is doing the biting, but not always'.

When a child has made an inference that is only partially right, he can get very bewildered. Partially correct rules often produce right results for the wrong reasons, as in sentences such as I DON'T WANT IT, where DON'T is treated as a single negative element. A further example of the confusion caused by a partially effective rule is seen in the Harvard child Adam's use of the pronoun IT. He produced 'odd' sentences such as MUMMY GET IT LADDER, SAW IT BALL, alongside correct ones such as GET IT, PUT IT THERE. He appeared to be treating IT as parallel in behaviour to THAT which can occur either by itself, or attached to a noun: BRING ME THAT, BRING ME THAT BALL.

Bring me	*it*	*(ball)*
Bring me	*that*	*(ball)*

( ) Parentheses denote optional items.

But this was not the only wrong conclusion Adam reached. He also wrongly assumed that IT had an obligatory s when it occurred at the beginning of a sentence, so he produced IT'S FELL, IT'S HAS WHEELS, as well as superficially correct utterances such as IT'S BIG. Presumably this error arose because Adam's mother used a large number of sentences starting with IT'S . . ., IT'S RAINING, IT'S COLD, and so on. When Adam's 'funny' rules produced correct results half the time, it is not surprising that he took time deciding when to abandon them.

We must conclude, then, that children are not just copying adult utterances when they speak. They seem to be following grammatical rules they devised themselves, and which produce systematic divergences from the adult output. Chomsky appears to be substantially correct in attributing to children an innate hypothesis-forming device which enables them to form increasingly complex theories about the rules which underlie the language they are exposed to. Like scientists, children are constantly testing new hypotheses. But, as we have seen, the scientist metaphor falls down in one vital respect. Scientists, once they have discarded a hypothesis, forget about it and concentrate on a new one. Children, on the other hand, appear to go through periods of experimentation and indecision in which two or more hypotheses overlap and fluctuate: each rule wavers for a long time, perhaps months, before it is finally adopted or finally abandoned.

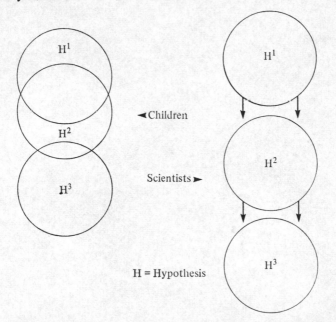

We can now summarize the main conclusions of this chapter.

In spite of difficulties connected with interpreting the data, we have seen that Chomsky is substantially correct when he assumes that children are 'wired' with an innate hypothesis-making device. They automatically 'know' that language is rule-governed, and they make a succession of hypotheses about the rules underlying the speech they hear around them. Chomsky's account falls down only in that he does not seem to take into consideration the fact that the hypotheses overlap and fluctuate in a way that the hypotheses of scientists do not. However, although we can see that children are following some type of rule even at the two-word stage, it is not clear how to encapsulate these rules in a grammar. Semantics and syntax seem to be entwined in quite complex ways, and the only hope of unravelling all this seems to be for psycholinguists of both types – linguistic and psychological – to co-operate in their research into the problem.

Meanwhile, we have not yet solved the problem of exactly *how* a child acquires his native language. In the next chapter, we consider whether Chomsky is right in his assumption that children make use of fairly specific outline facts which are somehow innate – or whether there are other ways of explaining language development.

7 Puzzling It Out

Exactly how do children learn language?

Teach your child to hold his tongue; he'll learn fast enough
to speak.

Benjamin Franklin

According to Chomsky, children learn language so efficiently and
so fast because they know in advance what languages look like. They
are wired, he argues, with an innate knowledge of language universals.

So far, it has not been very difficult to show that children have
some inkling of what languages are like. As we noted in the last
chapter, children seem to 'know' that language is rule-governed –
that a finite number of principles govern the enormous number of
utterances they hear going on around them. They also have an
instinctive awareness that languages are hierarchically structured –
the knowledge that several words can go in the same structural slot
as one. A child might say:

	I LOVE	TEDDY
or	I LOVE	MY TEDDY
or	I LOVE	MY OLD BLUE TEDDY

Furthermore, children realize that language makes use of operations
which are structure-dependent, so that each 'slot' in a sentence
functions as a unit which can be moved around, as in

WHERE	MY TEDDY?	
DON'T TAKE	MY TEDDY	AWAY
	MY TEDDY	HERE

However, an innate knowledge that language is rule-governed,
that it has a hierarchical structure, and that it makes use of structure-

dependent operations, combined with an inbuilt ability to make hypotheses about it, by no means explains the whole of language acquisition. In particular, we still need to know exactly *how* children develop language ability so efficiently. We would also like to find out *why* it is that English children follow such remarkably similar paths in the development of their language. These are mysteries which cannot just be swept aside with the vague explanation of 'innate programming'. We must investigate the matter more fully.

Content Cuthbert or Process Peggy?

Two types of explanation have been put forward to account for the mysterious nature of language acquisition. First of all, there is Chomsky's *content* approach. Secondly, an alternative *process* approach has been proposed. What is the difference between these two? Briefly, a content approach postulates that a child's brain naturally *contains* a considerable amount of specific information about language. A process approach, on the other hand, suggests that children have inbuilt puzzle-solving equipment which enables them to *process* the linguistic data they come across.

We have already outlined Chomsky's content proposals in Chapter 5. His most important claim is that children somehow 'know' that all sentences have a deep and surface structure, and that this knowledge enables them to infer abstract deep structures which are nowhere visible on the surface. He further claims that children somehow 'know' universal constraints on linguistic rules.

However, Chomsky's theory that children innately contain large chunks of specific information about language is disputed by a number of people. These researchers claim that, instead of possessing advance information, children are born with some sort of process mechanism which enables them to analyse linguistic data (Derwing, 1973; Slobin, 1971b). They suggest that 'the child's mind is somehow "set" in a predetermined way to process the sorts of structures which characterize human language. . . . That is not to say that the grammatical system itself is given as innate knowledge, but that the child has innate means of processing information and forming internal structures, and that when these capacities are applied to the speech he hears, he succeeds in constructing a grammar of his native language' (Slobin, 1971b:56).

The crucial point is this: is a child wired with a full set of linguistic universals, as Chomsky suggests? Or does he come equipped with

special techniques for performing linguistic analysis? Is his head
loaded with information? Or with puzzle-solving equipment? Are
we dealing with a 'Content Cuthbert' or a 'Process Peggy'?

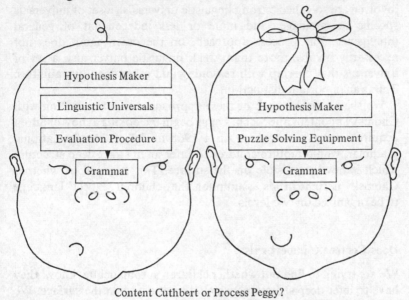

Content Cuthbert or Process Peggy?

In both the content and process approaches the child is likely to
end up with the same set of linguistic universals. But in the second
case they are the *result* of inbuilt analytic procedures. They are not
there at the beginning.

Because the end result may be the same in both cases, it is sometimes claimed that the two points of view are virtually indistinguish-
able, and should be regarded as two sides of one coin. Geoffrey
Sampson (1975:129), for example, has claimed that we are dealing
with 'a distinction without a difference'. He supports his argument
by suggesting that the development of language is in some sense
like the growth of teeth. 'I have thirty teeth, though I started life
with no teeth at all. Should I say that my genetic blueprint *contained*
a specification of (among other things) a set of thirty teeth, or rather
that my body was innately programmed to *process* the nourishment
that came my way from conception onwards in a way which caused
the growth of thirty teeth? Either way of speaking seems equally
appropriate; and to shift the discussion from acquisition of teeth
to acquisition of language does not make the process/content
distinction any more relevant.'

However, the two viewpoints are not as similar as Sampson suggests, because each approach implies different types of universals. Chomsky's content approach presupposes that the universals involved are so-called 'strong linguistic universals', a set of universals specific to language, and more or less independent of general intelligence. The process approach, on the other hand, does not necessarily involve more than 'weak linguistic universals', a set of universals that overlap with reasoning and other cognitive abilities. This is an important distinction.

We shall consider each of these approaches in turn, starting with Chomsky's content approach. Let us begin by looking at how children acquire constructions which, in a 1965 model of transformational grammar, would require children to infer an abstract deep structure which is nowhere visible on the surface. This may tell us whether Chomsky is right in his assumption that children 'expect' language to be organized on two levels.

Does Content Cuthbert exist?

We are trying to find out whether children automatically 'know' they have to infer deep structures which do not occur on the surface. We shall do this by examining three constructions in particular: the *progressive*, the *passive*, and *wh–question formation*. In order to acquire each of these, Chomsky claims that a child must first discover the deep structure.

First of all, let us consider the verb form known as the *progressive*. This describes an on-going action:

> POLLY IS SNORING
> ARTHUR IS WHISTLING.

It is a 'discontinuous' sandwich-like construction because the progressive sequence IS . . . ING is interpreted by the verb:

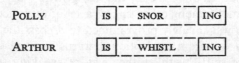

It is clear that IS . . . ING functions as a single unit, because when an on-going action is described we do not find one without the other. English does not have sentences such as

*POLLY IS SNORE

or   *ARTHUR WHISTLING.

Note, by the way, that the form IS, (AM, ARE) does not always occur joined to –ING in English. It occurs alone when it represents a so-called 'copula' or joining word, as in

HE IS A MENACE
I AM ILL.

However, when AM, (IS, ARE) is part of the progressive, it must always occur with an –ING which is attached to the verb.

In a 'classic' 1965 transformational grammar, IS . . . ING is presumed to be a single element in deep structure:

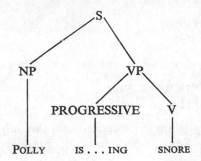

If this is a correct analysis, then in order to acquire progressives, a child must infer from the surface IS SNORING that the correct deep analysis of the string is IS . . . ING SNORE. In other words, if he meets a construction of the surface form

I X   J
IS SNOR – ING

he must be prepared to analyse it as

(I   J) (X)
IS–ING SNORE.

Fodor suggests that children may be 'naturally' programmed to recognize this type of sandwich construction. He proposes that 'the child comes to the language learning situation with the instruction that whenever he finds sets of terminals that satisfy the description IXJ one of the preferred hypotheses about their syntactic analysis is that their base structure contains (IJ) and that their transformational history contains the operation just c ted' (Fodor, 1966:16).

Is Fodor right when he proposes that the analysis of IXJ as (IJ) (X) is a 'preferred hypothesis'? In other words, do children find discontinuities easy to cope with? Let us look at how the Harvard children, Adam, Eve and Sarah, dealt with the progressive (Brown, 1973).

The Harvard children all used the –ING part of the progressive early. Both Adam and Eve acquired it earlier than any other ending. But they all omitted the IS (AM, ARE, etc) part:

WHAT COWBOY DOING?
WHY YOU SMILING?

There were two possible exceptions to this clear cut pattern: one child produced the sentences:

I'M TWIST HIS HEAD
I'M PLAY WITH IT.

But careful analysis showed that these sentences possibly meant:

I'M GOING TO TWIST HIS HEAD
I'M GOING TO PLAY WITH IT.

So these were not genuine exceptions and the only other inconsistency came from Adam, who once said, inexplicably:

DEY ARE STAND UP.

Apart from this, all three children omitted the IS, but inserted the –ING.

The full IS . . . ING construction appeared only after a long delay. In both Adam's and Sarah's speech, the gap was longer than twelve months. For a year, it seems, they just did not fully recognize the connection between the IS and the –ING. And there appears to be nothing inherently difficult about the phonetic forms AM, IS, ARE. This is shown by the fact that for all three children the copula IS (AM, ARE), as in

HE IS A COWBOY

occurred some time before AM, IS, ARE, in progressive constructions.

What conclusions can we draw from this? What we have discovered is that the recognition of IJ (IS . . . ING) as a discontinuous unit in a sequence IXJ (IS SINGING) is not a *preferred* analysis, but a last resort analysis. Adam, Eve and Sarah assigned –ING to the progressive early, but were baffled by the preceding IS. Far from expecting a deep structure that was different from the surface, they were thoroughly confused by this sandwich construction. Discontinuities seem to go against children's natural intuitions about what language is like. At least this seems to be the case in the Harvard study. Note, by the way, that we are not at the moment asking whather children acquire a Chomsky-like deep structure *after* they have developed the full progressive. The point being made is that children do not, so far, seem to be naturally geared to *looking for* two levels of structure.

The *passive* form presents similar difficulties for Chomsky's proposals. It is a construction acquired relatively late. Before the age of five or six, children tend to misinterpret passives as actives in the absence of contextual clues. For example,

THE VAN WAS BUMPED BY THE BUS

is likely to be interpreted as:

THE VAN BUMPED THE BUS.

But

THE VAN WAS DRIVEN BY THE POSTMAN

will possibly be interpreted correctly, because it is unlikely that vans drive postmen around (Slobin, 1966a). Children tend not to produce passives spontaneously, and they score low on tests which attempt to elicit the passive (Fraser, Bellugi and Brown, 1963; Hayhurst, 1967). However, this late development is not necessarily damaging to Chomsky's viewpoint. The passive occurs much less frequently than the active in normal English conversation, so it is not particularly surprising if children postpone the problem of coming to grips with it.

There are two types of passive sentence to take into consideration. Firstly, there are 'full' passives in which the agent or 'logical subject', the person who actually performed the action, is expressed, as in:

THE YETI WAS KNOCKED OVER BY A MAD SKIER.

Secondly, there are 'short' passives in which the agent is omitted as in

THE YETI WAS KNOCKED OVER.

If Chomsky is correct, and a deep structure which relates both the active and the passive has to be inferred, then we can make one crucial prediction. Passive sentences which are nearer to the underlying structure will occur first. This means that full passives with agents should develop earlier than short passives without agents, since the agent or 'logical subject' is always expressed in deep structure.

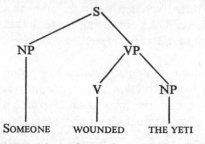

DEEP STRUCTURE (simplified) of

> SOMEONE WOUNDED THE YETI
> THE YETI WAS WOUNDED BY SOMEONE.

What is unfortunate for Chomsky's theory is that agentless passives actually occur first. Children produce sentences such as

> THE DOG WAS RUN OVER

before they say

> THE DOG WAS RUN OVER BY A BUS.

In other words, children learn 'short' passives as if they were dealing with a construction which is similar to a copula + adjective sequence (Hayhurst, 1967; Derwing, 1973; Watt, 1970):

Copula + Adjective	*Short Passive*
THE YETI WAS COLD	THE YETI WAS WOUNDED
THE YETI WAS DIRTY	THE YETI WAS KILLED

Passives with agents develop later, when the agent seems to be treated as an optional extra, parallel to other adverbial phrases which can be added to sentences:

THE YETI WAS CAUGHT	IN A TRAP
	BY A HUNTER
	LAST SATURDAY

There is no evidence at all that in order to acquire passive sentences children have to discover an abstract, underlying structure which relates them to actives. Actives and passives are learnt separately, and are related to one another at a later stage. To judge from the passive, it seems that during the period when children acquire the bulk of their language, they are not looking for deep structures. On the contrary, they seem to be happily oblivious of their possible existence.

The development of *wh-questions* (questions beginning with WHAT, WHO, WHY, etc) is also embarrassing to Chomsky's theory. All adults can relate a sentence such as

JEMIMA HAS BOUGHT A YAK

to the corresponding question

WHAT HAS JEMIMA BOUGHT?

According to Chomsky, these sentences are likely to be related to similar underlying structures:

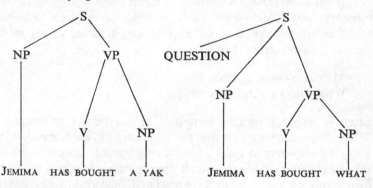

DEEP STRUCTURE (simplified) of

JEMIMA HAS BOUGHT A YAK
WHAT HAS JEMIMA BOUGHT?

If children had to infer deep structures, we would expect them to go through a stage in which they say:

JEMIMA HAS BOUGHT WHAT?

which is nearer the deep structure. But when we looked at the development of wh-questions in Chapter 4, we found no trace of such an intermediate stage. Children, from the very beginning, put the WH-word at the front:

WHAT COWBOY DOING?

It is true that they go through a second stage, which looks as if it is an intermediate phase between the deep structure and the surface sentence:

WHAT HE CAN RIDE ON?
WHY KITTY CAN'T STAND UP?

In these sentences, HE and CAN, and KITTY and CAN'T still need to be transposed to CAN HE, CAN'T KITTY. But this is flimsy evidence from which to conclude that the child has suddenly established a deep structure for himself. In fact, all the child may be doing is persisting in his original hypothesis, 'Questions are formed by putting a WH-word in front of the sentence', while at the same time adding the auxiliary CAN to his original sentence structure. In conclusion, there is no evidence that children relate questions to a Chomsky-like deep structure.

Perhaps here we need a word of warning about the ambiguity and looseness with which some authors speak of children 'acquiring transformations'. As soon as a child can manage to relate the following two sentences:

MY DINOSAUR ATE A JAM TART
WHAT DID MY DINOSAUR EAT?

Some authors say he has 'acquired the question transformation'. What they actually mean is that children can form questions. But it is only strictly correct to speak of 'acquiring transformations' if we can show that children have inferred a deep structure to which the trans-formations can apply. As we have tried to demonstrate, this is not the case. We have concluded that it is not necessary to infer deep struc-tures in order to be able to speak. Children grasp constructions such as passive and WH-questions by learning surface patterns, and how to manipulate them. It is still an open question whether at a later stage adults and older children have Chomsky-type deep structures. The acquisition of such underlying structures could occur months or even years later. They might do this 'by way of "inductive" inferences from an already acquired stock of surface structures. . . . The child learns at first only the surface structures which it can observe, and only subsequently he extrapolates from these to a more parsimoni-ous and effective set of rules' (Schlesinger, 1967:398).

In summary, Chomsky's assumption that a child looks at language expecting to find two levels of structure seems to be wrong. The child expects only regular, surface patterns. When he does not find these, he is puzzled, as in the case of progressives. After a long delay, he eventually realizes the existence of discontinuous elements. Furthermore, there is no evidence that in order to acquire passives and WH-questions the child necessarily acquires deep structures relating them. The child learns surface structures. Whether or not he *later* relates these surface structures to a Chomsky-like deep structure is a question which will be discussed in a later chapter.

How does Process Peggy work?

We have now rejected, in its extreme form, Chomsky's so-called content approach, the assumption that children are born containing large chunks of specific information about language universals. Let us now look at the alternative process approach, which suggests that instead of advance information about language, children have some sort of process mechanism which enables them to analyse and process linguistic data.

A process approach assumes that a child has a number of perhaps subconsciously applied 'strategies' or 'operating procedures', which he brings into play when he is learning to speak. An analogy might make this clearer. If an adult is asked to perform some type of mental task, he automatically thinks up 'strategies' or plans to help him achieve it. Suppose he is playing Kim's Game, the game in which you have to remember as many objects on a tray as you can. A possible strategy for this game might be the self-instruction, 'Use the biggest objects as landmarks'. The player might then mentally note that there is a milk bottle in the top left-hand corner, a grapefruit in the centre, and a hairbrush on the right. After that he might say to himself 'Remember the articles round the milk bottle going clockwise', then 'Remember the articles round the grapefruit going clockwise'. And so on, until he has memorized the whole tray. Children may subconsciously devise similar strategies for themselves in connection with language learning.

If such operating principles exist, what are they, and how do we find out about them? Unfortunately, we cannot ask children, 'How are you working it all out? How are you puzzling out a grammar?' Nevertheless, with a little ingenuity it is not impossible to discover which aspects of language a child finds difficult and which he finds easy. This can give clues to the ways in which a child is naturally pre-set to tackle language learning problems. There are three main methods. First of all, we can look at the order in which constructions are acquired, and see if we can notice any strategies behind this. Secondly, we can look at the kinds of mistakes children make. Thirdly, we can analyse the speech of bilingual children. Let us look at these methods more closely.

Looking at the order in which children acquire constructions is perhaps the least helpful of the three possibilities. It may not give us direct insight into a child's strategies. The order of acquisition could result from a number of other factors apart from linguistic complexity. One possibility is that it reflects the frequency with which the forms are uttered by the parents. Another is that it might indicate the cognitive complexity of the various ideas expressed. Several studies have tried to unravel these possibilities. Roger Brown looked at the acquisition of a number of grammatical endings and function words by the Harvard children, Adam, Eve and Sarah (1973), and a London University graduate student, Gisela Szagun, has recently done a study of the acquisition of tenses by English and German children (1975). Both of them tried to assess the relative importance to the order of acquisition of linguistic complexity, cognitive complexity, and frequency of parental usage.

Frequency seems the simplest factor to deal with. Both Brown and Szagun conclude, somewhat surprisingly, that the frequency with which the parents use various forms is not particularly important. Brown comments that although it is a truism that children do not develop constructions they do not normally hear, such as the full passive, he is 'prepared to conclude that frequency is not a significant variable' (Brown 1973:368). And Szagun records that the German children she studied all used the perfect tense (I HAVE COME) before the simple past (I WENT) – even though their parents showed a mild preference for the simple past.

The influence of the second factor, cognitive complexity, cannot be dismissed so quickly. It is not particularly easy to measure, so psycholinguists are uncertain how much stress to lay on it. However, it seems we cannot ignore its importance in connection with the acquisition of tenses. Children apparently start by using verb forms which describe a present, on-going action – that is, one that is true at the time of the utterance, such as MUMMY (IS) WASHING. They then move from this present-centred obsession to talk about the immediate past and the immediate future, e.g. IT SPILLED referring to a recently dropped mug of milk, and I'M GOING TO SMACK HIM, as the child walked across the room to smack the dog. Eve in Roger

Brown's study used HAFTA to express immediate intention, as in
I HAFTA EAT MY ICE CREAM and I HAFTA PEE-PEE JUST TO PASS THE
TIME AWAY. After the immediate past and future stage, children
gradually begin to talk about the more remote past and the
more remote future, as in

> WE LOCKED UNCLE DAVID OUT
> or DADDY CATCHED A MOUSE,

referring to an event which occurred days or weeks ago.

This moving-outwards approach to time seems to be reflected in
the form of the tenses used. It possibly explains why the –ING of the
present progressive occurs so early, and may also be why Szagun's
German children used the perfect before the superficially easier
simple past since the perfect in German often expresses a more recent
action.

Since certain aspects of language development such as the acquisition of tenses are clearly linked to cognitive development, some
psychologists have put forward an extreme viewpoint – that cognitive
development alone explains language acquisition. As children reach
each cognitive stage they feel a strong urge to express this in words.
But this approach is oversimple. Although cognitive development
perhaps explains why the present progressive (MUMMY (IS) WASH-
ING) occurs before the simple past (MUMMY WASHED), it does not
explain why English children at first say MUMMY WASHING rather
than MUMMY IS WASH, or even the full form, MUMMY IS WASHING.
It seems likely that linguistic factors are behind this phenomenon.

Can we then pinpoint any language learning strategies after we
have attempted to sift out other possible factors? Yes – we can make
tentative hypotheses about aspects of language acquisition which
cannot be accounted for by cognitive development. For example, we
can put forward five interdependent hypotheses to account for the
late development of the full progressive, and for the fact that progressive IS develops perhaps a year after the –ING. We can express
these hypotheses in the form of 'innate' self-instructions which a
child might subconsciously give himself as he attempts to analyse
linguistic data:

1. Allot one form only to each unit of meaning.
2. Linguistic units should not be interrupted.
3. Remember that the form of words may be consistently and
   meaningfully modified.

4. Pay attention to the ends of words.
5. Expect words to be modified by suffixes.

Of course, at the moment these are only hypotheses. But there seems to be additional evidence in their favour. For example, Instruction 2 (Linguistic units should not be interrupted) seems to be borne out by the way in which children develop relative clauses (clauses introduced by relative pronouns such as WHO, WHICH, THAT). Sentences in which a relative clause *interrupts* the main clause develop later than those in which the relative clause *follows* the main clause. For example, sentences of the type:

MUNGO SAW AN OCTOPUS [WHICH HAD 20 LEGS]

develop before those of the type:

THE OCTOPUS [WHICH HAD 20 LEGS] ESCAPED.

Moreover, if children are asked to repeat a sentence in which a main clause is interrupted by a relative clause, they tend to alter the sentence in order to avoid this happening. A child asked to repeat the sentence:

THE OWL [WHO EATS CANDY] RUNS FAST

repeated it as:

THE OWL EAT A CANDY AND HE RUN FAST
(Slobin and Welsh, 1967)

Similarly, Instruction 4 (Pay attention to the ends of words) seems to be subconsciously followed even when children are not dealing with specific inflectional endings. When English children confuse two different words, they often get the last part right: THE LION AND THE LEPRECHAUN instead of 'the lion and the unicorn', ICE CREAM TOILET, for 'ice cream cornet' (Aitchison, 1972). And it is well known that children tend to omit or confuse the first syllable of a word, particularly if it is unstressed, as in RITACK, RIDUCTOR, RIFECTION for 'attack', 'conductor', 'infection' (Smith, 1973:172). But this is not only because the syllable is unstressed. It is also because the syllable occurs at the beginning of a word. In Czech, where initial syllables are stressed, it is the unstressed final syllables which are better remembered by children, according to one researcher (Pačesova, 1968, reported in Slobin, 1973). And further evidence that suffixes are more salient than prefixes or items placed in front of a word comes from the fact that English children omit prepositions that are essential to the sentence (e.g. MUMMY GARDEN) at a time when they have already started using the correct endings on words (e.g. DADDY SINGING).

However, it is perhaps dangerous to draw too many conclusions about strategies solely from the order of acquisition. So let us now consider the second way in which we can find out about operating procedures – by analysing children's errors. We can look both at spontaneous errors, and at those made in repetition tests. Of course, repetition tests must be used with care, since sometimes they merely show that a child cannot handle all the information included in a sentence. A child tends to simplify a sentence which has too much compressed into it. For example:

THE OLD GRAY WOLF CHASED RABBITS

is likely to be repeated as

THE OLD WOLF CHASED RABBITS.

(Smith, 1967)

But with this proviso, mistakes made in repetition tests can, like spontaneous errors, prove a useful guide to those aspects of language the child finds difficult.

The similarity of mistakes produced independently by children learning English is impressive. They 'not only make the same kind of errors; they even make them with some of the identical words. The similarities across these children, despite differences in their home dialect, are too numerous to be dismissed, (Cazden, 1972:48). This type of consistency suggests that certain expectations of children as to what language is like are not being met. They must be following some procedure which is not working in their analysis of English.

For example, a common error found in almost all English children is a tendency to interpret passives as actives:

THE HEFFALUMP WAS CHASED BY THE DINOSAUR

is likely to be interpreted as:

THE HEFFALUMP CHASED THE DINOSAUR.

And a sentence such as:

THE FLEA WAS HARD TO SEE

is likely to be understood as:

THE FLEA FINDS IT HARD TO SEE.

Children seem to be assuming that English follows a consistent subject–verb–object word order. The operating principle which led them to this strategy seems to be an assumption that word order matters and is related consistently to meaning. In other words, children are following a basic operating rule: 'Pay attention to the order of words.' Furthermore, in imitation tests, children try to impose a subject–verb–object order on to superficially confusing sentences. For example:

THE BOY THE CHAIR HIT WAS DIRTY

was repeated as:

BOY HIT THE CHAIR WAS DIRTY

(Slobin and Welsh, 1973).

Further evidence in favour of this strategy is the observation that in some cases children try to impose a consistent order on their utterances even in languages where word order does not matter (Slobin, 1966). Slobin notes: 'One of the earliest and most pervasive operating principles has to do with attention to order of elements in an utterance. It seems that a basic expectation which the child brings to the task of grammatical development is that the order of elements in an utterance can be related to underlying semantic relations' (Slobin, 1973:197).

Another common mistake (already noted several times in this book) is the use by children of over-regularized forms of irregular verbs or nouns. A child tends to say COMED instead of CAME, TAKED instead of TOOK, FOOTS instead of FEET, in spite of frequent exposure to the correct form. This provides further evidence in favour of an operating principle already proposed: 'Allot one form only to each unit of meaning.' Possibly, when a child considers he has unambiguously identified a plural ending –s and a past tense ending –D, he feels confident in generalizing these to all plurals and past tenses – so producing forms such as FOOTS, COMED and TAKED.

However, in spite of the illumination into possible acquisition 'strategies' suggested by errors, it is the third method, the study of bilingual children, which seems to be the most reliable guide to a child's operating procedures. This method has been pioneered by Dan Slobin (1973), a psychologist at the University of California at Berkeley, and it eliminates the confusing possibility that the child might merely be having difficulties with the concepts he is trying to express. Slobin points out that children who grow up learning two languages together do not normally acquire parallel constructions simultaneously in both languages. For example, children who are acquiring Hungarian and Serbo-Croatian as twin native languages produce Hungarian locatives such as INTO THE BOX, ON THE TABLE, long before they produce the equivalent Serbo-Croatian ones. Clearly, there cannot be any conceptual difficulty connected with the notion of locative, because the Hungarian ones are used in the correct circumstances. We conclude that there must be something intrinsically difficult about Serbo-Croatian locatives from the linguistic point of view. They must go against a child's natural expectations about his language, since his operating procedures do not produce the correct analysis. Let us consider the Hungarian and Serbo-Croatian examples in turn. The Hungarian locative, on the one hand, is formed by means of a suffix attached to a noun. Each locative expression, INTO, ON, and so on, is a single unambiguous syllable, placed after a noun.

e.g. HAJÓBAN 'Boat-in, in the boat'
HAJÓBÓL   'Boat-out-of, (getting) out of the boat'.

The Serbo-Croatian locatives, on the other hand, are not nearly as clear-cut. The Serbo-Croatian word U can mean either 'into' or 'in' (just as the English word IN can mean either 'into' or 'within' – you can say 'put it in (into) the cupboard', or 'It is in (within) the cupboard'. You can tell the difference between the two uses of Serbo-Croatian U by looking at the end of the following noun:

U KUĆU   'into the house'
U KUĆI   'in the house'

But the situation is further complicated because the noun endings are not only used in conjunction with this preposition, but have other uses as well. Worse still, another preposition K 'towards' which you might expect to be followed by the same suffix as U 'into' in fact takes a quite different noun ending. So in Serbo-Croatian we find the same prepositional form with more than one meaning, and followed by more than one noun ending. And we find prepositions with similar meaning followed by different noun endings, as well as the same noun endings used for a variety of purposes. No wonder that children get confused!

Apart from the obvious and rather naive comment that the Hungarian locative is 'simpler' than the Serbo-Crotian one, we can go somewhat further. First of all, we note that the 'simple' Hungarian

locative is expressed by means of consistent noun suffixes. This is
further evidence in favour of three operating principles already
mentioned: 'Remember that the form of words may be consistently
and meaningfully modified'; 'Pay attention to the ends of words'
and 'Expect words to be modified by suffixes'. But the 'difficult'
Serbo-Croatian locatives, on the other hand, which have both a
preposition and a noun-ending to express a single directional concept, go contrary to two other likely expectations that (as we noted
earlier) children possibly bring to the task of language acquisition:
'Allot one form only to each unit of meaning'; and 'Linguistic units
should not be interrupted'. In brief, it seems that Hungarian locatives
fulfil a child's likely expectations about language, and Serbo-
Croatian locatives go against them.

So far, then, we have looked at three ways in which we can find out
what aspects of language a child finds difficult: we can look at the
order of acquisition, we can analyse children's errors and we can
study the speech of bilinguals. As a result we have suggested a number of 'self-instructions' which a child might subconsciously bring to
the task of language acquisition:

1. Allot one form only to each unit of meaning.
2. Linguistic units should not be interrupted.
3. Remember that the form of words may be consistently and
   meaningfully modified.
4. Pay attention to the ends of words.
5. Expect words to be modified by suffixes.
6. Pay attention to the order of words.

But this is only a beginning. Slobin has made some further tentative suggestions about children's operating procedures (1973). But
considerably more work needs to be done on bilingual children and
languages other than English before we can confidently propose a
universal set of acquisition strategies.

To summarize: in this chapter we have tried to see exactly how a
child extracts grammar from the data he hears around him. Chomsky's
suggestion that the child comes equipped with the knowledge that
language is organized into two layers – a deep level and a surface
level – seems to be false. In the place of a 'Content Cuthbert', a child
whose mind contains knowledge of language universals, we should
perhaps substitute a 'Process Peggy' – a child whose mind is set up
with puzzle-solving equipment.

Process Peggy treats language as a puzzle she has to solve. In order to find a solution to it, she uses a number of inbuilt 'operating procedures' or strategies which tell her how to set about it. Exactly what these strategies are is not yet clear – though we have been able to make some outline suggestions, such as 'Pay attention to the order of words – Pay attention to the ends of words'.

Content Cuthbert and Process Peggy are not mere notational variants – Cuthbert's language universals are specific to language, and unrelated to general cognitive development, whereas Peggy's are likely to be related to other aspects of intelligence. However, both Cuthbert and Peggy have to go through a process of making successive hypotheses to account for the data they hear around them. As Slobin notes: 'While we can disagree about the extent to which this process of developing grammars requires a richly detailed innate language faculty, there can be no doubt that the process requires a richly structured and active child mind' (Slobin 1973:208).

Although we have now completed our discussion of language acquisition, there is one point which remains quite open. What kind of internal grammar does someone who has completed the acquisition of language have? In other words what does the internalized grammar of an adult look like? Is it a transformational grammar? This is the next question to be considered. But before that, we have a brief excursus in which we discuss the following topic: how did Chomsky conceive the idea of a transformational grammar in the first place?

8 Celestial Unintelligibility

Why propose a transformational grammar?

'If any one of them can explain it,' said Alice, 'I'll give him sixpence. *I* don't believe there's an atom of meaning in it.'
'If there's no meaning in it,' said the King, 'that saves a world of trouble, you know, as we needn't try to find any. And yet I don't know,' he went on, 'I seem to see some meaning after all.'

Lewis Carroll
Alice in Wonderland

Linguists, particularly transformational linguists, are sometimes accused of being 'too abstract' and 'removed from reality'. For example, one reviewer has condemned 'that celestial unintelligibility which is the element where the true student of linguistics normally floats and dances' (Philip Toynbee, *Observer*). Yet almost all linguists, not just psycholinguists, are trying to find out about a speaker's mental 'grammar' – the internalized set of rules which enables someone to speak and understand his language. As Chomsky notes: 'The linguist constructing a grammar of his language is in effect proposing a hypothesis concerning this internalized system' (Chomsky, 1972a:26).

So the question which naturally arises is this: if linguists are really trying to form theories about an internalized system, why did they hit on something as complex and abstract as transformational grammar? Surely there are other types of grammar which do not seem as odd? Some of the reasons for setting up a transformational grammar were mentioned in Chapter 1. But the question will be considered again from a different angle here.

Jupiter's stick insects

Suppose . . . a space ship full of English speakers had landed on Jupiter. They found the planet inhabited by a race of green stick insects who communicated by sitting down and wiggling their stick-like toes. The English speakers learned the Jupiter toe-wiggle language easily. It was a sign language like Washoe's in which signs stood for words, with no obvious structure. So communication was not a serious problem. But the Emperor of Jupiter became highly envious of these foreigners who were able to walk about *and* communicate at the same time. They did not have to stop, sit down, and wiggle their toes. He decided to learn English.

At first, he assumed the task was easy. He ordered his servants to record all the sentences uttered by the English speakers, together with their meanings. Each morning he locked himself into his study and memorized the sentences recorded on the previous day. He carried out this routine unswervingly for about a year, dutifully learning every single sentence spoken by the foreigners. As he was an inhabitant of Jupiter, he had no natural ability for understanding the way a language worked. So he did not detect any patterns in the words, he simply memorized them. Eventually, he decided he knew enough to start testing his knowledge in conversation with the Englishmen.

But the result was a disaster. He didn't seem to have learnt the sentences he needed to use. When he wanted to ask the Englishmen if they liked sea-urchin soup, the nearest sentence he could remember having learnt was 'This is funny-tasting soup. What kind is it?' When it rained, and he wanted to know if rain was likely to harm the foreigners, the most relevant sentence was 'It's raining, can we buy gumboots and umbrellas here?'

He began to have doubts about the task he had set himself of memorizing all English sentences. Would it ever come to an end? He understood that each sentence was composed of units called words, such as JAM, SIX, HELP, BUBBLE which kept recurring. But although he now recognized most of the words which cropped up, they kept appearing in new combinations, so the number of new sentences did not seem to be decreasing. Worse still, some of the sentences were extremely long. He recalled one in which an English speaker had been discussing a greedy boy: 'Alexander ate ten sausages, four jam tarts, two bananas, a Swiss roll, seven meringues, fourteen oranges, eight pieces of toast, fourteen apples, two icecreams, three trifles and then he was sick.' The Emperor wondered despairingly what would have happened to the sentence if Alexander hadn't been sick. Would it have gone on for ever? Another sentence worried him, which an English speaker had read out of a magazine. It was a summary of previous episodes in a serial story: 'Virginia, who is employed as a governess at an old castle in Cornwall, falls in love with her employer's son Charles who is himself in love with a local beauty queen called Linda who has eyes only for the fisherman's nephew Philip who is obsessed with his half-sister Phyllis who loves the handsome young farmer Tom who cares only for his pigs.' Presumably the writer ran out of characters to describe, the Emperor reasoned. Otherwise, the sentence could have gone on even further.

The king had therefore deduced for himself two fundamental facts about language. There are a finite number of elements which can be combined in a mathematically enormous number of ways. And it is *in principle* impossible to memorize every sentence because there is no linguistic bound on the length of sentence. Innumerable 'sub'-sentences can be joined on to the original one, a process known as *conjoining*:

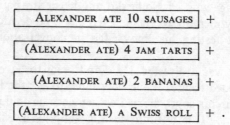

ALEXANDER ATE 10 SAUSAGES +

(ALEXANDER ATE) 4 JAM TARTS +

(ALEXANDER ATE) 2 BANANAS +

(ALEXANDER ATE) A SWISS ROLL + . . .

Alternatively, sub-sentences can be inserted or *embedded* inside the original one:

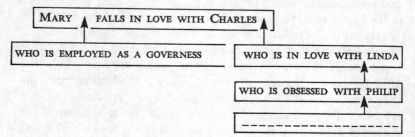

MARY FALLS IN LOVE WITH CHARLES

WHO IS EMPLOYED AS A GOVERNESS

WHO IS IN LOVE WITH LINDA

WHO IS OBSESSED WITH PHILIP

This property of language is known as RECURSIVENESS from the Latin to 'run through again' – you can repeatedly apply the same rule to one sentence, a process which could (in theory) go on for ever. Of course, in practice you would fall asleep, or get bored or get a sore throat. But these are not *linguistic* reasons for stopping. This means that no definite set of utterances can ever be assembled for any language.

The Emperor of Jupiter eventually concluded that memorization of all English sentences was impossible. He realized it was the *patterns* behind the utterances which mattered.

How should he discover what these were? One way would be to make a list of all the English words he had collected, and to note whereabouts in the sentence each one occurred. He started to do this. But he hit on problems almost immediately. He had a feeling that some of his sentences had mistakes in them, but he was not sure which ones. Was 'I hic have hic o dear hic hiccups' a well-formed English sentence or not? And what about 'I mean that what I wanted I think to say was this'?

His other problem was that he found gaps in the patterns, and he didn't know which ones were accidental, and which not. For example, he found four sentences containing the word ELEPHANT:

> THE ELEPHANT CARRIED TEN PEOPLE
> THE ELEPHANT SWALLOWED TEN BUNS
> THE ELEPHANT WEIGHED TEN TONS
> TEN PEOPLE WERE CARRIED BY THE ELEPHANT.

But he *did not* find

> TEN BUNS WERE SWALLOWED BY THE ELEPHANT
> TEN TONS WERE WEIGHED BY THE ELEPHANT.

Why not? Were these gaps accidental? Or were the sentences ungrammatical? The Emperor did not know, and grew very depressed. He had discovered another important fact about language: collections of utterances must be treated with caution. They are full of false starts and slips of the tongue. And they constitute only a small subset of all possible utterances. In linguistic terms, a speaker's *performance* is likely to be a random sample bespattered with errors, and does not necessarily provide a very good guide to his *competence*, the internalized set of rules which underlie them.

The Emperor of Jupiter realized that he needed the help of the foreigners themselves. He arrested the spaceship captain, a man called Noam, and told him that he would free him as soon as he had written down the rules of English. Noam plainly knew them, since he could talk.

Noam was astounded. He pleaded with the Emperor, pointing out that speaking a language was an ability like walking which involved knowing *how* to do something. Such knowledge was not necessarily conscious. He tried to explain that philosophers on earth made a distinction between two kinds of knowing: knowing *that* and knowing *how*. Noam knew *that* Jupiter was a planet, and factual knowledge of this type was conscious knowledge. On the other hand, he knew *how* to talk and *how* to walk, though he had no idea how to convey this knowledge to others, since he carried out the actions required without being aware of how he actually managed to do them.

But the king was adamant. Noam would not be freed until he had written down an explicit set of rules, parallel to the system internalized in his head.

Noam pondered. Where could he begin? After much thought he made a list of all the English words he could think of, then fed them into a computer with the instructions that it could combine them in any way whatsoever. First it was to print out all the words one by one, then all possible combinations of two words, then three words, then four words, and so on. The computer began churning out the words as programmed, and spewed out (in the four-word cycle) sequences such as:

> DOG INTO INTO OF
> UP UP UP UP
> GOLDFISH MAY EAT CATS
> THE ELEPHANT LOVED BUNS
> DOWN OVER FROM THE
> SKYLARKS KISS SNAILS BADLY.

Sooner or later, Noam reasoned, the computer would produce every English sentence.

Noam announced to the Emperor that the computer was programmed with rules which made it potentially capable of producing all possible sentences of English. The Emperor was suspicious that the task had been completed so quickly. And when he checked with the other foreigners, his fears were confirmed. The others pointed out that although Noam's computer programme could in theory generate *all* English sentences, it certainly did not generate *only* the sentences of English. Since the Emperor was looking for a device which paralleled a human's internalized grammar, Noam's programme must be rejected, because humans did not accept sentences such as:

> DOG INTO INTO OF.

It was also unlikely that they would accept

> GOLDFISH MAY EAT CATS
> or   SKYLARKS KISS SNAILS BADLY.

But there was nothing really wrong with these grammatically: these were accidental facts about the diet of goldfish and the amatory preferences of skylarks which need not be included in the grammar.

So Noam went away again and thought hard. It dawned on him that all sentences were straightforward word 'strings': they were composed of words strung together, one after the other. And the order in which they occurred was partially predictable. For example, THE had to be followed either by an adjective such as GOOD, LITTLE or by a noun such as FLOWER, CHEESE, or occasionally an adverb such as CAREFULLY as in

THE CAREFULLY NURTURED CHILD SCRIBBLED OBSCENE GRAFFITI ON THE WALLS.

Perhaps, he pondered, one's head contained a network of associations such that each word was in some way attached to the words which could follow it in a sentence. He started to devise a grammar which started with one word, which triggered off a choice between several others, which in turn moved to another choice, until the sentence was complete:

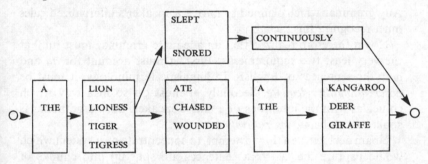

This simple device could account for quite a number of different sentences:

A LION ATE A KANGAROO
THE TIGRESS CHASED THE GIRAFFE,

and so on. If he continued to elaborate it, perhaps it could eventually include all possible sentences of English.

He presented it to the king, who in turn showed it to the other Englishmen. They pointed out a fatal flaw. Such a device could not possibly account for a speaker's internalized rules for English, because English (and all other languages) has sentences in which non-adjacent words are dependent on one another. For example, you can have a sentence:

THE LIONESS HURT HERSELF.

If each word triggered off the next only, then you would not be able to link the word following HURT with LIONESS, you would be just as likely to have

*THE LIONESS HURT HIMSELF.

Similarly, a sentence starting with EITHER, as in

EITHER BILL STOPS SINGING OR YOU FIND ME EAR PLUGS

would not fit into this system, since there would be no means of triggering the OR. Furthermore, in this left to right model, all the words had equal status, and were linked to one another like beads on a necklace. But in language, speakers treat 'chunks' of words as belonging together:

THE LITTLE RED HEN / WALKED SLOWLY / ALONG THE PATH / SCRATCHING FOR WORMS.

Any grammar which claimed to mirror a speaker's internalized rules must recognize this fact.

Noam therefore realized that an adequate grammar must fulfil at the very least two requirements. First, it must account for *all* and *only* the sentences of English. In linguistic terminology, it must be *observationally adequate*. Secondly, it must do so in a way which coincides with the intuitions of a native speaker. Such a grammar is spoken of as being *descriptively adequate*.

Noam decided, as a third attempt, to concentrate on a system which would capture the fact that sentences are split up into chunks of words which go together. He decided that a multi-layered, 'downward branching' system was the answer. At the top of the page he wrote the letter S to represent 'sentence'. Then he drew two branches forking from it, representing the shortest possible English sentence (not counting commands).

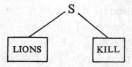

Then each branch was expanded into a longer phrase which could optionally replace it:

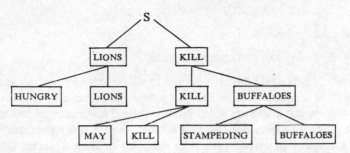

This tree diagram clearly captured the *hierarchical* structure of language, the fact that whole phrases can be the structural equivalent of one word. It diagrammed the fact that HUNGRY LIONS functions as a single unit in a way that KILL STAMPEDING does not.

The Emperor of Jupiter was delighted. For the first time he began to have an inkling of the way language worked. 'I want some soup . . . some seaweed soup . . . some hot seaweed soup . . . some steaming hot seaweed soup', he murmured to himself, realizing the importance of Noam's new system.

The other Englishmen praised the system, but grudgingly. They admitted that the tree diagram worked very well for sentences such as

HUNGRY LIONS MAY KILL STAMPEDING BUFFALOES.

But they had one major objection. Did Noam realize just how many trees might be required for the whole language? And did he realize that sentences which speakers felt to be closely related would have quite different trees? For example

HUNGRY LIONS MAY KILL STAMPEDING BUFFALOES

would have a tree quite different from

STAMPEDING BUFFALOES MAY BE KILLED BY HUNGRY LIONS.

And a sentence such as

TO CHOP DOWN LAMP-POSTS IS A DREADFUL CRIME

would have a different tree from

IT IS A DREADFUL CRIME TO CHOP DOWN LAMP-POSTS.

Worse still, had Noam noticed that sentences which were felt to be quite different by the speakers of the language had exactly the *same* trees?

THE BOY WAS LOATH TO WASH

had exactly the same tree as

THE BOY WAS DIFFICULT TO WASH.

Surely Noam could devise a system in which sentences felt by speakers to be similar could be linked up, and dissimilar ones separated?

After much contemplation, Noam realized he could economize on the number of trees needed, and he could also capture the intuitions of speakers that certain sentences were similar if he regarded similar sentences as belonging to the same basic tree! Actives and passives, for example, could be related to a tree that was as yet neither active nor passive.

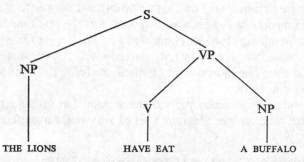

Then this 'deep structure' tree could be 'transformed' by operations known as transformations into different surface structure trees. In the case of an eventual active sentence, the words are already in the right order, though we need a verb agreement transformation, which checks that the verb 'agrees' with the previous noun, so that we get

THE LIONS HAVE EATEN A BUFFALO

instead of the ungrammatical sequence

*THE LIONS HAS EATEN A BUFFALO.

But for a passive sentence the word order has to be altered, and the items BE and BY inserted before the application of the verb agreement transformation. If, wrongly, the passive transformation had been applied second, the sentence would have ended up as

*A BUFFALO HAVE BEEN EATEN BY THE LIONS

instead of the correct

A BUFFALO HAS BEEN EATEN BY THE LIONS.

Using the same principle, Noam realized that he could explain the similarity of

TO CHOP DOWN LAMP-POSTS IS A DREADFUL CRIME

and

IT IS A DREADFUL CRIME TO CHOP DOWN LAMP-POSTS.

Conversely, the difference between

THE BOY WAS LOATH TO WASH

and

THE BOY WAS DIFFICULT TO WASH

could be explained by suggesting that the sentences are connected to different deep structure strings.

The Emperor of Jupiter was delighted with Noam's latest attempt, and the other Englishmen agreed that Noam seemed to have hit on a very good solution. He appeared to have devised a clear, economical system which was able to account for *all* and *only* the sentences of English, and which also captured the intuitions of the speakers about the way their language worked. A further important bonus was that the system could possibly be used for French, Chinese, Turkish, Arawak, or any other language in the strange human world.

However, the Emperor was still somewhat puzzled. Had Noam explained to him how to actually *produce* English sentences? Or had he merely drawn him a map of the way in which related sentences were stored in an Englishman's head? Noam was rather vague when asked about this. He said that although the map idea seemed nearer the truth, the map nevertheless had important implications for the way in which sentences were produced and recognized. The Emperor was extremely puzzled by this statement. However, he decided that Noam had done some splendid work, and so should be set free, and rewarded handsomely. Meanwhile, the Emperor made a mental note that when he had some more spare time, he would have to contemplate more thoroughly the question of how Noam's proposals related to the way humans produced and recognized sentences.

Let us summarize what the Emperor of Jupiter had discovered about the nature of human language and the type of 'grammar' which can account for it. Firstly, he discovered that it is in principle impossible to memorize every sentence of a language, because there is no linguistic limit on the length of a sentence.

Secondly, he found that any collection of utterances must be treated with the utmost care. It contains slips of the tongue, and represents only a random sample of all possible utterances. For this reason it is important to focus attention on a speaker's underlying system of rules, his 'competence' rather than on an arbitrary collection of his utterances, or his 'performance'. Thirdly, the Emperor realized that a good grammar of a language will not only be observationally adequate – one which can account for all the possible sentences of a language. It will also be descriptively adequate – that is, it will reflect the intuitions of the native speaker about his language. This meant that a simple, left to right model of language, in which each word was triggered by the one before it, was unworkable. It was observationally inadequate because it did not allow for non-adjacent words to be dependent on one another. And it was descriptively inadequate because it wrongly treated all words as being of equal value and linked together like beads on a string, when in practice language is hierarchically structured with 'chunks' of words going together.

Fourthly, the Emperor of Jupiter noted that a hierarchically structured top-to-bottom model of language was a reasonable proposal – but it did not link up sentences which were felt by the speakers to be closely related, such as

TO BURN DOWN LAMP-POSTS IS A DREADFUL CRIME

and

IT IS A DREADFUL CRIME TO BURN DOWN LAMP-POSTS.

On the other hand it wrongly linked up sentences such as

THE BOY WAS LOATH TO WASH

and

THE BOY WAS DIFFICULT TO WASH,

which seemed to be quite different. So finally, he became convinced that the most satisfactory system was a transformational model of language, in which sentences felt to be similar share the same deep structure. He came to believe that all sentences had both a hidden, deep structure and an obvious surface structure which might look quite different, and he accepted that these two levels were linked by processes known as transformations.

However, the Emperor remained puzzled about how this model of an internalized grammar tied in with the way humans produce and comprehend sentences. He felt that Noam had been quite unclear on the topic.

Several of the things discovered by the mythical Emperor of Jupiter are points made by Noam Chomsky in his early, slim, but extremely influential work, *Syntactic Structures* (1957). In this, he explains why a left to right or 'finite-state' model of language is deficient, and also why a top-to-bottom or 'phrase structure' model is inadequate. He then justifies the need for a transformational grammar. However, he does not discuss in any coherent way how a transformational grammar relates to the way we actually *use* a language. Let us look at Chomsky's views on this topic.

Linguistic knowledge

Chomsky claims that the grammar he has proposed 'expresses the speaker-hearer's knowledge of the language'. This knowledge is latent or 'tacit', and 'may well not be immediately available to the use of the language' (Chomsky 1965:21).

The notion of tacit or latent knowledge is a rather vague one, and appears to cover more than Chomsky intended. It seems to cover two types of knowledge. On the one hand, it consists of knowing *how* to produce and comprehend utterances. This involves using a rule system, but it does not necessarily involve any awareness of the rules – just as a spider can spin a web successfully without any awareness of the principles it is following. On the other hand, knowledge of a language also covers the ability to make various kinds of judgements about the language. The speaker does not only know the rules, but in addition, he knows something about that knowledge. For example, speakers can quickly distinguish between well-formed and deviant sentences. An English-speaker would unhesitatingly accept

HANK MUCH PREFERS CAVIARE TO SARDINES

but would quickly reject

*HANK CAVIARE TO SARDINES MUCH PREFERS.

In addition, mature speakers of a language can recognize sentence relatedness. They 'know' that

FADING FLOWERS LOOK SAD

is closely related to

FLOWERS WHICH ARE FADING LOOK SAD

and that

IT ASTONISHED US THAT BUZZ SWALLOWED THE OCTOPUS WHOLE

is related to

THAT BUZZ SWALLOWED THE OCTOPUS WHOLE ASTONISHED US.

Moreover, they can distinguish between sentences which look superficially alike but in fact are quite different, as in

EATING APPLES CAN BE GOOD FOR YOU.

(Is it good to eat a type of apple called an eating apple, or is any type of apple good to eat?), or

SHOOTING STARS CAN BE FRIGHTENING
SHOOTING BUFFALOES CAN BE FRIGHTENING.

(How do you know who is doing the shooting?)

There seems to be no doubt whatsoever that a transformational grammar encapsulates this second type of knowledge, the speaker's awareness of language structure. People *do* have intuitions or knowledge of the type specified above, and a transformational grammar *does* seem to describe this. However, it is by no means clear how a transformational grammar relates to the first type of knowledge – the knowledge of how to actually *use* language. Although Chomsky claims that a speaker's internal grammar has an important bearing on the production and comprehension of utterances, he makes it quite clear that this grammar 'does not, in itself, prescribe the character or functioning of a perceptual model or a model of speech production (Chomsky, 1965:9). And he even labels as 'absurd' any attempt to link the grammar directly to processes of production and comprehension (Chomsky, 1967:399).

In Chomsky's words, 'We must make a fundamental distinction between *competence* (the speaker-hearer's knowledge of his language) and *performance* (the actual use of language in concrete situations)' (Chomsky, 1965:4).

Let us put the matter in another way. Anyone who knows a language can do three things:

1.	Produce sentences or 'encode'	LANGUAGE
2.	Comprehend sentences or 'decode'	USAGE
3.	Store linguistic knowledge	LANGUAGE KNOWLEDGE

We are saying that a transformational grammar seems undoubtedly to cover (3), but appears to be separate from, or only indirectly related to (1) and (2).

LANGUAGE		LANGUAGE
USAGE		KNOWLEDGE

This is a rather puzzling state of affairs. Is it possible for linguistic knowledge to be completely separate from language usage? If not, what could possibly be meant by saying that the two are 'indirectly related'? This is the topic of the next chapter.

9 The White Elephant Problem

Do we need a transformational grammar in order to speak?

'I have answered three questions, and that is enough,'
Said his father; 'don't give yourself airs!
Do you think I can listen all day to such stuff?
Be off, or I'll kick you downstairs!'

Lewis Carroll
Old Father William

In the last chapter we noted that a transformational grammar appears to 'capture' a speaker's abstract knowledge of his language in an intuitively satisfying way. But it is not yet clear how knowledge relates to usage. At first sight, the two seem rather distant. First of all, Chomsky denies that linguistic knowledge is directly related to the way we understand and produce utterances. And secondly, we saw in Chapter 7 that children can apparently learn to talk quite happily *without* the kind of intuitions encapsulated in a transformational grammar. They can, for example, use active and passive sentences quite happily without necessarily linking up the two.

This leads to a crucial and rather startling question: is a transformational grammar actually *irrelevant* to the problem of understanding speech? Are we suggesting that language usage, consisting of encoding and decoding, must be separated from language knowledge?

If we put this question to a hard-core linguist, he would probably answer: 'Of course language knowledge and language usage are not totally separate, they just have to be studied separately, because the relationship between them is indirect.'

If we persisted, and said, 'What exactly do you mean by an indirect relationship?' he would probably say: 'Look, please stop bothering me with silly questions. The relationship between language usage and language knowledge is not my concern. Let me put you straight. All normal people seem to have a tacit knowledge of their language. If that knowledge is there, it is my duty as a linguist to describe it. But it is not my job to tell you how that knowledge is used. I leave that to the psychologists.'

This, to a psycholinguist, seems an extremely unhappy state of affairs. He is just as much interested in language usage as language knowledge. In fact, he finds it quite odd that anybody is able to concentrate on one rather than the other of these factors, since they seem to him to go together rather closely. Consequently, in this chapter, we shall be briefly examining attempts made by psycholinguists over the last fifteen years to assess the relationship between a transformational grammar and the way someone produces and comprehends sentences. We shall start by looking at the earliest psycholinguistic experiments on the topic, which were carried out in the early 1960s.

The years of illusion

When Chomsky's ideas spread across into the field of psychology in the early 1960s they made an immediate impact. Psychologists at once started to test the relevance of a transformational grammar to the way we process sentences. Predictably, their first instinct was to test whether there was a direct relationship between the two.

At this time, two different but similar viewpoints were put forward. The first is sometimes known as the 'correspondence hypothesis', and the second as the 'derivational theory of complexity' or DTC for short.

Supporters of the correspondence hypothesis postulated a close correspondence between the form of a transformational grammar, and the operations employed by someone when he produces or comprehends speech. They suggested that 'the sequence of rules used in the grammatical derivation of a sentence . . . corresponds step by step to the sequence of psychological processes that are executed when a person processes the sentence' (Hayes, 1970:5). The assumption was that when someone produces a sentence he first of all assembles the deep structure:

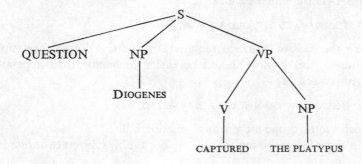

He then 'winds on' the transformations one by one, so that as an intermediate stage he might get:

QUESTION – THE PLATYPUS WAS CAPTURED BY DIOGENES

and finally

WAS THE PLATYPUS CAPTURED BY DIOGENES?

Decoding was thought to be the reverse of this procedure – a hearer was assumed to 'unwind' the transformations one by one. And finally, deep structure and transformations were presumed to be stored separately in the brain.

Supporters of DTC put forward a slightly weaker hypothesis. They suggested that the more complex the transformational derivation of a sentence – that is, the more transformations were involved – the more difficult it would be to produce or comprehend. They did not, however, assume a one-to-one correspondence between the speaker's mental processes and grammatical operations.

A number of experiments were devised to test these claims. Perhaps the two best-known are a sentence-matching experiment by George Miller of Harvard University (Miller, 1962; Miller and McKean, 1964), and a memorization experiment by Harris Savin and Ellen Perchonock, two psychologists from the university of Pennsylvania (Savin and Perchonock, 1965).

George Miller reasoned that if the number of transformations significantly affected processing difficulty, then this difficulty should be measurable in terms of time. In other words, the more transformations a sentence had, the longer it should take to cope with. For example, a passive sentence such as

THE OLD WOMAN WAS WARNED BY JOE

should be harder to handle than a simple active affirmative declarative (or SAAD for short) such as

JOE WARNED THE OLD WOMAN,

since the passive sentence required an additional transformation. However, this passive should be easier to handle than a passive negative such as

THE OLD WOMAN WASN'T WARNED BY JOE

which required one more transformation still.

In order to test this hypothesis, Miller gave his subjects two columns of jumbled sentences, and asked them to find pairs which went together. The sentences to be paired differed from one another in a specified way. For example, in one section of the experiment actives and passives were jumbled, so that a passive such as

THE SMALL BOY WAS LIKED BY JANE

had to be matched with its 'partner'

JANE LIKED THE SMALL BOY.

And

JOE WARNED THE OLD WOMAN

had to be paired with

THE OLD WOMAN WAS WARNED BY JOE.

Miller assumed that the subjects had to strip the sentences of their transformations in order to match them up. The more they differed from each other, the longer the matching would take, he predicted.

Miller carried out this experiment twice, the second time with strict electronic time-controls (a so-called 'tachistoscopic' method). His results delighted him. Just as he had hoped, it took nearly twice as long to match sentences which differed by *two* transformations as it took to match sentences which differed by only one transformation. When he added the time needed to match actives with passives (approximately 1·65 seconds) to the time taken to pair affirmatives with negatives (approximately 1·40 seconds), the total added up to almost the same as that required for matching active with passive negative sentences (approximately 3·12 seconds).

Active ◄1·65► *Passive*	
JOE WARNED THE OLD WOMAN	THE OLD WOMAN WAS WARNED BY JOE
Affirmative ◄1·40► *Negative*	
JOE WARNED THE OLD WOMAN	JOE DIDN'T WARN THE OLD WOMAN
Active ◄3·12► *Passive Negative*	
JOE WARNED THE OLD WOMAN	THE OLD WOMAN WASN'T WARNED BY JOE

Miller seemed to have proved that transformations were 'psychologically real', since each transformation took up a measurable processing time – and his claim appeared to be strengthened by Savin and Perchonock's memorization experiment.

Savin and Perchonock asked their subjects to memorize short sentences followed by strings of unrelated words:

> THE BOY HIT THE BALL – BUSH – COW – BUS – HOUR – CHAIR – RAIN – HAT – RED.
> THE BOY DIDN'T HIT THE BALL – TREE – HORSE – SHIP – DAY – DESK – SNOW – COAT – GREEN.

The reason behind the experiment was as follows: a person's immediate memory has a small constant capacity. It seems likely that sentences which involve several transformations will take up more memory space than those which involve only one or two. So they predicted that the more transformations were added, the fewer random words would be remembered. This prediction turned out to be correct. With a straightforward SAAD sentence such as

> THE BOY HIT THE BALL

subjects remembered on average five unrelated words. When one extra transformation (such as passive or negative) was involved, they remembered on average four words. When two extra transformations were added, subjects remembered only three words. The conclusion drawn by Savin and Perchonock was that subjects remembered sentences in their underlying form, with transformations tacked on separately as 'footnotes' which took up measurable memory space.

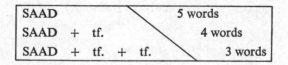

SAAD		5 words
SAAD + tf.		4 words
SAAD + tf. + tf.		3 words

Many psychologists were overjoyed at the results of these experiments. Miller, it seemed, had shown that transformations took up time in sentence matching experiments, and Savin and Perchonock had demonstrated that they occupied memory space, and similar experiments by other psychologists all pointed in the same direction (e.g. Mehler, 1963). Several people optimistically assumed that the correspondence hypothesis was correct, and claimed that a new era had dawned for psycholinguistics.

But this period of illusion was shortlived. A time of disappointment and disillusion followed. Fodor and Garrett (1966) gave a crushing paper at the Edinburgh University conference on Psycholinguistics in March 1966, in which they clearly showed the emptiness of the 'correspondence hypothesis' and DTC. They gave detailed theoretical reasons why hearers do not 'unwind' transformations when they decode speech. For example, the correspondence hypothesis entails the consequence that people do not begin to decode what they are hearing until a sentence is complete. It assumes that, after waiting until he has heard all of it, a hearer then undresses the sentence transformation by transformation. But this is clearly wrong, it would take much too long. In fact, it can be shown that hearers start to decode as soon as a speaker begins talking.

In addition, Fodor and Garrett pointed out flaws in the experiments carried out by Miller and Savin and Perchonock. The transformations, such as passives and negatives, on which their results crucially depended, are atypical. Negatives change the meaning, and passives move the actor away from its normal place at the beginning of an English sentence. Passives and negatives are also longer than SAADs, so it is not surprising that they take longer to match and are more difficult to memorize. The difficulty of these sentences need not have anything to do with transformational complexity. Fodor and Garrett pointed out that there are other transformations which make no difference to processing difficulty. There is no detectable difference in the time taken to comprehend

> JOHN PHONES UP THE GIRL

and

> JOHN PHONES THE GIRL UP.

If the correspondence hypothesis or DTC was correct, the second should be more difficult, because a 'particle separation' transformation has been applied, separating PHONES and UP. Worse still for the theory are sentences such as

> BILL RUNS FASTER THAN JOHN RUNS
> BILL RUNS FASTER THAN JOHN.

The second sentence has one more transformation than the first, because the word RUNS has been deleted. In theory it should be more difficult to comprehend, but in practice it is easier.

Fodor and Garrett followed their 1966 conference paper with another article in 1967 where they pointed out more problem constructions (Fodor and Garrett, 1967). For example DTC wrongly predicts that

THE TIRED SOLDIER FIRED THE SHOT

should be more complex to process than

THE SOLDIER WHO WAS TIRED FIRED THE SHOT

which is closer to the deep structure. It also counter-intuitively treats 'truncated' passives such as

THE BOY WAS HIT

as more complex than full passives such as

THE BOY WAS HIT BY SOMEONE.

After this, researcher after researcher came up with similar difficulties. According to DTC,

THERE'S A DRAGON IN THE STREET

should be more difficult to process than

A DRAGON IS IN THE STREET.

Yet the opposite is true. Similarly,

DEE IS HARD TO PLEASE

should be more complex than

FOR ANY ONE TO PLEASE DEE IS HARD.

Yet in practice the first sentence is much simpler (Watt, 1970).

It seems, then, that both the correspondence hypothesis and DTC must be abandoned. Transformational grammar is *not* a model of the production and comprehension of speech, and derivational complexity as measured in terms of transformations does not correlate with processing complexity. Sentences that are transformationally complex are often simpler to produce and comprehend than those that are transformationally simpler, and complexity itself is a far more complicated notion than was originally supposed. Clearly, Chomsky is right when he denies that there is a direct relationship between language knowledge, as encapsulated in a transformational grammar, and language usage.

The deep structure hypothesis

By the mid-sixties, the majority of psycholinguists had realized quite clearly that transformations had no direct relevance to the way a person produces and understands a sentence. However, the irrelevance of transformations does not mean that other aspects of transformational grammar are also irrelevant. So in the late 1960s another hypothesis was put forward – the suggestion that when people process sentences, they mentally set up a Chomsky-like deep structure. In other words, when someone produces, comprehends or recalls a sentence, 'the speaker-hearer's internal representation of grammatical relations is mediated by structures that are isomorphic to those that the grammatical formalism employs' (Fodor, Bever and Garrett, 1974:262). The experiments that are of most relevance to this hypothesis are of two types: recall experiments and click experiments.

A number of recall experiments have produced interesting results. Two of these will be described here. One was carried out by Blumenthal (1967) and the other by Wanner (1974).

Blumenthal asked his subjects to memorize pairs of sentences such as

GLOVES WERE MADE BY TAILORS
GLOVES WERE MADE BY HAND.

He then asked them to recall each sentence by prompting them with either the word TAILORS or the word HAND. When prompted by the word TAILORS, the subjects recalled the first sentence fairly well. But they were not nearly so successful with the second when prompted by the word HAND. What do we conclude from this? Blumenthal himself was fairly cautious in his assessment. He merely claimed that the experiment proves that simple slot-filling operations do not explain language, and that speakers are able to recognize the fundamentally different functions of TAILORS and HAND, although the sentences are superficially similar: 'Apparently the implicit semantic and grammatical abilities of the Ss enabled them to infer different relational characteristics for sentences that were otherwise the same in observed phrase stucture' (Blumenthal 1967:206). But this is not particularly surprising, and tells us nothing new. More interesting are subsequent speculations as to why TAILORS was a better prompt than HAND. One suggestion is that subjects were remembering the deep structure configuration of the sentences.

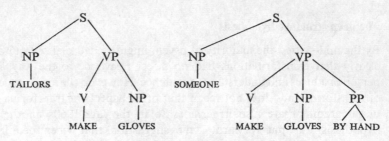

In the deep structure, TAILORS is considerably more prominent. It is directly underneath, or 'dominated' by the S-node. In other words, it is one of the basic components of the sentence, and is essential to its intrinsic structure. But HAND is far less important. It appears relatively low down on the deep structure tree. If subjects remember sentences in terms of their deep structures, then it makes sense that they should reconstruct them from the top of the tree downwards. But this is not the only possible explanation. TAILORS occurs frequently in speech without an accompanying BY, while HAND is often part of a set phrase BY HAND, so splitting up BY and HAND may have caused confusion, and hindered rather than aided recall.

The results of the recall experiment carried out by Wanner are less easy to explain away. He showed his subjects pairs of sentences such as

THE GOVERNOR ASKED THE DETECTIVES TO CEASE DRINKING
THE GOVERNOR ASKED THE DETECTIVES TO PREVENT DRINKING.

When prompted with the word DETECTIVES, the subjects tended to recall the first sentence more readily than the second. Why? It cannot be because the first sentence is more inherently memorable, since there was no difference in the level of recall of the two sentences when the word GOVERNOR was used as a prompt. One possible

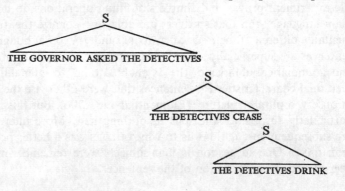

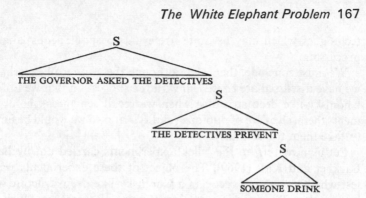

explanation is that the word DETECTIVE occurs three times in the proposed deep structure of the first sentence, but only twice in that of the second sentence.

This is an intriguing result. At first sight it seems strongly to support the notion of a Chomskyan deep structure. But we must not be too optimistic, because the nature of the experiments themselves may have falsified the results. The subjects were told in advance that the experiments involved memorization, and this may have affected their attitude. One psychologist found that he got quite different results in a memorization experiment when he did not tell his subjects that they would be expected to recall the sentences (Johnson-Laird and Stevenson, 1970). Furthermore, a number of psychologists have found that all memory of syntax and vocabulary normally fades very fast indeed, unless a subject is specifically told that he will be asked to recall the sentence. Memory for syntax of any kind is near to chance approximately half a minute after a sentence has been spoken (Sachs, 1967). In normal circumstances, it seems, people remember only the gist of what has been said, and they often confuse this with a number of extra beliefs and expectations about the topic under discussion (Fillenbaum, 1973). So it may be unrealistic to expect to find any syntax retained in normal recall. Johnson-Laird notes, 'No one knows how meaning is represented within memory, but there is no evidence to show that any form of syntactic structure is directly involved' (Johnson-Laird, 1970:269).

In brief, many psychologists now consider that recall experiments are irrelevant to the study of deep structure because of the natural tendency of humans to 'wipe away' the syntax and exact words of a sentence, unless they are carefully instructed to the contrary – in which case the experiment will reflect conscious memorization techniques which may be quite irrelevant to spontaneous language processing.

We must conclude, then, that although the two recall experiments we have discussed are *consistent* with the suggestion that we utilize a Chomsky-like deep structure when we recall sentences, the experiments themselves are of dubious validity – and so we would be unwise to take them too seriously.

Let us now turn to the 'click' experiments carried out by Bever, Lackner and Kirk (1969). The object of these experiments was to test whether a person recovers a Chomsky-like deep structure when he decodes. The experimenters took pairs of sentences which had similar surface structures, but different deep structures. For example:

THE CORRUPT POLICE CAN'T BEAR CRIMINALS TO CONFESS QUICKLY
THE CORRUPT POLICE CAN'T FORCE CRIMINALS TO CONFESS QUICKLY.

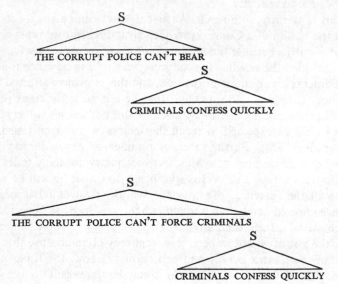

In the first sentence, the word *criminals* only occurs once in the deep structure, but in the second sentence it occurs twice, according to a 'classic' transformational model. If anyone doubts that these sentences have a different deep structure, try turning them round into the passive, and the difference becomes clear: the first sentence immediately becomes quite ungrammatical, though there is nothing wrong with the second:

*CRIMINALS CANNOT BE BORN BY THE POLICE TO CONFESS QUICKLY

CRIMINALS CANNOT BE FORCED BY THE POLICE TO CONFESS QUICKLY.

In the experiment, the subjects were asked to wear headphones. Then the sentences were played into one ear, and a 'click' which occurred during the word CRIMINALS was played into the other. Subjects were asked to report whereabouts in the sentence they heard the click. In the first sentence, subjects tended to hear the click *before* the word CRIMINALS, where a Chomskyan deep-structure suggests a structural break:

◀— •

THE CORRUPT POLICE CAN'T BEAR / CRIMINALS TO CONFESS QUICKLY

But in the second sentence, the click stayed still, as if the hearers could not decide where the structural break occurred. They behaved as if CRIMINALS straddled the gap between the two sections of the sentence. Since in deep structure CRIMINALS occurs twice, with the structural break between the two occurrences, this is a very encouraging result:

THE CORRUPT POLICE CAN'T FORCE CRIMINALS/
CRIMINALS TO CONFESS QUICKLY

This suggests quite strongly that people recover a 'classic' deep structure when they decode a sentence.

But we must be cautious. One swallow does not make a summer, and one experiment does not prove the validity of deep structure. (In any case, as will be discussed below, any science proceeds by *disproving* hypotheses, not by proving them.) Moreover, the significance of this particular experiment has been disputed. Both its design and interpretation have been challenged. The results may be due to the unusual experimental situation, or they may be connected with meaning rather than with an underlying deep structure syntax (Fillenbaum, 1971; Johnson-Laird, 1974). The 'muddled history of clickology' (Johnson-Laird, 1974:138) is still a source of considerable controversy.

What are we to conclude so far? The experiments described in this section are *consistent* with the suggestion that we recover a Chomsky-like deep structure when we recall or understand sentences. But they are consistent with other hypotheses also. All that we can be sure about is that underlying every sentence is a set of internal relations which may well not be obvious on the surface. As Bever notes (1970:

286): 'The fact that every sentence has an internal and external structure is maintained by all linguistic theories – although the theories may differ as to the role the internal structure plays within the linguistic description. Thus talking involves actively mapping internal structures onto external sequences, and understanding others involves mapping external sequences onto internal structures.' In other words, although it may seem rather *unlikely* that we always recover a Chomskyan deep structure when we understand sentences, we have not yet disproved this possibility. No one has yet shown that the suggestion is totally false.

The point is, science proceeds by *disproving* hypotheses. Suppose you were interested in flowers. You might formulate a hypothesis, 'All roses are white, red, pink, orange or yellow.' There would be absolutely no point at all in collecting hundreds, thousands, or even millions of white, red, pink, orange and yellow roses. You would merely be collecting additional evidence consistent with your hypothesis. If you were genuinely interested in making a botanical advance, you would send people in all directions hunting for black, blue, mauve or green roses. Your hypothesis would stand until somebody found a blue rose. Then, in theory, you should be delighted that botany had made progress, and found out about blue roses. Naturally, when you formulate a hypothesis it has to be one which is capable of disproof. A hypothesis such as 'Henry VIII would have disliked spaceships' cannot be disproved, and consequently is useless. A hypothesis such as 'The planet Mars is made of chalk' would have been useless in the year 100 AD, when there was no hope of getting to Mars – but it is a perfectly legitimate, if implausible, one in the twentieth century when planet probes and space travel are feasible.

This leads us back to Chomsky. Some people have claimed that deep structures cannot be disproved, and so are useless as a scientific hypothesis. It is true that, at the moment, it is difficult to see how to test them. But psycholinguistic experimentation is, in some ways, still in its infancy. Every year new techniques are introduced. In the last ten years or so an enormous amount of progress has been made. Perhaps with the development of further new techniques, ways will be found of definitively disproving theories about the 'inner structure' of a language. At the moment, as one psycholinguist notes, 'Presently available evidence on almost any psycholinguistic point is so scanty as to blunt any claim that this or that hypothesis has truly been disconfirmed' (Watt, 1970:138).

To sum up, the suggestion that people utilize a Chomskyan deep structure when they recall, comprehend or produce sentences seems unlikely, but the hypothesis has not been truly disconfirmed, and at the moment it is not clear how to do this.

The linguistic archive

We have now come to the conclusion that transformations are irrelevant to sentence processing, and that deep structure is not necessarily relevant. The few clues we have are consistent with the deep structure hypothesis – but we can think up alternative explanations.

We are coming round to the view that transformational grammar represents a kind of archive which sit in the brain ready for consultation, but is possibly only partially consulted in the course of a conversation. Perhaps it could be likened to other types of knowledge, such as the knowledge that four times three is the same as six times two. This information is mentally stored, but is not necessarily directly used when checking to see if the milk bill is correct.

Of course, the information may be represented in the brain in a rather different way from that suggested in a transformational grammar. But once again we are not in a position to *disprove* the transformational model. Until we *have* disproved it, we may say that a transformational grammar represents a linguistic archive which encapsulates a speaker's latent knowledge of his language.

Note that we are *not* proposing a clean break between language knowledge and language usage. In practice the two overlap to a quite considerable extent, and the extent of the overlap varies from sentence to sentence.

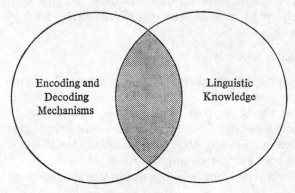

Let us take a simple example:

AUNT AGATHA WAS RUN OVER LAST THURSDAY.

We note that a short passive of this type is generally simpler and quicker to comprehend than a full passive such as

AUNT AGATHA WAS RUN DOWN BY SOMEONE (OR SOMETHING) LAST THURSDAY.

It therefore seems quite unnecessary to suppose that, in order to understand this sentence, a hearer has to recover a Chomsky-like deep structure which includes the agent SOMEONE (or SOMETHING):

SOMEONE (OR SOMETHING) RAN OVER AUNT AGATHA LAST THURSDAY.

Instead, he may not pay attention to the agent; he may be too busy thinking about Aunt Agatha. However, if he *did* spend rather longer pondering about the sentence, he could recover not only the agent SOMEONE (or SOMETHING) which the 'classic' deep structure suggests, but much more information in addition (Watt, 1970). He could suggest that Aunt Agatha was run over by SOMETHING, rather than SOMEONE, and that this something was probably a MOVING VEHICLE. He obtained all this information from his knowledge of the lexical item RUN OVER – but it is optional whether he uses it or not when he comprehends the sentence.

And RUN OVER is not an isolated example. Other verbs from which a person could also extract a considerable amount of information if necessary are DEFLOWER and GORE. In

MARIGOLD WAS DEFLOWERED

he knows that SOMEONE deflowered Marigold, and that the deflowerer was likely to be male and human (Watt, 1970). Similarly, in the sentence

CHARLIE WAS GORED

he can assume that the gorer was male and bovine. This information is *potentially* recoverable, though it *need* not be recovered.

In other words, someone who knows a language has an enormous amount of knowledge which he *could* use when he encodes or decodes, but he does not have to. Or rather, he usually has to use some of it, but often only a rather small proportion.

Another perhaps more obvious example is the sentence

PALE PEOPLE EAT PINK PILLS.

It is quite unlikely that anyone recovers the full deep structure when he decodes or encodes this sentence, which is something like:

PEOPLE WHO ARE PALE EAT PILLS WHICH ARE PINK.

There is no doubt that speakers of English *can* relate PINK PILLS to PILLS WHICH ARE PINK – but there is no need for them to do so when they produce or hear this sentence. However, there may be other occasions when speakers *do* need to utilize rather more knowledge in their interpretation of a sentence which starts out in a similar fashion:

DROWNING HEFFALUMPS CAN CAUSE A TERRIBLE COMMOTION.

Here, the hearer might well subconsciously have to query, 'Are we dealing with heffalumps who are drowning, or someone who is drowning heffalumps?' And he might even put this query into words.

This again suggests that a transformational grammar represents a linguistic archive whose contents are available for use when a person processes a sentence. In principle, someone could, if he wanted to, recover *all* the knowledge stored in connection with a sentence when he decodes or encodes it. This may be what Chomsky meant when he wrote that 'the generative grammar represents the information concerning sentence structure that is available, in principle, to one who has acquired a language. It indicates how, ideally . . . he would understand a sentence' (Chomsky, 1963:326). The word 'ideally' may mean perfect understanding of the sentence as far as is possible within the limits of grammatical knowledge. Of course, in practice, no one has the time or the need to unravel every sentence in this way. Most people make a quick decision about the sentences they hear, and do not consider all the ramifications. In Bever's words, they rely on 'perceptual strategies' or short cuts, rather than on full utilization of 'epistemological structures' or beliefs about language structure (Bever, 1970:281).

But it would be a mistake to assume that 'epistemological structures' are an optional extra. A person who could not detect ambiguities, who could not make judgements of grammaticality, and who could not link up related sentences would only 'know' his language in a very limited way. There is no clear-cut line between knowing *how* to utter and comprehend sentences, and knowing *that* these sentences are grammatical and how they are related to other sentences. Humans do not behave like spiders, who can weave webs without any conscious knowledge about their skill. Humans need knowledge about their language in order to function properly as articulate mammals. As far as language is concerned, the distinction between knowing *how* (as in knowing how to walk) and knowing *that* (as in knowing that the world is round) is a fuzzy one, because the two types of knowledge overlap.

Let us summarize what we have just said. We have concluded that a transformational grammar incorporates mainly 'archival knowledge' or 'epistemological structures' – a set of beliefs or intuitions about one's language which may not necessarily be recoverable at a conscious level. These beliefs are not merely optional extras, they are an essential part of anyone's ability to speak and understand a language.

We need to ask a further question about these 'epistemological structures', and that is, how are they acquired? Do children learn how to use language, then later build up full knowledge about it, as Bever suggests (1970)? Or do the two learning processes go on simultaneously? This question has been studied by three psychologists from the University of Pennsylvania (Gleitman, Gleitman and Shipley, 1972). They concluded that the process of learning how to speak was intertwined with that of acquiring beliefs about one's language. Both types of knowledge progress simultaneously, though the latter develops considerably more slowly. Even two-year-olds have *some* notion of grammaticalness, though this is rather shaky. And children's judgements about their language remain shaky even when they can speak fluently. It is between the ages of five and eight that children start to have intuitions about their language that parallel those of an adult (and this agrees with the conclusions which we reached in Chapter 7 concerning a child's attitude to the relationship of actives and passives: he can use them both before he relates them). Let us illustrate these points.

The fact that even quite young children have some beliefs about their language is shown by two-year-old Allison, who judged the sequence

*BALL ME THE THROW

to be 'silly', and corrected it to

THROW ME THE BALL.

Similarly, two-year-old Sarah amended

SONG ME A SING

to

SING ME A SONG.

However, Sarah's judgements were not consistently reliable, since she found

WASH THE DISHES

an odd sentence, and corrected it to

WASH THE DISHES (!)

It was easier to elicit responses from the older children, and the results were more clear-cut. For example, when seven children between the ages of five and eight were asked whether the sentence

I AM KNOWING YOUR SISTER

sounded 'sensible' or 'silly', the five- and six-year-olds found nothing wrong with it, but the seven- and eight-year-olds disapproved of it, though they could not always say why it was odd. The following is the response given by seven-year-old Claire:

R (Researcher): How about this one: I AM KNOWING YOUR SISTER
C (Claire): No. I KNOW YOUR SISTER
R: Why not I AM KNOWING YOUR SISTER? You can say I AM EATING YOUR DINNER.
C: It's different! (shouting) You say different sentences in different ways. Otherwise it doesn't make sense!

But for other sentences, Claire not only gave adult judgements concerning grammaticalness, she also gave an adult-type reason:

R: How about this one: BOY IS AT THE DOOR.
C: If his name is BOY. You should – the kid is named John, see? JOHN IS AT THE DOOR or A BOY IS AT THE DOOR.

The researchers note: 'The ability to reflect upon language dramatically increases with age. The older children were better not only in noting deviance but also in explaining where the deviance lies' (Gleitman, Gleitman and Shipley, 1972:160).

We can now summarize the conclusions we have reached in this chapter. We have been examining the relationship between language knowledge (as 'captured' by a transformational grammar) to the way in which we produce and comprehend sentences. In the first section we noted that transformations are irrelevant to the way in which we encode and decode. In the second section, we saw that the hypothesis that we recover a Chomsky-like deep structure when we comprehend a sentence has not been disproved, but is on the whole unlikely. In the final section we concluded that a transformational grammar represents a person's linguistic archive – a store of knowledge about his language that is only partially utilized in the course of conversations. This archive develops simultaneously with, though rather more slowly than, the ability to speak and comprehend sentences.

In the next two chapters we shall deal with the encoding and decoding mechanisms which overlap with this linguistic archive.

10 The Case of the Missing Fingerprint

How do we understand speech?

'It seems very pretty,' Alice said, 'but it's rather hard to understand.' You see, she didn't like to confess, even to herself, that she couldn't make it out at all. 'Somehow it seems to fill my head with ideas – only I don't know exactly what they are!'

Lewis Carroll
Through the Looking Glass

In the last chapter we noted that a transformational grammar could not give us any direct insights into the way a person understands or produces speech. It merely represents the knowledge that is potentially available to someone when he encodes or decodes. The extent to which this knowledge is used varies from sentence to sentence, and probably from speaker to speaker. So we now need to find out about the processes of comprehension and production.

Finding out about encoding and decoding is more difficult than it might appear at first sight. One basic problem is that the link between the two may not be straightforward. Although it would be simpler for psycholinguists if they were directly related, we have no reason for assuming this is so, and must allow for at least four possibilities:

1. Encoding and decoding are totally different.
2. Decoding is encoding in reverse.
3. Decoding is the same as encoding: that is, a decoder reconstructs the message for himself in the same way as he would construct it if he were the speaker.
4. Decoding and encoding are partially the same, and partially different.

This range of options means that we must deal with comprehension and production separately. As will become clear, possibility (4) is perhaps nearest to the truth.

178 *The Articulate Mammal*

Let us look at decoding first. How should we begin? One useful way is to note down utterances which hearers find difficult to comprehend, and then find out why. Let us give some examples.

A card pinned to the door of a Bayswater flat said: 'Milkman, please stop milk until July 3. If you do not see this, THE WOMAN WHO HAS THE FLAT ON THE GROUND FLOOR'S SISTER will tell you.' It possibly took the milkman some time to realise who was supposed to be telling him about the milk. Yet there is nothing actually *wrong* with this sentence grammatically. It just takes a long time to process.

A similar example is

THE PIG PUSHED IN FRONT OF THE PIGLETS ATE ALL THE FOOD.

Again, there is nothing really wrong with this sentence. Compare:

THE GIRL PUSHED IN FRONT OF THE BUS ESCAPED WITH MINOR INJURIES.

A more extreme example is:

THE CAT THE DOG THE MAN THE BABY TRIPPED UP BIT SCRATCHED COLLAPSED.

(The baby tripped up the man, the man bit the dog, the dog scratched the cat, the cat collapsed).

This is an exceptionally difficult sentence to cope with. Some people find it impossible. But, again, there is nothing tangibly *wrong* with it grammatically. Somehow or other, it is just too complex to be dealt with easily.

If we can satisfactorily account for why these sentences are difficult to understand, we shall have discovered quite a lot about decoding mechanisms.

Broadly speaking, a hearer is likely to find a sentence hard to comprehend for one or both of the following reasons. It will be difficult if

1. It goes against his linguistic expectations
2. It goes beyond certain 'psychological' limits.

Let us consider each of these. But we will first of all show that decoding is not the simple matter it was once thought to be. People do not passively 'register' the sentences uttered by a speaker. Instead they hear what they *expect* to hear. They actively reconstruct both the sounds and syntax of an utterance in accordance with their expectations.

Hearing what we expect to hear

Until relatively recently, psycholinguists assumed that the process
of understanding or decoding speech was a simple one. The hearer
was envisaged, metaphorically, as a secretary sitting at a typewriter
taking down a dictation. She mentally 'typed out' the sounds she
heard one by one, then 'read off' the words formed by them. Or,
taking another metaphor, the hearer was envisaged as a detective
solving a crime by matching fingerprints to known criminals. All
the detective had to do was match a fingerprint found on the
scene of the crime against one in his files, and see who it belonged
to. Just as no two people's fingerprints are the same, so each sound
was regarded as having a unique acoustic pattern.

Unfortunately, this simple picture turns out to be wrong. A
series of experiments conducted by phoneticians and psycholinguists
have disproved the 'passive secretary' or 'fingerprints' approach.
There are a number of problems.

First of all, it is clear that hearers cannot 'take down' or 'match'
sounds one by one. Apart from anything else, the speed of utterance
makes this an impossible task. If we assume an average of four
sounds per English word, and a speed of five words a second, we
are expecting the ear and brain to cope with around twenty sounds
a second. But humans cannot process this number of separate
signals in that time – it is just too many (Liberman *et al.*, 1967).

A second reason why the 'passive secretary' or 'fingerprint'
approach does not work is that there is no fixed acoustic representation of, say, a T, parallel to the fixed typewriter symbol T. The
acoustic traces left by sounds are quite unlike the fingerprints left
by criminals. In actual speech, each sound varies considerably
depending on what comes before and after it. The T in TOP differs
from the T in STOP or the T in BOTTLE. In addition, a sound varies
from speaker to speaker to a quite surprising extent. So direct 'copy-
typing' or 'matching' of each sound is impossible. (If it were feasible,
cheap machines which could do this would long ago have flooded
the market and made audio-typists an irrelevant luxury.)

A third, related problem is that sounds are acoustically on a
continuum: B gradually shades into D which in turn shades into G.
There is no definite borderline between acoustically similar sounds,
just as it is not always possible to distinguish between a flower vase
and a mug, or a bush and a tree (Liberman *et al.*, 1957).

These findings indicate that there is no sure way in which a human can 'fingerprint' a sound or match it to a mental 'typewriter symbol', because the acoustic patterns of sounds are not fixed and distinct. And even if they were, people would not have time to identify each one positively. The information extracted from the sound waves forms 'no more than a rough guide to the sense of the message, a kind of scaffolding upon which the listener constructs or reconstructs the sentences' (Fry, 1970:31).

In interpreting speech sounds, hearers are like detectives who find that solving a crime is not a simple case of matching fingerprints to criminals. Instead, they find a situation where 'a given type of clue might have been left by any of a number of criminals or where a given criminal might have left any of a number of different types of clue' (Fodor, Bever and Garrett, 1974:301). What they are faced with is 'more like the array of disparate data from which Sherlock Holmes deduces the identity of the criminal'. In such cases, the detectives' background information must come into play.

In other words, deciphering the sounds of speech is an *active* not a passive process. Hearers have to compute *actively* the possible phonetic message by using their background knowledge of the language. This is perhaps not so astonishing. We have plenty of other evidence for the active nature of this process. We all know how difficult it is to hear the exact sounds of a foreign word. This is because we are so busy imposing on it what we expect to hear, in terms of our own language habits, that we fail to notice certain novel features.

However, it is not only a person's expectation of sound patterns that influences what she hears, but perhaps to an even greater extent, her expectation of syntactic and semantic patterns. We cannot yet be completely sure how we disentangle these, since 'almost every aspect of sentence recognition remains unsettled despite the experimental attention that the problem has recently received' (Fodor, Bever, and Garrett, 1974:374). But at the moment the evidence seems to point in one direction. When someone hears a sentence, she latches on to outline clues, and 'jumps to conclusions' about what she is hearing. An analogy might make this clearer. Suppose someone found a large foot sticking out from under her bed one night. She would be likely to shriek 'There's a man under my bed', because past experience has led her to believe that large feet are usually attached to male human beings. Instead of just reporting the actual situation, 'There is a foot sticking out from under the bed', she has jumped to the conclusion that this foot belongs to a man, and this man is lying under the bed. All the evidence suggests that we make similar 'informed guesses' about the material we hear.

The kind of guesses a person makes depends very much on what she expects to hear. So this is the next question we must tackle. What kind of expectations do people bring to the task of sentence comprehension? And what kind of clues do they look for? One person who has worked on this is Tom Bever, a psychologist at Columbia University, New York. The next section is based to a large extent on suggestions made by him (1970).

Informed guesses

When someone sets about decoding an utterance he does so in accordance with a number of assumptions or expectations about the probable structure and content of the sentences of his language. Sentences which fit in with these expectations are likely to be easy to understand, and those which do not, less so. Let us suggest what these assumptions are likely to be. The following four seem basic to English speakers.

Assumption 1. 'Every sentence consists of one or more sentoids or sentence-like chunks, and each sentoid normally includes a noun-phrase followed by a verb, optionally followed by another noun-phrase.' That is, every sentence will either be a simple one such as

> DO YOU LIKE CURRY?
> TADPOLES TURN INTO FROGS
> DON'T TOUCH THAT WIRE

or it will be a 'complex' one containing more than one sentence-like structure or sentoid. For example, the sentence

> IT IS NOT SURPRISING THAT THE FACT THAT PETER SINGS IN HIS BATH UPSETS THE LANDLADY

contains three sentoids:

> IT IS NOT SURPRISING ▲
> THAT THE FACT ▲ UPSETS THE LANDLADY
> THAT PETER SINGS IN HIS BATH

Within a sentence, each sentoid normally contains either a noun-phrase – verb sequence such as

THE LARGE GORILLA GROWLED

or a noun-phrase – verb – noun-phrase sequence such as

COWS CHEW THE CUD.

Assumption 2. 'In a noun-phrase–verb–noun-phrase sequence, the first noun is usually the actor and the second the object.' That is, an English sentence normally has the word order actor–action–object with the person doing the action coming first as in

GIRAFFES EAT LEAVES
DIOGENES BOUGHT A BARREL.

Assumption 3. 'When a complex sentence is composed of a main clause and one or more subordinate clauses, the main clause usually comes first.' That is, it is more usual to find a sentence such as

NERO FIDDLED   [WHILE ROME BURNED]

than

[WHILE ROME BURNED]   NERO FIDDLED.

Similarly,

PETRONELLA EXPECTED [THAT PERICLES WOULD SCRUB THE FLOOR]

is considerably more likely than

*[THAT PERICLES WOULD SCRUB THE FLOOR] PETRONELLA EXPECTED

Assumption 4. 'Sentences usually make sense.' That is, people generally say things that are sensible. They utter sequences such as

HAVE YOU DONE THE WASHING UP?
THE TRAIN GOES AT EIGHT O'CLOCK

rather than

HAPPINESS SHOOTS LLAMAS
THE HONEY SPREAD MOTHER WITH A KNIFE.

Guided by these assumptions, which are possibly common to all English speakers, people devise 'strategies' for dealing with the sentences they come across. When a person hears a sentence, he looks for clues which will confirm that his expectations are correct. When he finds them (or thinks he has found them) he jumps to conclusions about what he is hearing. Let us briefly consider the strategies linked to the four assumptions mentioned above. Although we shall be labelling the strategies 'first', 'second', 'third', and 'fourth', this is not meant to refer to the order in which they are used. When we decode sentences all four seem to be working simultaneously.

The first strategy or working principle follows from assumption 1, and seems to be: 'Divide each sentence up into sentoids by assuming that each noun-phrase–verb (–noun-phrase) sequence represents a sentoid.' This is sometimes referred to as the *canonical sentoid* strategy, since noun-phrase–verb–noun-phrase is the 'canonical' or standard form of an English sentence. It is clear that we need such a strategy when we distinguish sentoids, since there are often no acoustic clues to help us divide a sentence up. We noted in Chapter 1 that subjects could not possibly have been using acoustic information when they correctly divided into two clauses the sentence:

IN ORDER TO CATCH HIS TRAIN/GEORGE DROVE FURIOUSLY TO THE STATION.

Fodor, Garrett and Bever note: 'An early stage in the perceptual analysis of linguistic material is the identification of the sentoids of which the input sentence is composed. By hypothesis, each such sentoid will consist of a subject NP and a verb which may or may not have an object' (Fodor, Bever and Garrett, 1974:344).

The clearest confirmation of this strategy comes from so-called 'centre embeddings' – sentences which have a Chinese box-like structure, one lying inside the other. The following is a double centre embedding – one sentence is inside another which is inside yet another:

THE MAN THE GIRL THE BOY MET BELIEVED LAUGHED.

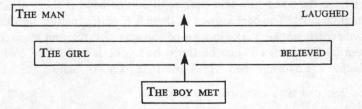

(The man, whom the girl believed the boy met, laughed.)

Blumenthal tested to see what happened when sentences of this type were memorized (1966). He noted that subjects tended to recall them as noun–verb sequences:

THE MAN, THE GIRL AND THE BOY MET, BELIEVED AND LAUGHED.

Their immediate reaction to being presented with an unusual sentence was to utilize the canonical sentoid strategy even though it was, strictly speaking, irrelevant. In a later experiment, Bever found to his surprise that subjects imposed an NP–V–NP sequence on sentences of this type *even after practice*. He comments, 'the NVN sequence is so compelling that it may be described as a 'linguistic illusion' which training cannot readily overcome' (Bever, 1970:295).

The canonical sentoid strategy seems to start young. Bever notes that by around the age of two children are already looking out for noun–verb sequences – though they tend to assume that the first noun goes with the first verb, and interpret

THE DOG THAT JUMPED FELL

as

THE DOG JUMPED.

Let us now turn to the second strategy. This one stems from assumption 2, and seems to be as follows: 'Interpret an NP–V–NP sequence as actor–action–object unless you have strong indications to the contrary.'

NP	V	NP
actor	action	object
PENGUINS	EAT	FISH

A number of experiments have shown that sentences which do not have the actor first take longer to comprehend if there are no semantic clues. The best known of these is Slobin's 'picture verification' experiment (1966a). He showed subjects pictures, and also read them out a sentence. Then he timed how long it took them to say whether the two matched. He found that passives such as

THE CAT WAS CHASED BY THE DOG

took longer to verify than the corresponding active

THE DOG CHASED THE CAT.

Another picture verification experiment showed that actor–action–object structures are comprehended more quickly than other structures which would fit the NP–V–NP sequence (Mehler and Carey, 1968):

THEY	ARE KIDNAPPING	BABIES
actor	action	object

was verified more quickly than

THEY	ARE	NOURISHING LUNCHES
subject	copula	complement

Bever (1971) has studied the development of the actor–action–object strategy in children by testing capacity to understand simple passive sentences which do not have semantic clues, such as

THE HORSE IS KISSED BY THE COW.

The result was somewhat surprising. Between the ages of two and four there was a steady improvement in the child's ability to understand these passives. But at the age of four there seemed to be a backward step. Suddenly there was a strong tendency to treat the first noun as actor and the second as object, even by children who had appeared to comprehend passives earlier. Why is this? Bever suggests that the temporary decrease in understanding is due to the development and over-generalization of the strategy, NP–V–NP equals actor–action–object. Why? Bever links the answer to the development of cerebral dominance. Around this time, one hemisphere shows definite signs of 'taking over' as far as speech is concerned. He claims that perceptual strategies of this type are firmly linked with the speech capacity of the left hemisphere.

We now come to the third strategy, which follows from assumption 3. It seems to be, 'Interpret the first clause as the main clause unless you have clear indications to the contrary.' The existence of this strategy accounts for the correct interpretation of

IT WAS OBVIOUS HE WAS DRUNK FROM THE WAY HE STAGGERED ACROSS THE ROAD.

Here, the subordinate clause is not marked in any way, but the hearer automatically assumes that it comes after the main clause. This strategy also accounts for the difficulty of

THE ELEPHANT SQUEEZED INTO A TELEPHONE BOOTH COLLAPSED.

Until he comes across the unexpected word COLLAPSED at the end of the sentence the hearer probably assumes that THE ELEPHANT SQUEEZED . . . was the beginning of the main clause. Further evidence in support of this strategy is the fact that sentences in which the subordinate clause occurs first are relatively hard to memorize. Subjects remembered

HE TOOTED THE HORN BEFORE HE SWIPED THE CABBAGES

more accurately than

AFTER HE TOOTED THE HORN HE SWIPED THE CABBAGES
(Clark and Clark, 1968).

We now come to the fourth strategy, which is perhaps the most powerful of all – though from the linguistic point of view, it is the least satisfactory because it is so vague. It says: 'Use your knowledge of the world to pick the most likely interpretation of the sentence you are hearing.' In certain circumstances this can override all other strategies, and reverse well-attested aspects of language behaviour. For example, under normal circumstances people find it much easier to remember sentences that are superficially grammatical than random strings of words. It is considerably easier to learn the apparently grammatical

THE YIGS WUR VUMLY RIXING HUM IN JEGEST MIV

than the shorter string

THE YIG WUR VUM RIX HUM IN JEG MIV (Epstein, 1961).

But this well-attested result can be *reversed* if the subjects are presented with semantically strange grammatical sentences and ungrammatical strings of words which appear to make sense. Subjects remember more words from strings such as:

NEIGHBOURS SLEEPING NOISY WAKE PARTIES
DETER DRIVERS ACCIDENTS FATAL CARELESS

than they do from sentences such as:

RAPID BOUQUETS DETER SUDDEN NEIGHBOURS

PINK ACCIDENTS CAUSE SLEEPING STORMS
(Marks and Miller, 1964).

This expectation that the world will make sense is brought into play in decoding. In the picture verification experiment mentioned above, Slobin (1966a) found that a sentence such as

THE CHEESE WAS EATEN BY THE MOUSE

(where the passive is 'irreversible' since cheeses do not eat mice) was understood as quickly as the active – though normally, passive sentences take longer.

However, knowledge of the world is more relevant to adult decoding than to that of young children. Children only gradually acquire a set of expectations as to which words go together. Youngsters do not necessarily find anomalous sentences more difficult to recall than normal ones. One psychologist concludes: 'It makes little difference whether one says to a child

WILD INDIANS SHOOT RUNNING BUFFALOES

or

WILD ELEPHANTS SHOOT TICKING RESTAURANTS.

The sentences are equally remarkable, and both have a meaning that cannot be totally grasped' (McNeill, 1970:118). A similar observation was made by Bever. He found no significant difference in the reaction of young children to

THE MOTHER PATS THE DOG

and

THE DOG PATS THE MOTHER. (Bever, 1970)

So far, then, we have listed a number of assumptions which a speaker appears to have about his language, and suggested a number of so-called 'perceptual strategies' which they give rise to. Let us now summarize what we have said by going through the possible steps by which a hearer might decode a fairly straightforward sentence such as

SEBASTIAN DISCOVERED THAT THE GORILLA HAD ESCAPED.

As soon as someone begins to speak, the hearer automatically prepares to bring strategy 1 into play. He mentally gets ready for at least one sentoid consisting of an NP–V(–NP) sequence. In other words, he begins to reconstruct a mental 'tree' of the sentence from the top downwards before a message has been received (Kimball, 1973). In setting up this tree he also possibly gets ready to use strategies 2 and 3 – he expects that what he is about to hear will be the main clause, and that it will begin with the actor.

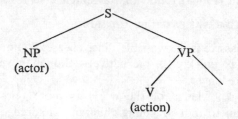

As soon as he hears the words SEBASTIAN DISCOVERED . . . he checks them against his expectations, and finds that they are fulfilled. (If they had not been fulfilled, he would have had to hastily revise his tree, which would have caused a brief delay in decoding.) He can mentally 'fill in' these words on his tree:

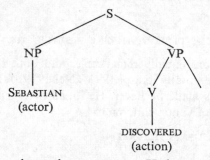

Then he waits to hear what comes next. He knows that DISCOVERED must be followed by either a noun, or a subordinate clause, but he does not yet know which option is being chosen. He possibly waits until he is quite sure which alternative is being selected before he fills in further items on his tree (Kimball, 1973). If he started constructing more branches too soon, he would have to make two alternative trees. He would not know whether SEBASTIAN DISCOVERED THAT . . . was going to lead to a noun or a new sentoid. It could end up as

SEBASTIAN DISCOVERED THAT GORILLA   (THAT + noun)

or

SEBASTIAN DISCOVERED THAT THE GORILLA HAD ESCAPED (that + S).

As soon as he hears the words THAT THE . . . he mentally starts another sentoid:

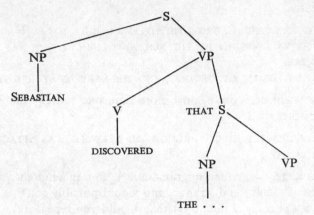

He then listens for the rest of the sentence . . . GORILLA HAD ESCAPED which again complies with the tree he had expected.

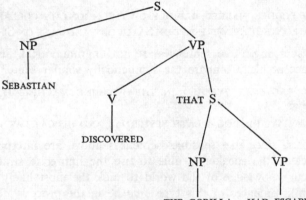

The whole sentence has complied with his expectations, and his strategies have worked.

Even quite odd sentences seem easy to understand if they fit in with the strategies:

THE KANGAROO SQUEEZED THE ORANGE AND THE KOOKABURRA ATE THE PIPS.

But sentences which do not fulfil the hearer's expectations are a little more difficult to comprehend. Each of the following go against one of the four basic strategies. The sentences can be understood reasonably easily, but they do need marginally more attention from the hearer:

> AFTER RUSHING ACROSS THE FIELD THE BULL TOSSED HARRY
> THE VAN WAS HIT BY THE BUS, AND THE CAR WAS RAMMED BY
> A TAXI
> THE POSTMAN BIT THE DOG, AND THE BABY SCRATCHED THE CAT.

When a sentence goes against more than one strategy the effect is rather worse:

> THE SHARK PUSHED THROUGH THE SEAWEED WAS ATTACKED BY
> A TADPOLE.

The sentence is neither ungrammatical, nor incomprehensible. It just seems clumsy and strange, and would possibly cause a hearer to say: 'I'm sorry, I didn't get that. Could you repeat it?'

It is an interesting fact that speakers tend to avoid sentences which go against perceptual strategies to too great an extent. People just do not *say* things such as

> THE POODLE WALKED RAPIDLY UP THE MOUNTAIN COLLAPSED
> JOAN GAVE JUNE A PRESENT ON SATURDAY AND JANE ON SUNDAY.

Strictly speaking, these sentences are not ungrammatical, just odd and unacceptable. Compare the syntactically similar sentences:

> THE RAG DOLL WASHED IN THE WASHING MACHINE FELL TO
> PIECES
> MAX GAVE HIS DOG A BATH YESTERDAY AND HIS CAT LAST WEEK.

However, since the 'sensible' sentences above are interpretable *only* because the speaker is able to use the imprecise strategy 4 ('Use your knowledge of the world to pick the most likely interpretation'), sentences of this type *may* be in the process of being eliminated from the English language – since perceptual needs can often influence linguistic rules. To quote Bever: 'The syntax of a language is partly moulded by grammatical responses to behavioural constraints' (1970:321).

Of course, the four strategies noted so far are not the only ones we use when we decode, and we could continue by listing more assumptions and more linked strategies. But there seems little point in doing this, once the general idea of perceptual strategies has been made clear. What we have said so far is that sentences which go against a hearer's expectations are more difficult to comprehend since the strategies he is utilizing do not work. Let us now consider some further reasons why a sentence may be difficult to comprehend.

Further difficulties

So far we have suggested that a hearer approaches the task of decoding with certain expectations about what he is going to hear – expectations that a sentoid will have a noun-phrase and a verb, that the actor will come first, that the main clause will come before the subordinate clause, and that the sentence will make sense. Sentences which go against these expectations will be more difficult, though by no means impossible, to comprehend. These are all *linguistic* expectations. But sentences may also be difficult to understand for general psychological reasons. The factors which affect them relate not only to language, but to other aspects of human ability, such as visual perception and mathematical skills.

Some of the factors we shall discuss seem to be 'purely' psychological, others to be linguistic and psychological combined. Let us consider these factors, starting with the most general ones.

To begin with, an obvious and also relatively trivial problem is one of length. For example, it is often difficult on a journey to follow the route directions of a passer-by. People tend to say things like: 'Take the third turning on the left-hand side past the fourth pub just before the hairdressers next door to the church.' Apart from anything else, this sentence is just too long to be retained in the memory. Before the speaker gets to the end, the hearer is likely to have forgotten the first part. Fodor, Bever and Garrett (1974:342) point out that we have only a limited amount of short-term memory available for the perceptual processing of sentences. Therefore, it is likely that we deal with only one sentoid at a time. As soon as we have decoded one, we probably forget the syntax, and remove the 'gist' of it to another, less accessible, memory space. This hypothesis seems to be supported by a number of psycholinguistic experiments. For example, in one experiment subjects were asked to report as soon as they heard a 'click' which occurred during the sentence (Abrams and Bever, 1969). It was found that they reacted more quickly to clicks coming at the beginning of sentoids than they did to clicks placed at the end. This suggests that the hearer's mind is cluttered up with information towards the end of a sentoid, leaving him with little spare attention for noticing clicks. As soon as a sentoid is completed, he 'wipes the slate clean', and starts afresh.

In other words, because humans have a limited immediate memory space, they deal with sentences sentoid by sentoid. This limited space would explain not only why unusually long sentoids are difficult (as in the direction-finding example given earlier), but also, perhaps, why sentences which cannot easily be divided into sentoids are a problem. For example,

THIS IS THE BUS THAT THE CAR THAT THE PROFESSOR THAT THE GIRL KISSED DROVE HIT

is more difficult than

THIS IS THE GIRL THAT KISSED THE PROFESSOR THAT DROVE THE CAR THAT HIT THE BUS

even though the second sentence has exactly the same number of words and almost the same meaning. Part of the trouble with the first is that you have to carry almost all of it unanalysed in your head. You have to wait until the end for the verb HIT that goes with CAR before you can divide it into sentoids.:

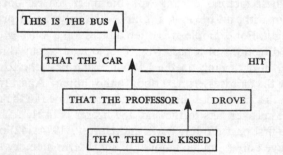

So far, then, we have said that sentences which overload short-term memory are difficult to cope with. However, memory by itself is possibly not as important as other factors. In dealing with sentences which cannot easily be divided into sentoids like the one above, it is not only the memory load, but also the difficulty of processing three sentoids simultaneously which causes problems. Three are not impossible (as some people have suggested, e.g. Kimball, 1973) because we can often (after some thought) compose sentences such as:

THE NEW BORN CROCODILE [WHICH THE KEEPER [YOU WERE TALKING TO THIS AFTERNOON] LOOKS AFTER] IS BEING MOVED TO ANOTHER ZOO.

But in general it is unusual to find more than two sentoids being coped with easily (and two are more difficult than one). It seems to be a fact about human nature that a person can only deal with a limited number of things at one time.

This leads us on to another difficulty, which overlaps with the simultaneous processing problem – that of interruptions. An interrupted structure is only slightly more difficult to process than an uninterrupted one, providing there are clear indications that you are dealing with an interruption. For example, the following sentence has a seventeen word interruption:

> THE GIRL [WHOM CUTHBERT KISSED SO ENTHUSIASTICALLY AT THE PARTY LAST NIGHT WHEN HE THOUGHT NO ONE WAS LOOKING] IS MY SISTER.

It is not particularly difficult to understand because the hearer knows (from the opening sequence THE GIRL WHOM . . .) that he is still waiting for the main verb. However, if there are no indications that an interruption is in progress, the sentence immediately increases in difficulty and oddness:

> CUTHBERT PHONED THE GIRL [WHOM HE KISSED SO ENTHUSIASTI-CALLY AT THE PARTY LAST NIGHT WHEN HE THOUGHT NO ONE WAS LOOKING] UP.

Here UP goes with PHONED, but the hearer has already 'closed off' that branch on his mental tree. He has not left it 'open' and ready for additional material:

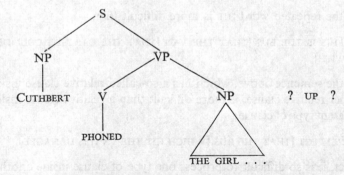

A fourth general difficulty concerns compression of information. Humans need thinking space to let things 'sink in', and they comprehend things best if they are presented only with a small amount of new information at one time. This is why Longfellow's poem

The Song of Hiawatha is so easy to follow. Each line repeats some information from the previous one, so there is only a small amount of new material in each one:

> By the shores of Gitche Gumee,
> By the shining Big-Sea-Water,
> Stood the wigwam of Nokomis,
> Daughter of the Moon, Nokomis.
> Dark behind it rose the forest,
> Rose the black and gloomy pine-trees,
> Rose the firs with cones upon them;
> Bright before it beat the water,
> Beat the clear and sunny water,
> Beat the shining Big-Sea-Water.

This slow dropping of information contrasts strikingly with the over-compressed:

THIS IS THE BUS THAT THE CAR THAT THE PROFESSOR THAT THE GIRL KISSED DROVE HIT.

We now come to a number of difficulties that seem to be partly psychological, partly linguistic. The first of these is repetition of items and structures. It is difficult to process a sentence which contains the same word twice, or more than one instance of the same type of structure, especially if the similar constructions are one inside the other. For example,

THIS IS THE BUS [THAT THE VAN [THAT THE CAR HIT] HIT]

with the repeated word HIT is more difficult than

THIS IS THE BUS [THAT THE VAN [THAT THE CAR HIT] COLLIDED WITH].

And the sentence above, which has a so-called relative clause inside another relative clause, is more difficult than a relative clause inside a different type of clause:

I EXPECT [THAT THE BUS [WHICH HIT THE VAN] IS DAMAGED].

In fact, it is so difficult to process one type of clause inside another similar one, that at least one linguist has suggested excluding such sentences from a grammar altogether (Reich, 1969). But this is not a workable suggestion, because it would also exclude perfectly good sentences such as

THE OCTOPUS [WHICH THE FISHERMAN [YOU WERE TALKING TO] HAD CAUGHT] LOOKED QUITE REVOLTING.

This a relative clause inside another relative clause.

Another difficulty, which seems to be partly a general psychological one, and partly a linguistic one, is the difficulty of backward processing (Grosu, 1974). In English we normally move from left to right when we process sentences. For example, it is easy to comprehend.

MARY, PETER AND PRISCILLA PLAY THE FLUTE, THE PIANO AND THE GUITAR RESPECTIVELY.

In this, the order of the people and the instruments they play moves from left to right:

```
    1       2        3          1      2       3
MARY PETER PRISCILLA – FLUTE PIANO GUITAR
```

It is considerably more difficult to understand

MARY, PETER AND PRISCILLA PLAY THE GUITAR, THE PIANO AND THE FLUTE REVERSELY.

Here, the instruments are given backwards, and you have to reverse the order in which they occur before you can sort out who is playing what:

```
    1       2        3          3      2       1
MARY PETER PRISCILLA – GUITAR PIANO FLUTE
```

The same kind of reversal occurs in the sentence:

THE CAR THAT THE PROFESSOR THAT THE GIRL KISSED DROVE CRASHED.

```
    1       2        3          3      2       1
CAR PROFESSOR GIRL – KISSED DROVE CRASHED
```

Backward processing (and compression) may also be why it is difficult to understand

MY AUNT'S EMPLOYER'S SON'S UMBRELLA'S COLOUR IS YELLOW

compared with the left-to-right uncompressed sentence

THE COLOUR OF THE UMBRELLA OF THE SON OF THE EMPLOYER OF MY AUNT IS YELLOW

– though alternative explanations are possible (Yngve, 1961; Miller and Chomsky, 1963).

Yet another problem which straddles the gap between general psychological and specific linguistic problems is that of ambiguity. Just as some trick drawings can be interpreted in two ways, as in the famous trick sketch which can be either a beautiful young girl or an old crone depending on how you look at it, so (as we have already noted) sentences can sometimes be interpreted in two ways. Like an ambiguous picture, an ambiguous sentence such as

JUMPING KANGAROOS CAN BE DANGEROUS

takes longer to process if the hearer notices the ambiguity – is it dangerous to jump kangaroos, or are kangaroos which jump dangerous? At first sight it seems that there is no more to be said. But on closer inspection, the matter is considerably more complicated – at least according to some psychologists, who claim that an ambiguous sentence is normally more difficult to process *even if* the hearer does not consciously notice the ambiguity. Briefly, there is a raging controversy going on over ambiguous sentences between those who support a so-called 'garden path' theory, and those who support a 'suppression of meaning theory'.

According to the 'garden path' proponents, the ambiguity problem is straightforward. Hearers normally perceive only *one* meaning of an ambiguous sentence, and they stick to that meaning unless something occurs to make them change their mind – in which case they realize they have been 'led up the garden path', and they re-process the sentence in accordance with their new information. In other words, according to this view, ambiguous sentences which are not consciously noticed to be ambiguous take no longer to process than utterances having only a single meaning.

But supporters of the 'suppression of meaning' theory disagree with this, and suggest that hearers actually consider, without realizing it, *both* possible meanings of an ambiguous sentence, then suppress the less appropriate one. They point out that there is so much ambiguity in every day speech, and so few misunderstandings, that 'normal sentence processing routines must deal routinely with ambiguity. There is just too much of it to ignore. . . . We bumble along in ordinary conversation through an incredible melange of sentence fragments rife with opportunities for misunderstanding and scarcely ever find ourselves in serious structural error' (Garrett, 1970:51). The following are examples of the type of ambiguity we must encounter and deal with, but do not consciously notice:

VISITING RELATIVES CAN BE A NUISANCE
THEY'RE COOKING APPLES
THE BOY RUSHED AT THE DOG WITH THE FIREWORK
HE FIRED HIS SECRETARY WITH ENTHUSIASM
ASPASIA WAS ENJOYABLY SEDUCED BY PERICLES
ANGUS BOUGHT A LIGHT SWEATER.

It is difficult, at the moment, to decide between these two viewpoints. Both the 'garden party' and the 'suppression of meaning' supporters appear to have convincing experimental evidence in their favour. For example, Carey, Mehler and Bever (1970) suggest that 'subjects know what they are doing.' They found that subjects took longer to process ambiguous sentences such as

THEY ARE VISITING SAILORS

when they consciously noticed the ambiguity, but not otherwise. But Foss (1970) found that subjects who were asked to check for the presence of a given sound in a sentence ('Press a button if you come to a word starting with B') reacted more slowly in ambiguous sentences, even when they claimed not to have noticed the ambiguity. They responded more slowly to the B in a sentence such as

THE SEAMEN STARTED TO DRILL BEFORE THEY WERE ORDERED TO DO SO

(drill holes or take part in a life-boat drill?)
than in one such as

THE SEAMEN STARTED TO MARCH BEFORE THEY WERE ORDERED TO DO SO.

We do not yet know who is right. We can point out, however, that there may not be as much ambiguity to cope with in ordinary conversations as some psychologists suggest. In the majority of cases, the context so predisposes the hearer to expect one interpretation, that he does not need to consider the other alternative one. In addition, there may be more misunderstandings than we realize. A person rarely checks that a hearer has interpreted what he said in the correct way. Only on rare occasions is there any consistent feedback. For example, in examinations students sometimes think they are repeating back what has been said to them – and then the level of misunderstanding is often quite horrifying. These comments indicate that the 'garden path' theory may be slightly more plausible, though the 'suppression of meaning' theory has by no means been disproved.

We must make one final point in connection with ambiguity: some types of ambiguity may be easier to recognize than others. Lexical ambiguities are noticed more easily than surface structure ambiguities, and deep structure ambiguities take longest of all, according to Mackay and Bever (1967). That is, people see both interpretations of

THE SAILORS LIKE THE PORT

(wine or town?)
more quickly than the two in

SMALL BOYS AND GIRLS ARE FRIGHTENED EASILY

(small boys and small girls, or small boys and *all* girls?).
And they see the two meanings in the sentence above more quickly than those in

THE MAYOR ASKED THE POLICE TO STOP DRINKING

(is it the police or other people who are to cease drinking?).
This means that if the 'garden path' theory is correct, it may be quicker to re-process a misinterpreted sentence which involves a lexical ambiguity than one containing a syntactic ambiguity.

The fourth partly linguistic, partly psychological factor which increases comprehension difficulty is the deletion of surface structure 'markers'. These are items which help to identify the various constructions. The fewer clues available for recognizing a structure, the more difficult it will be to identify. This is true whether we are dealing with a sentence in a language, or a partly hidden object in front of our eyes. Just as a picture of a face which lacks a nose may take longer to recognize than one with eyes, nose and mouth all complete, so a sentence with a word seemingly missing will take longer to comprehend (Fodor, Garrett and Bever, 1968; Hakes, 1971; Fodor, Bever and Garrett, 1974). For example,

THE CROW THE FOX FLATTERED LOST ITS CHEESE

is more difficult than

THE CROW WHICH THE FOX FLATTERED LOST ITS CHEESE.

In the second sentence WHICH is retained, enabling speakers to note more quickly that they are dealing with a relative clause. Similarly,

SEBASTIAN NOTICED THE BURGLAR HAD LEFT FOOTPRINTS

takes longer to comprehend than

SEBASTIAN NOTICED THAT THE BURGLAR HAD LEFT FOOTPRINTS.

Here, the word THAT gives an immediate clear indication to the hearer that he is dealing with a so-called 'complement structure'.

Yet another factor which straddles the gap between psychological and linguistic difficulties is the presence of a negative. In general, negative sentences take longer to comprehend than affirmative ones. However, within negative sentences there are some strange discrepancies which relate to the hearer's expectations about his world. For example, it is easier and quicker to negate an expected fact than an unexpected one: it takes less time to comprehend the sentence

THE TRAIN WAS NOT LATE THIS MORNING

if you had *expected* the train to be late. If the train was normally on time, the same sentence would take longer to process. Similarly,

A WHALE IS NOT A FISH   and   A SPIDER IS NOT AN INSECT

are simpler, and take less time to understand, than

A WHALE IS NOT A BIRD   and   A SPIDER IS NOT A MAMMAL

because hearers had *expected* the whale to be a fish and the spider an insect (Wason, 1965).

Let us now turn to a final and somewhat disputed factor which may increase the difficulty of decoding sentences – the inclusion of a 'versatile verb'. This factor is somewhat more linguistic than the others we have considered, but it is still partly psychological because it concerns the time taken to look up lexical items in a mental dictionary.

When Alice met Humpty Dumpty in Lewis Carroll's *Through the Looking Glass*, he claimed that adjectives were easier to deal with than verbs: 'They've a temper, some of them – particularly verbs, they're the proudest – adjectives you can do anything with, but not verbs.' This fanciful comment reflects a feeling which is shared by some psycholinguists – that verbs are in some sense the 'key' to the sentence, and impose a structure on it. Fodor, Garrett and Bever (1968) suggest that when someone hears a sentence, he pays particular attention to the verb. The moment he hears it, he looks up the entry for this verb in a mental dictionary. The dictionary will contain a list of the possible constructions associated with that verb. For example,

KICK	+NP	HE KICKED THE BALL
EXPECT	+NP	HE EXPECTED A LETTER
	+TO	HE EXPECTED TO ARRIVE AT SIX O'CLOCK
	+THAT	HE EXPECTED THAT HE WOULD BE LATE

If Fodor, Garrett and Bever are correct in their claim, then sentences containing verbs which give no choice of construction should be easier to process than those which contain 'versatile verbs' – verbs associated with multiple constructions. In the case of a verb such as KICK, the hearer only has a simple lexical entry to check. But in the case of a verb such as EXPECT, he mentally activates each of the possible constructions before picking on the correct one. This suggestion is sometimes known as the 'verbal complexity hypothesis'.

Several psycholinguists have tried to test this theory – though so far the results have been inconclusive. Fodor, Garrett and Bever (1968) tried to test it in two ways. Firstly, they gave undergraduates pairs of sentences which were identical except for the verb. A single construction verb was placed in one sentence (e.g. MAIL), and a multiple construction verb in the other (e.g. EXPECT).

THE LETTER THE SECRETARY THE MANAGER EMPLOYED MAILED WAS LATE
THE LETTER THE SECRETARY THE MANAGER EMPLOYED EXPECTED WAS LATE.

They then asked the students to paraphrase each sentence. The result was that the sentences with the single construction verbs were marginally (but not significantly) easier to paraphrase than those with the multiple construction verbs. The second experiment was more encouraging. Once again, the experimenters used pairs of sentences. As before, each pair differed only in that one had a single construction verb, and the other a multiple construction one:

THE LETTER WHICH THE SECRETARY MAILED WAS LATE
THE LETTER WHICH THE SECRETARY EXPECTED WAS LATE.

Fodor, Garrett and Bever jumbled up the words in each, and then asked the students to unscramble them. They found what they had hoped to find – that it was much easier to sort out the single construction verb sentences. But both these experiments have been criticized. The problem is that they do not test comprehension directly: they assess the difficulty of a task which occurs *after* the sentence has been originally processed. This led another psychologist to test single versus multiple construction verbs while comprehension was actually in progress (Hakes, 1971). He used the 'phoneme monitoring' technique mentioned earlier in this chapter in connection with ambiguity. That is, he asked the subjects to report as soon as they heard a specified sound or 'phoneme'. To his surprise, he found that the type of verb did not seem to affect the subjects' performance of this task. He had expected that 'versatile verbs' would be more difficult to cope with, and so would distract a hearer's attention from the sound he had been asked to report. So the verbal complexity hypothesis may be wrong.

In fact a number of theoretical criticisms can be levelled against this hypothesis (Watt, 1970; Gough, 1971). Why should hearers activate a verb's structures in advance? Surely they just wait patiently to hear what comes next in a sentence? And why are verbs so special? If hearers mentally look up the structures which can follow a verb in advance, why do they not mentally look up the constructions which can occur at any point in the sentence where a multiple option is possible? For example, a multiple option occurs after the word BY in the sentence

FLOYD THURSBY WAS SHOT BY . . .

You could have

FLOYD THURSBY WAS SHOT BY A STREETLIGHT
FLOYD THURSBY WAS SHOT BY MIDNIGHT
FLOYD THURSBY WAS SHOT BY MISADVENTURE
FLOYD THURSBY WAS SHOT BY A VIXEN.

But there is no evidence that the presence of the multiple option after BY increases the difficulty of comprehending the sentence.

At present, the verbal complexity hypothesis is still under discussion. On balance, the evidence is against it. We noted earlier in this chapter that hearers listen to sentences with certain expectations. It is quite likely that they have these expectations concerning verbs also. That is, they might mentally expect a verb to take one construction rather than others. I THINK THAT . . . is more common than I THINK AS . . . (e.g. I THINK AS I GO ALONG). Similarly, I EXPECT THAT . . . may be more likely than I EXPECT + NP (e.g. I EXPECT A

LETTER). In other words, hearers may activate in advance one favoured construction for a given verb, but there is no need for them to activate mentally all possible constructions associated with it. If only one favoured construction is activated per verb, then 'versatile' verbs are no more difficult than 'non-versatile' ones – except when an odd or unexpected option is chosen.

Let us now summarize this section. We have listed nine possible factors which can make a sentence more difficult to understand. Four of these are purely general psychological difficulties: we noted that short-term memory space is limited, that there appears to be a constraint on the number of sentoids that can be processed simultaneously, that unmarked interruptions are difficult to deal with, and so is a sentence which contains too much compressed information. The next five were partly linguistic, and partly psychological: we saw that the repetition of items and structures causes problems, and so does backward processing. Ambiguities that are consciously noticed delay comprehension (and so perhaps do unnoticed ambiguities). The deletion of surface structure clues slows down syntax recognition, and negatives delay sentence processing. The final factor, the possibility that 'versatile verbs' cause processing difficulties was found to be unproven, and even unlikely. So at the moment we should perhaps disregard it.

Since all the factors discussed in this section are background psychological ones which relate in addition to abilities other than linguistic ones, we do not need to incorporate them into grammar, which is concerned *only* with language. That is, we need to incorporate into a grammar rules for say, joining up sentoids – but we do *not* need to incorporate a rule saying 'Don't make any one sentoid too long' or 'Don't jumble up too many sentoids together'. This will be dealt with by a more general psychological theory of human capacity. Of course, linguists must be aware of this more general theory. They can even help to write it. The important point is that factors such as short-term memory constraints need not be written into a linguist's grammar, no matter whether he is dealing with a universal grammar (a model of language that covers every possible actual language) or the grammar of one particular language.

Conclusion

Let us now conclude this chapter by looking again at the three sentences that seemed so difficult at the beginning. The first was a note to the milkman: 'Milkman, please stop milk until July 3. If you do not see this, THE WOMAN WHO HAS THE FLAT ON THE GROUND FLOOR'S SISTER will tell you.' The primary difficulty in this sentence is the presence of an unmarked interruption. The hearer has already mentally closed off the branch in the structure ending with the word WOMAN. Suddenly, he is presented with the phrase 'S SISTER which he is unable to fit in. In addition, there are several subsidiary problems. The intertwined sentoids are relatively long, and the information is compressed.

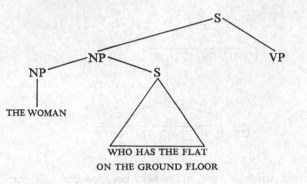

The second sentence

> THE PIG PUSHED IN FRONT OF THE PIGLETS ATE ALL THE FOOD

is difficult because it goes against the hearer's linguistic expectations. He assumes that the first noun will go with the first verb in an NP–VP (actor–action) sequence as part of the main clause (strategies 1, 2, and 3). So he understandably makes the wrong guesses when he hears the words THE PIG PUSHED . . ., especially as his knowledge of the world (strategy 4) tells him that pigs are not usually pushed, they generally do the pushing.

But the difficulty of decoding the sentences above is trivial compared with that of:

> THE CAT [THE DOG [THE MAN [THE BABY TRIPPED UP] BIT] SCRATCH-ED] COLLAPSED.

(The baby tripped up the man, the man bit the dog, the dog scratched the cat, the cat collapsed.)

This sentence is about as difficult as any sentence could possibly be. It goes against the speaker's basic linguistic expectations. The

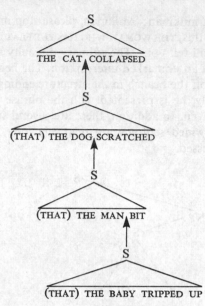

canonical sentoid strategy does not work, because the sentence is not in the form NP–VP–NP, and the objects CAT, DOG, MAN come before the actors DOG, MAN, BABY. From the point of view of meaning the sentence seems topsy-turvy: people do not expect dogs to scratch cats and men to bite dogs. It also involves most of the psychological difficulties we discussed. It puts an intolerable strain on short-term memory, it requires the simultaneous processing of three sentoids inside one another, it requires some degree of backward processing, and the word THAT has been omitted, which means that clues to the structure are missing. It is no wonder that most people, when faced with it, say: 'Sorry, it's just not English' – even though, strictly speaking, no grammatical rule has been broken.

Of course, a great deal of work still needs to be done before we fully understand what is happening when we comprehend sentences. But, as we have seen, it seems that we can usefully approach the problem in two ways. We can build up a list of basic assumptions that speakers make about their language, and note the linked strategies which hearers utilize when they decode sentences. Secondly, we can work on discovering the general psychological difficulties which affect sentence processing. A next step is for linguists to incorporate the assumptions and strategies into a grammar, and to co-operate with psychologists in producing a general theory of human ability.

Let us now turn to the topic of sentence production. As we shall see, this presents us with even more problems than sentence comprehension.

11 The Cheshire Cat's Grin

How do we plan and produce speech?

'I wish you wouldn't keep appearing and vanishing so suddenly,' said Alice, 'You make one quite giddy.'
   'All right,' said the Cat; and this time it vanished quite
slowly, beginning with the end of the tail, and ending with
the grin, which remained some time after the rest of it had
gone.
   'Well! I've often seen a cat without a grin,' thought Alice;
'but a grin without a cat! It's the most curious thing I ever
saw in all my life!'

Lewis Carroll
Alice in Wonderland

In the last chapter we discussed decoding. Although much work
remains to be done, we were able to gain some insights into how
people understand sentences. We now come to a rather trickier
problem – that of finding out about encoding.

It is tantalizingly difficult to observe how anyone actually plans
and produces speech. It is equally hard to devise experiments to
test it. When somebody utters a sentence, we have very little idea
how long it actually took to plan it, and what processes were involved.
Consequently, we shall be very tentative over any conclusions we
draw. As Fodor, Bever and Garrett comment: 'Practically anything
that one can say about speech production must be considered speculative, even by the standards current in psycholinguistics' (Fodor,
Bever and Garrett, 1974:434).

Clues as to what is happening are infuriatingly elusive. In fact,
there seems to be only one situation in which we can actually catch
a speaker as he mentally prepares an utterance, and that is when
someone is trying to recall a forgotten name. The name is often on
'the tip of his tongue', but he cannot quite remember it. His mind
is not completely blank as far as the word is concerned. A teasing
and seemingly uncatchable wraith of it remains. He is left with a
'kind of disembodied presence, a grin without the Cheshire Cat'
(Brown, 1970:234).

Apart from this, we have to rely on indirect evidence. This is of two types. First of all, we can look at the pauses in spontaneous speech. The object of this is to try to detect patterns in the pausing which may give us clues as to when speech is planned. Secondly, we can examine speech errors, both the slips of the tongue found in the conversation of normal people (e.g. HAP-SLAPPILY for 'slap-happily', CANTANKEROUS for 'contentious'), and the more severe disturbances of dysphasics – people whose speech is impaired due to some type of brain damage (e.g. TARIB for 'rabbit', RABBIT for 'apple'). Hopefully, breakdown of the normal patterns may give us vital information about the way we plan and produce what we say.

Pauses

It may seem rather paradoxical to investigate speech by studying non-speech. But the idea is not as irrelevant as it may seem at first sight. Around 40 to 50 per cent of an average spontaneous utterance consists of silence, although to the hearer the proportion does not seem as high because he is too busy listening to what is being said.

The pauses in speech are of two main types: *breathing* pauses and *hesitation* pauses of the er . . . um variety. The first type are relatively easy to cope with. There are relatively few of them (partly because we slow down our rate of breathing when we speak), and they account for only about 5 per cent of the gaps in speech. They tend to come at grammatical boundaries, although they do not necessarily do so (Henderson *et al.*, 1965).

Hesitation pauses are more promising. There are more of them, and they do not have any obvious physical purpose comparable to that of filling one's lungs with air. Normally they account for one-third to one-half of the time taken up in talking. Speech in which such pausing does not occur is 'inferior' speech (Jackson, 1932). Either it has been rehearsed beforehand, or the speaker is merely stringing together a number of standard phrases he habitually repeats, as when the mother of the seven-year-old who threw a stone through my window rattled off at top speed, 'I do apologize, he's never done anything like that before, I can't think what came over him, he's such a good quiet little boy usually, I'm quite flabbergasted'. (Unfortunately, we tend to over-value the fluent, glib speaker who may not be thinking what he is saying, and often condemn a hesitant or stammering speaker who may be thinking very hard.)

Hesitation pauses are rather difficult to measure, because a

long-drawn-out word such as WE . . . ELL, IN FA . . . ACT may be substituted for a pause. This type of measurement problem may account
for the extraordinary differences of view found among psycholinguists
who have done research on this topic. The basic argument is about
where exactly the pauses occur. One researcher claims that hesitations
occur mainly after the first word in the clause or sentoid (Boomer,
1965). But another psycholinguist, whose experiments seem equally
convincing, finds pauses mainly before important lexical items
(Goldman–Eisler, 1964). It seems impossible, from just reading
about their experiments, to judge who is right.

But in spite of this seemingly radical disagreement we can glean
one important piece of information. *Both* researchers agree that
speakers do not normally pause between clauses, they pause *inside*
them. This means that there is overlapping in the planning and
production of clauses. That is, instead of a simple sequence

Plan	*Utter*	*Plan*	*Utter*
clause A	clause A	clause B	clause B

we must set up a more complicated model:

Plan clause A	*Plan* clause B	
	Utter clause A	*Utter* clause B

In other words, it is quite clear that we do not cope with speech
one clause at a time. We begin to plan the next clause while still
uttering the present one.

Armed with this vital piece of information, we can now attempt
to elaborate the picture by looking at the evidence from speech
errors.

Speech errors: the nature of the evidence[1]

Linguists are interested in speech errors because they hope that
language in a broken-down state may be more revealing than
language which is working perfectly. It is possible that speech is
like an ordinary household electrical system, which is composed
of several relatively independent circuits. We cannot discover very
much about these circuits when all the lamps and sockets are working
perfectly. But if a mouse gnaws through a cable in the kitchen, and

fuses one circuit, then we can immediately discover which lamps and sockets are linked together under normal working conditions. In the same way, it might be possible to find selective impairment of different aspects of speech.

The errors we shall be dealing with are, firstly, '*slips of the tongue*', and, secondly, the speech of *dysphasics* – people with some more serious type of speech disturbance. Because the evidence is rather unusual, let us consider its nature a little more fully.

Everybody's tongue slips now and again, most often when the tongue's owner is tired, a bit drunk, or rather nervous. So errors of this type are common enough to be called normal. However, if you mention the topic of slips of the tongue to a group of people at least one of them is likely to smirk knowingly and say 'Ah yes, tongue slips are sexual in origin, aren't they?' This fairly popular misconception has arisen because Sigmund Freud, the great Viennese psychologist, wrote a paper suggesting that words sometimes slipped out from a person's subconscious thoughts, which in his view were often concerned with sex. For example, he quotes the case of a woman who said her cottage was situated ON THE HILL-THIGH (BERGLENDE) instead of 'on the hillside' (Berglehne), after she had been trying to recall a childhood incident in which 'part of her body had been grasped by a prying and lascivious hand' (Freud, 1901). In fact, this type of example occurs only in a relatively small number of tongue slips. It is true, possibly, that a percentage of girls have the embarrassing experience of sinking rapturously into, say, Archibald's arms while inadvertently murmuring 'Darling Algernon'. It is also perhaps true that anyone talking about a sex-linked subject may get embarrassed and stumble over his words, like the anthropology professor, who red to the ears with confusion, talked about a PLENIS-BEEDING CEREMONY (penis-bleeding ceremony) in New Guinea. But otherwise there seems little to support the sexual origin myth. Perhaps one might add that people tend to notice and remember sexual slips more than any other type. During the anthropology lecture mentioned above, almost everybody heard and memorized the PLENIS-BEEDING example. But few people afterwards, when questioned, had heard the lecturer say, YAM'S BOOK ON YOUNG-GROWING (Young's book on yam-growing). So laying aside the sex myth, we may say that slips of the tongue tell us more about the way a person plans and produces speech than about his or her sexual fantasies.

Dysphasia is rather different from slips of the tongue, in that it is far from 'normal'. The name *dysphasia* comes from a Greek word which means 'bad speech', and so differs from *aphasia*, which means literally 'without speech'. Unfortunately, several writers on the subject use the two words almost interchangeably. They use both to mean 'speech disturbance', though they often reserve the term aphasia for more severe varieties. Here we shall keep to the more strictly correct term dysphasia.

Dysphasia covers an enormous range of speech problems. At one end of the range we find people who can only say a single word such as O DEAR, O DEAR, O DEAR, or more usually, a swear word such as DAMN, DAMN, DAMN. (One unproved theory is that people who have had a severe stroke sometimes find their speech 'petrified' into the word they were uttering as the stroke occurred.) At the other end of the scale are people with only occasional word-finding difficulties – it is not always clear where true dysphasia ends and normal slips of the tongue begin. The fact that one merges into the other means that we can examine both types of error together in our search for clues about the planning and production of speech.[2]

The typology of dysphasia (attempts to classify dysphasia into different kinds of disturbance) is a confused and controversial topic, and is beyond the scope of this book. Here we shall be looking mainly at name-finding difficulties, which is perhaps the most widespread of all dysphasic symptoms. Although it affects some patients more than others, it is usually present to some degree in most types of speech disturbance. A vivid description of this problem occurs in Kingsley Amis's novel *Ending Up* (1974). The fictional dysphasic is a retired university lecturer, Professor George Zeyer, who had a stroke five months previously:

'Well, anyway, to start with he must have a, a, thing, you know, you go about in it, it's got, er, they turn round. A very expensive one, you can be sure. You drive it, or someone else does in his case. Probably gold, gold on the outside. Like that other chap. A bar – no. And probably a gold, er, going to sleep on it. And the same in his . . . When he washes himself. If he ever does, of course. And eating off a gold – eating off it, you know. Not to speak of a private, um, uses it whenever he wants to go anywhere special, to one of those other places down there to see his pals. Engine. No. With a fellow to fly it for him. A plate. No, but you know what I mean. And the point is it's all because of us. Without us he'd be nothing, would he? But for us he'd still be living in his, ooh, made out of . . . with a black woman bringing him, off the – growing there, you know. And the swine's supposed to be some sort of hero. Father of his people and all that. A plane, a private plane, that's it.'

It was not that George was out of his mind, merely that his stroke had afflicted him, not only with hemiplegia, but also with that condition in which the sufferer finds it difficult to remember nouns, common terms, the names of familiar objects. George was otherwise fluent and accurate and responded normally to other's speech. His fluency was especially notable; he was very good at not pausing at moments when a sympathetic hearer could have supplied the elusive word. Doctors, including Dr Mainwaring, had stated that the defect might clear up altogether in time, or might stay as it was, and that there was nothing to be done about it.

Of course, not every dysphasic is as fluent as George. And sometimes a patient is in the disquieting situation of thinking she has found the right word – only to discover to her dismay, when she utters it, that it is the wrong one. A description of this unnerving experience occurs in Nabokov's *Pale Fire:*

> She still could speak. She paused and groped and found
> What seemed at first a serviceable sound,
> But from adjacent cells imposters took
> The place of words she needed, and her look
> Spelt imploration as she sought in vain
> To reason with the monsters in her brain.

Perhaps the following two extracts will give a clearer picture of the problem. They are taken from tape-recordings of a severely dysphasic patient in her seventies who had had a stroke two months earlier.

The patient (P) has been uttering the word RHUBARB, apparently because she is worried about her garden which is going to rack and ruin while she is in hospital. The therapist (T) tries to comfort her then says:

T: NOW THEN, WHAT'S THIS A PICTURE OF? (showing a picture of an apple).
P: RA- RA- RABBIT.
T: NO, NOT A RABBIT. IT'S A KIND OF FRUIT.
P: FRUIT.
T: WHAT KIND OF FRUIT IS IT?
P: O THIS IS A LOVELY RABBIT.
T: NOT A RABBIT, NO. IT'S AN APPLE
P: APPLE, YES.
T: CAN YOU NAME ANY OTHER PIECES OF FRUIT? WHAT OTHER KINDS OF FRUIT WOULD YOU HAVE IN A DISH WITH AN APPLE?
P: BEGINNING WITH AN A?

T: NO, NOT NECESSARILY.
P: O WELL, RHUBARB.
T: PERHAPS, YES.
P: OR RHUBARB.

In the second extract, the same type of phenomenon occurs, but in a different context.

T: WHAT'S THIS BOY DOING? (showing a picture of a boy swimming)
P: O HE'S IN THE SEA.
T: YES.
P: DRIVING . . . DRIVING. IT'S NOT VERY DEEP. HE'S DRIVING WITH HIS FEET, HIS LEGS. DRIVING. WELL DRIVING, ER DIVING.
T: IN FACT HE'S . . .
P: SWIMMING.
T: GOOD, WHAT ABOUT THIS ONE? (showing a picture of a boy climbing over a wall)
P: DRIVING, ON A . . . ON A WALL.
T: HE'S WHAT?
P: DR . . . DRIVING, HE'S CLIMBING ON A WALL.

Most of the mistakes in these passages represent an extension of the selection problems seen in ordinary slips of the tongue. That is, the same kind of mistakes occur as in normal speech, but they occur more often and seem less obvious.

Broadly speaking, we may categorize speech errors into two basic types. First, we have those in which a wrong item (or items) is chosen, where something has gone wrong with the *selection* process. For example,

> DID YOU REMEMBER TO BUY SOME TOOTHACHE? (Did you remember to buy some toothpaste?)

Note, by the way, that although generally classified as 'slips of the tongue', selection errors are more accurately 'slips of the brain'.

Secondly, we find errors in which the correct choice of word has been made, but the *programme* set up for utterance by the speaker has been faultily executed as in

> SOMEONE'S BEEN WRITENING THREAT LETTERS (Someone's been writing threatening letters).

Let us look at these two categories, *selection errors* and *programming errors* more carefully, and attempt to subdivide them.

Errors in which wrong items have been chosen are most commonly whole word errors. There are three main types: *semantic errors* (or similar meaning errors), *malapropisms* (or similar sound errors) and *blends*.

So-called *semantic* or *similar meaning* errors are fairly common. In fact, they are so usual that they often pass unnoticed. We are talking about naming errors in which the speaker gets the general 'semantic field' right, but uses the wrong word, as in

DO YOU HAVE ANY ARTICHOKES? I'M SORRY, I MEAN AUBERGINES.

This kind of mistake often affects linked pairs of words. People say LEFT when they mean 'right', UP when they mean 'down', and EARLY instead of 'late', as in

IT'S SIX O'CLOCK. WON'T THAT BE TOO EARLY TO BUY BREAD?

Mistakes like this occur repeatedly in the speech of some dysphasics, and in its extreme form the general condition is sometimes rather pompously labelled 'conceptual agrammatism' (Goodglass, 1968). Such patients repeatedly confuse words like YESTERDAY, TODAY, and TOMORROW. They seem able to find names connected with the general area they are talking about, but unable to pinpoint particular words within it, so that a 'garden roller' is likely to be called a LAWN MOWER, a 'spade' maybe called a FORK, and a 'rake' may be called a HOE. A mistake like this occurred in one of the dysphasic passages quoted above: the patient said DIVING when she meant 'swimming'. At other times, a patient may use a paraphrase such as WATER COMPARTMENT for 'drinking trough', or HORSE HUT for 'stable'.

The second type of word selection error, so-called *malapropisms* occur when a person confuses a word with another, similar sounding one. The name comes from Mrs Malaprop, a character in Thomas Sheridan's play *The Rivals*, who continually confused words which sounded alike, as in

SHE'S AS HEADSTRONG AS AN ALLEGORY ON THE BANKS OF THE NILE (She's as headstrong as an alligator in the banks of the Nile),

and

A NICE DERANGEMENT OF EPITAPHS (A nice arrangement o epithets).

Not only in Sheridan's play, but in real life also, the results are sometimes hilarious, as when a lady lecturer claimed that

> YOU KEEP NEW-BORN CHICKS WARM IN AN INCINERATOR (You keep new-born chicks warm in an incubator).

Equally funny was a man's statement that he had NUBILE TOES instead of 'mobile' ones.

So far, we have mentioned selection errors connected with meaning, and selection errors connected with the sound of the word. But it would be a mistake to assume that we can easily place mistakes into one or the other category. Often the two overlap. Although children's mistakes are usually purely phonetic ones, as in

> MUSSOLINI PUDDING (semolina pudding)
> NAUGHTY STORY CAR PARK (multi-storey car park),

the majority of adult ones have some type of semantic as well as phonetic link. The malapropism INCINERATOR for 'incubator' is a case in point, since in addition to the phonetic similarity both words are connected with the idea of heat. Another example is the statement

> YOU GO UNDER A RUNWAY BRIDGE (You go under a railway bridge),

where, in addition to the similar sounds, both words describe a track for a means of transport. Yet another example is the error

> COMPENSATION PRIZE (consolation prize).

However, the semantic connection does not always have to be between the two words that are being confused. Sometimes the intruding idea comes in from the surrounding context, as in the statement

> LEARNING TO SPEAK IS NOT THE SAME THING AS LEARNING TO TALK (Learning to speak is not the same thing as learning to walk).

Another example of this type of confusion was uttered by a nervous male involved in a discussion on BBC's *Woman's Hour* about a cat who never seemed to sleep, because it was perpetually chasing mice. He said:

> HOW MANY SHEEP DOES THE CAT HAVE IN ITS HOUSE THEN? I'M SORRY, I MEAN MICE, NOT SHEEP.

The speaker correctly remembered that he was talking about an animal of some kind, but the animal had somehow become contaminated by the sound of the word SLEEP, resulting in SHEEP! He may also have been influenced by the fact that humans reputedly count sheep jumping over fences in order to get to sleep.

The third type of selection error, so-called *blends*, are an extension and variation of semantic errors. They are fairly rare, and occur when two words are 'blended' together to form one new one. For example,

NOT IN THE SLEAST

contains a mixture of 'slightest and least'. And

PLEASE EXPLAND THAT

is a mixture of 'explain and expand'. A rather more bizarre example of a blend occurs in the first of the passages of dysphasic speech quoted on P. 211. The patient had been talking about RHUBARB, and was trying to think of the word APPLE. What came out was a mixture of the two, RABBIT! Such mixes are also known as *contaminations* since the two words involved 'contaminate' one another. Normally, in this kind of mistake, both the items chosen are equally appropriate. It is just that the speaker seems to have accidentally picked two together – or rather failed to choose between two equally appropriate words in time. He has not so much picked the wrong word, as not decided which of the right ones he needed.

Note, by the way, that two items are sometimes intentionally blended together in order to create a new word. Lewis Carroll makes Humpty Dumpty explain in *Alice Through the Looking Glass* that SLITHY means 'lithe and slimy', commenting, 'You see, it's like a portmanteau – there are two meanings packed up into one word' – though Lewis Carroll's made-up words may not be as intentional as they appear. Apparently, he suffered from severe migraine attacks, and it has been pointed out that many of his strange neologisms are uncannily like the kind of temporary dysphasia produced by some migraine sufferers (Livesley, 1972). Perhaps better examples of intentional blends are SMOG from 'smoke and fog', and BRUNCH from 'breakfast and lunch'. There are sometimes interesting parallels of this type to be spotted between slips of the tongue and language change.

Let us now turn to *programming errors* – errors in which the correct word choice had been made, but the programme set up has been faultily executed. There are three main types: *transpositions, antici-pations*, and *repetitions*, which may affect words, syllables or sounds.[3]

Transpositions are not, on the whole, very common (Cohen, 1966; Nooteboom, 1969). Whole words can switch places, as in

DON'T BUY A CAR WITH ITS TAIL IN THE ENGINE (Don't buy a car with its engine in the tail)

I CAN'T HELP THE CAT IF IT'S DELUDED (I can't help it if the cat's deluded)

and so can syllables:

I'D LIKE A VIENEL SCHNITZER (I'd like a Viener Schnitzel).

But perhaps the best known are the sound transpositions known as spoonerisms. These are named after a real-life person, the Reverend William A. Spooner, who was Dean and Warden of New College, Oxford, around the turn of the century. Reputedly, he often transposed the initial sounds of words, resulting in preposterous sentences, such as

THE CAT POPPED ON ITS DRAWERS (The cat dropped on its paws)

YOU HAVE HISSED ALL MY MYSTERY LECTURES (You have missed all my history lectures)

YOU HAVE TASTED THE WHOLE WORM (You have wasted the whole term).

However, there is something distinctly odd about these original spoonerisms. One suspects that the utterances of the Reverend Spooner were carefully prepared for posterity. The odd features are that they always make sense, they affect only initial sounds, and there is no discernible phonetic reason for the transposed sounds. In real life, spoonerisms do not usually make sense, as in

TILVER SILLER (silver tiller).

They can affect non-initial sounds, as in

A COP OF CUFFEE (a cup of coffee).

And they frequently occur between phonetically similar sounds, as

LEAK WINK (weak link).

Anticipations, particularly sound anticipations, are the most widespread type of programming error (Cohen, 1966; Nooteboom,

1969). Here, a speaker anticipates what he is going to say by bringing in an item too early. Note that it is not always possible to distinguish between anticipations and potential transpositions if the speaker stops himself half-way through, after realizing his error. This may partially account for the high recorded proportion of anticipations compared with transpositions. For example, the following could be a prematurely cut off transposition:

> I WANT YOU TO TELL MILLICENT . . . I MEAN, I WANT YOU TO TELL MARY WHAT MILLICENT SAID.

But the following sound anticipations are clearly just simple anticipations. A participant in a television discussion referred, much to his embarrassment, to:

> THE WORST GERMAN CHANCELLOR (The West German Chancellor).

Here he had anticipated the vowel in GERMAN. The same thing happened to the man, who interrupting over-eagerly, begged to make

> AN IMPOITANT POINT (an important point).

Repetitions (or *perseverations*) are rather rarer than anticipations, though commoner than transpositions. We find repeated words, as in:

> A: ISN'T IT COLD? MORE LIKE A SUNDAY IN FEBRUARY.
> B: IT'S NOT TOO BAD – MORE LIKE A FEBRUARY IN MARCH I'D SAY. (It's not too bad – more like a Sunday in March).

An example of a repeated sound occurred when someone referred to:

> THE BOOK BY CHOMSKY AND CHALLE (Chomsky and Halle)

– perhaps an indication of the mesmerizing effect of Chomsky on a number of linguists! Repetitions are relatively unusual because normal people have a very effective 'wipe the slate clean' mechanism. As soon as they have uttered a word, the phonetic form no longer remains to clutter up the mind. This is perhaps the greatest single difference between ordinary people and dysphasics, who often, to their frustration and despair, repeatedly repeat sounds and words from the sentence before. A dysphasic had been shown a picture of an apple. After some prompting, she said the word APPLE. She was then shown a picture of a blue ball. When asked what it was, she replied without hesitation APPLE. The therapist pointed out that she was confusing the new object with the previous one. 'Of course, how stupid of me', replied the patient. 'This one's an APPLE. No, no, I didn't mean that, I mean APPLE!' A similar example occurs in the dialogue on P. 211 where the patient keeps repeating the word RHUBARB.

We have now outlined the main types of selection and programming errors:

Selection Errors	Programming Errors
Semantic errors	Transpositions
Malapropisms	Anticipations
Blends	Repetitions

In the next section we shall see what kind of information we can glean from this disparate array of mistakes.

Planning and producing utterances

What (if anything) can we learn from this seemingly strange array of errors? In fact, quite a lot. First of all, we can suggest what are the units of planning – in other words, the size of chunk we prepare in advance ready for utterance. Secondly, we can make hypotheses as to how words and syntax are planned and assembled. Thirdly, we can look at the process of word selection.

Let us begin with the unit of planning. This appears to be what is sometimes called a *tone group* or *phonemic clause* – a short stretch of speech spoken with a single intonation contour. For example,

> WHAT TIME IS IT?
> DEBORAH BOUGHT SOME SNAILS.
> MAX TOOK A BATH/BEFORE HE WENT TO THE PARTY.

Note, by the way, that a so-called *phonemic* clause (or tone group) should not be confused with a *syntactic* clause (or sentoid). The two quite often coincide, but do not necessarily do so. For example,

> I WANT TO BUY SOME BUNS

is a single phonemic clause, though it is regarded in transformational grammar as containing two underlying syntactic clauses. In this chapter the word *clause* refers to a phonemic clause, unless otherwise stated.

The main reason for confidently asserting that the tone group is the unit of planning is that slips of the tongue almost always occur within a single tone group. For example:

WE'LL GO TO TAXI IN A CHOMSKY   (We'll go to Chomsky in a taxi)

WE FORGED THIS CONGRESS . . . CONTRACT IN OUR OWN CONGRESS-ES   (We forged this contract in our own congresses).

This strongly suggests that each tone group is planned and executed as a whole. If larger units were prepared, we would expect to find frequent contamination between clauses. As it is, such interference is rare, so much so that Boomer and Laver (1968) regard it as a tongue slip 'law' that 'The target and the origin of a tongue-slip are both located in the same tone-group' (with 'law' to be understood in a statistical rather than in an absolute sense).

Assuming, then, that the tone group is the unit of planning, we now need to ask *when* each tone group is planned. We partially solved this problem in our discussion of hesitation pauses (p. 207). There we noted that hesitation pauses (which may represent planning pauses) occur *within* clauses rather than between them. This indicates that speakers do not follow a simple sequence: *Pause and plan – utter. Pause and plan – utter.* Instead, they must prepare each new tone group while the previous one is being spoken.

But this vague assumption that we 'plan in advance' is not very satisfactory. We need to be more precise. This leads us on to the second topic in this section – the planning and assemblage of words and syntax. Let us begin by making a fairly sweeping statement, and then justifying it. Briefly we, may divide the planning of an utterance into *two* main stages: firstly, *outline planning*, which begins while the previous clause is being uttered. Secondly, *detailed planning*, which takes place while the clause is actually in progress. Outline planning means the choice of key words, syntax and intonation pattern, whereas detailed planning involves the fitting together of previously chosen words and syntax.

Let us look at outline planning first. The most straightforward evidence for the existence of this stage comes from anticipations and transpositions. If a person anticipates or transposes an item, clearly he is already thinking about it before it actually needs to be used. We note the general fact that the larger an item is, the further ahead it can be anticipated (Nooteboom, 1969; Hotopf, 1972). That is, the bigger the item, the bigger the gap between its actual occurrence and the place where it ought to be. The gap between confused words is normally greater than that between confused sound segments. However, the actual size of the gap is not the crucial point. The important thing to notice is this: although slips of the tongue normally occur within the tone group, on the rare occasions when this 'law' is broken it is whole *words* which slip into the preceding clause, rather than sound segments. That is, words can cross clause boundaries, whereas sounds generally do not. For example:

WHEN YOU BUY THE LAUNDRY . . . (When you take the laundry, please buy me some cigarettes)
WHEN YOU TAKE THE ROSES OUT, ADMIRE . . . (When you take the garbage out, admire the roses).
EXTINGUISH YOUR SEATBELTS . . . (Extinguish your cigarettes and fasten your seatbelts)

Compare these with the following sound transpositions and anticipations, which all occur within the same clause:

SHE WROTE ME A YETTER . . . (letter yesterday)
TWAPTER CHELVE (chapter twelve)
A COP OF CUFFEE (a cup of coffee)
DOG WAS . . . (Doug was a doctor).

The phenomenon described above indicates that key words are thought out while the preceding clause is being uttered – whereas the detailed organization of a tone group is left till later. Other types of advance planning are less easy to pin down. Of course, in many cases, common sense tells us that outline syntactic planning occurs well in advance of the actual utterance of a clause. In the sentence

IF HE WERE TO SEDUCE LOLITA, SHE WOULD BE DELIGHTED

the phrase IF HE WERE immediately indicates that the second clause has been thought about to some extent. However, this 'common sense' notion is rather vague. Evidence that is somewhat more useful comes from looking at intonation patterns. Here, we find a surprising phenomenon: errors which occur within the tone group do not normally disrupt the intonation pattern. For example:

TAKE THE FREEZES OUT OF THE STEAKER

has the same intonation pattern as the 'target' sentence: 'Take the steaks out of the freezer'.

Assuming, then, that we are correct in saying that the planning of key words and outline syntax (including the intonation pattern) begins during the preceding clause, we are now faced with a tricky and much disputed question: which comes first, the words or the syntactic pattern? Those who argue that the words come first point out quite simply that it is 'key' words which determine the choice of syntax, and by 'key' words they mean above all nouns, verbs and sometimes adjectives. Clearly, verbs influence the choice of syntax more than the nouns – but the noun may, in some cases, influence the choice of verb.

Those who suggest that the syntax comes first put forward an equally strong argument. They note that when a speaker makes a word selection error, he almost always picks a wrong word belonging to the same word class as the target word. That is, nouns are confused with other nouns, verbs with other verbs, and adjectives with other adjectives. Even dysphasic speech, which is often quite garbled, tends to follow this pattern (though exceptions do occur). People say UP instead of 'down', JELLY instead of 'blancmange', TRANSLATION instead of 'transformation'. But there is no reason for parts of speech to cling together like this. Why shouldn't verbs and nouns get confused? The fictional Mrs Malaprop gets her word classes confused much of the time, which is why many of her malapropisms are essentially implausible. She says things such as:

YOU WILL PROMISE TO FORGET THIS FELLOW – TO ILLITERATE HIM, I SAY, QUITE FROM YOUR MEMORY. (You will promise . . . to obliterate him . . . from your memory).

But in real life, it is extremely unusual to find adjective-verb confusions of the ILLITERATE for 'obliterate' type uttered by Mrs Malaprop. Even malapropisms uttered by children generally follow this similar word-class pattern:

YOU TAKE AN ANTELOPE IF YOU SWALLOW POISON (You take an antidote if you swallow poison)
I'M LEARNING TO PLAY THE ELBOW (I'm learning to play the oboe).

According to the 'syntax first' supporters, the most likely explanation for this phenomenon is that the syntax has already been chosen, and the words are then slotted in: 'Unless the syntactic structure is already constructed, word selection would not be constrained to proper word classes' (Fromkin, 1973:30). 'The very fact that a mistakenly selected word always or nearly always belongs to the same word class as the intended word indicates that the grammatical structure of the phrase under construction imposes imperative restrictions on the selection of words' (Nooteboom, 1969:130).

How are we to solve this controversy between the 'words first' and 'syntax first' supporters? Who is right? Possibly both sides, to some extent. On the one hand, it is extremely unlikely that the key word advocates are entirely correct. There is no evidence whatsoever that we assemble *all* the key words, and then bind them together with joining words. On the other hand, it is quite impossible to plan the syntax with no idea of the lexical items which are going to be used. For example, the syntax of

JOHN CLAIMED TO BE ABLE TO EAT A LIVE FROG

must depend to some extent on the word CLAIM, since other words with a similar meaning take a different construction. We cannot say

*JOHN ASSERTED TO BE ABLE TO EAT A LIVE FROG.

or

*JOHN DECLARED TO BE ABLE TO EAT A LIVE FROG

It is possible then, that we start by picking perhaps *one* key verb or noun, and then build the syntax around it. Later we slot other words into the remaining gaps.

If one key word triggers off the syntax, then we must assume that words in storage are clearly marked with their word class or part of speech (e.g., noun, verb) as well as with information about the constructions they can enter into. For example:

EAT	VERB
	NP – EAT – NP

We are, therefore, hypothesizing that when people plan utterances they build syntactic trees from the bottom upwards (see p. 223).

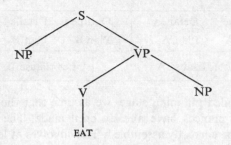

However, one problem remains. If we are correct in assuming that certain key words come first, how do we account for the fact that we often get the syntax right, but cannot remember key words, even though the forgotten item has clearly influenced the choice of syntax? For example:

HE TOOK A LOT OF . . . WHAT'S THE WORD I WANT? . . . PERSUASION.

This type of example suggests that we possibly plan with the 'idea of a word' (for want of a better way of putting it), then only later fit it to a phonetic form. This is supported by slips of the tongue such as

WHEN IS IT GOING TO BE RECOVERED BY?

In this sentence the syntax was picked for 'mend', but the phonetic form activated was RECOVERED.

Note, by the way, that a 'word idea' which (we are claiming) is selected before its phonetic form is not just an intangible 'concept', but a definite and firmly packaged lexical item. It includes both an understanding of what is being referred to and a firm word class label (noun, verb, adjective, etc.), as well as information about the syntactic configurations it can enter into.

So far, then, we have dealt with outline planning. We have hypothesized that, while still uttering the previous clause, speakers begin to prepare key words (usually in non-phonetic form), then build the syntax round them, and this also involves selection of an intonation pattern. The second, detailed planning state probably takes place while the clause is actually being uttered. One plausible suggestion is that we carry out the detailed planning during a hesitation pause which occurs near the beginning of a tone group. Boomer (1965) claims that he found a significantly high proportion of pauses *after* the first word of a clause. This suggests a picture like this:

Outline Plan A	Detailed Plan A	Outline Plan B	Detailed Plan B
Utter Clause A		Utter Clause B	

By the detailed planning stage, we assume that the major lexical and syntactic choices have already been made. The items chosen now have to be correctly assembled. This involves at least two types of manoeuvre: on the one hand, lexical items have to be put into their correct slots in the sentence. This has been wrongly carried out in

> IT'S BAD TO HAVE TOO MUCH BLOOD IN THE ALCOHOL STREAM (It's bad to have too much alcohol in the blood stream)
> A FIFTY-POUND DOG OF BAG FOOD (A fifty-pound bag of dog food).

The slotting in of lexical items must also include the slotting in of negatives, since these can get disturbed as in

> IT'S THE KIND OF FURNITURE I NEVER SAID I'D HAVE (It's the kind of furniture I said I'd never have)
> I DISREGARD THIS AS PRECISE (I regard this as imprecise).

In addition, detailed planning involves adding on word endings in the appropriate place. This has been done incorrectly in:

> SHE WASH UPPED THE DISHES (She washed up the dishes)
> SHE COME BACKS TOMORROW (She comes back tomorrow)
> HE BECAME MENTALIER UNHEALTHY (He became mentally unhealthier).

However, we can say rather more about the assemblage of words and endings than the vague comment that they are 'slotted together'. We noted in Chapter 3 that speakers seem to have an internal neural 'pacemaker' – a biological 'beat' which helps them to integrate and organize their utterances, and we saw that this pacemaker may utilize the syllable as a basic unit. If we look more carefully, we find that syllables are organized into *feet* – a foot being a unit which includes a 'strong' or stressed syllable. And we see that feet are organized into tone groups. In other words, we have a hierarchy of rhythmic units: tone groups made up of feet, and feet made up of syllables:

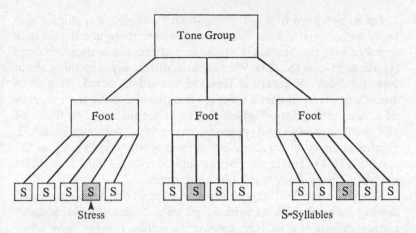

So within each tone group an utterance is planned foot by foot. This is indicated by the fact that transposed words are normally similarly stressed, and occupy similar places in their respective feet. For example:

HE FOUND A WÍFE : FOR HIS JÓB   (He found a job for his wife)

THE QUÁKE CAUSED : EXTENSIVE VÁLLEY : IN THE DÁMAGE   (The quake caused extensive damage in the valley).

Within each foot, the stressed or 'tonic' word may be activated first, since tonic words are statistically more likely to be involved in tongue slips than unstressed ones (Boomer and Laver, 1968). Finally, the importance of the syllable as a 'psychologically real' unit is shown by the fact that tongue slips 'obey a structural law with regard to syllable place' (Boomer and Laver, 1968:7). That is, the initial sound of a syllable will affect another initial sound, a final sound will affect another final, and vowels affect vowels, as in:

JAWFULLY LOINED   (lawfully joined)
HASS OR GRASH   (hash or grass)
BUD BEGS   (bed bugs).

Let us recapitulate; at the outline planning stage, the key words, syntax, and intonation of the tone group as a whole are set up. At the detailed planning stage, words and endings are slotted in foot by foot, with the stressed word in each foot possibly activated first. Finally, the remaining unstressed syllables are assembled.

Let us now turn to word selection and storage – our third major topic within this section. We can say rather more about this than merely noting the fact that the basic lexical item can be detached from its phonetic form (p. 223). We can, in addition, say something about how the 'idea' or semantic form of a word is stored, as well as something about phonetic storage. We can also posit the existence of a 'monitoring device' which checks to see that the two forms of the word, semantic and phonetic, have been correctly matched. Our most direct information comes from Roger Brown's 'tip of the tongue' (TOT) experiment (Brown and McNeill, 1966). Less direct evidence comes from word selection errors.

Roger Brown's TOT experiment was a simple one, which produced fascinating results. He assembled a group of students, and read them out definitions of relatively uncommon words. For example, when the 'target' word was SEXTANT, the students heard the definition: 'A navigational instrument used in measuring angular distances, especially the altitude of sun, moon and stars at sea'. Some of the students recognized the right word immediately. But others went into a TOT ('tip of the tongue') state. They felt they were on the verge of getting the word, but not quite there. In this state Brown asked them to fill in a questionnaire about their mental search. To his surprise, he found that the students could provide quite a lot of information about the elusive missing name. Sometimes the information was semantic, and sometimes it was phonetic. For example, in response to the definition of SEXTANT, several of them provided the similar meaning words ASTROLABE, COMPASS and PRO-TRACTOR. Others remembered that it had two syllables and began with an S, and made guesses such as SECANT, SEXTON, and SEXTET.

Semantically, this suggests that words are stored in 'semantic fields' – that is, all words of a similar meaning are found together. When we select the 'idea' of a word for utterance we enter the general area where it 'lives', before pinpointing one word in particular. When errors occur we have been insufficiently precise in locating the exact one needed – as with YESTERDAY instead of 'tomorrow', SHIRT instead of 'blouse', and (another example from Brown's TOT experiment) BARGE, HOUSEBOAT, JUNK instead of 'sampan'.

Phonetically, word storage is not quite so straight-forward. Children seem to store words above all by their rhythm, but adults pay at least as much attention to the initial letter, to judge by the evidence from TOT guesses and malapropisms.

When children confuse similar sounding words, they almost

invariably get the word rhythm right, and usually the stressed vowel as well, as in VIVACIOUS BORDER (herbacious border), HARVEST VEGETABLE (harvest festival). Adults also tend to get the rhythm right in malapropisms, as in the NATIVE APE for the 'naked ape', and COMPETENCE instead of 'confidence'. Furthermore, Roger Brown noted that his TOT subjects could often tell him the number of syllables of the target word, and also seemed aware of the position of the main stress. However, with adults, there is merely a *tendency* to get the rhythm right, and a number of exceptions are found, as in COMPETITIVE for 'combative', and TRANSLATION for 'transformation'. On the other hand, adults nearly always get the initial letter right in malapropisms and TOT guesses, whereas children often get it wrong, as in MUSCLE SPROUTS for 'brussel sprouts', MISTAKE CAR for 'estate car', and ICE-CREAM TOILET for 'ice-cream cornet'.

So tentatively we may suggest that children search for and identify phonetic word forms above all by their rhythm, then later 'load' the sounds on to the underlying pattern. But adults (perhaps as a result of learning to read) tend to identify word forms by their initial letter as well as their rhythm.[4]

In addition to our suggestions about separate phonetic storage, we can (as we noted above) postulate the existence of a 'monitoring device' which checks to see that each word has been fitted to the correct phonetic form:

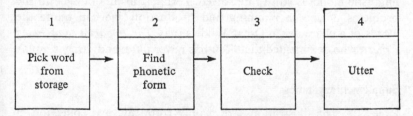

1	2	3	4
Pick word from storage	Find phonetic form	Check	Utter

The existence of a monitoring device is indicated by the fact that in adult speech 'pure' errors are rare: as noted earlier, there is usually both a phonetic *and* a semantic reason for a mistake, as with INCINERATOR for 'incubator', which is both phonetically and semantically relevant to some extent. If such a check did not exist, we would possibly find many more purely phonetic malapropisms which had no obvious connection with the topic under discussion. Presumably, many quite weird potential malapropisms are 'caught' by the check barrier and never uttered. Most of those which are uttered have passed a check which was clearly not thorough enough. In other words, a speaker who is not concentrating may accidentally let through a word that has some phonetic and some semantic appropriateness, even when it is in fact the wrong one. In dysphasic speech especially, the check mechanism seems particularly weak. Dysphasics seem to let through a far wider range of inappropriate words, providing there is at least some sound and meaning link, however flimsy (as in DRIVING for 'swimming', caused by DRIVING for 'diving' and DIVING for 'swimming'). Of course, even if the first 'check' lets a word through, then there is a second 'check' after a person has uttered it. If a speaker realizes his mistake, he says, 'Sorry, I mean . . .' and starts the phrase again.

Where does all this leave us? Still fairly much in the dark, compared with what we were able to find out about decoding. There are still enormous gaps in our knowledge, and much of what we have said is hypothetical. We have realized that, for every clause uttered, a human speaker must be carrying out a number of complex overlapping tasks, a feat he manages by relying on a rhythmic principle. Utterances are organized tone group by tone group. Within the tone group they are organized foot by foot, and within the foot syllable by syllable. As far as word storage and selection is concerned, the 'idea' of a word is possibly selected first, then later attached to its phonetic form.

The question of to how all this can be fitted into a coherent linguistic model is still to be solved. Perhaps, as an epilogue to the problems of speech planning and production, we can quote the words of a character in Oscar Wilde's play *The Importance of Being Ernest*, who commented that 'Truth is never pure, and rarely simple'.

Supplementary notes

Page 208 [1]The illustrations are mainly from my own collection of tongue slips, supplemented with examples from Fromkin (1971), Fromkin, (1973), Boomer and Laver (1968).

Page 210 [2]The view taken here, that the word selection errors of dysphasics are quantitatively (rather than qualitatively) different from the slips of the tongue of normal speakers, is not shared by all psycholinguists.

Page 216 [3]Whole sound segments may be affected, or only certain components or 'features' of sound, as in PIG AND VAT (big and fat), with transposition of the feature 'voiced'.

Page 227 [4]This clear-cut picture can be disturbed in both child and adult speech by factors such as the presence of a 'chunked suffix' as in the child malapropisms OPERATED MILK (evaporated) and the adult one ACCUMULATOR for 'incubator'. Here both child and adult seem to be influenced by the suffix, which seems to have been memorized as a rhyming 'chunk' (Brown and McNeill, 1966; Aitchison, 1972).

12 Banker's Clerk or Hippopotamus?

The Future of Psycholinguistics

He thought he saw a Banker's Clerk
  Descending from a bus:
He looked again, and found it was
  A Hippopotamus.
                              Lewis Carrol
                              Sylvie and Bruno

We are now nearing the end of *The Articulate Mammal*. But obviously this is not the end as far as psycholinguistics is concerned. Psycholinguistics is, as this book has shown, a field of study riddled with controversies. Frequently, apparently simple data can be interpreted in totally different ways. The psycholinguist often finds that he is in the same situation as the Lewis Carroll character who is not sure whether he is looking at a banker's clerk or a hippopotamus.

In this general situation, it would be over-optimistic to predict the future of the subject with any confidence. However, certain lines of inquiry are beginning to emerge as important, some of which are mentioned or foreshadowed in this book. What are these? Perhaps a useful way to introduce them is to outline briefly the conclusions we have reached so far, and show the issues which arise from them.

General conclusions

As we noted in the Introduction, three psycholinguistic topics can be singled out as particularly important: the innateness question, the relationship of linguistic knowledge (as encapsulated in a transformational grammar) to language use, and the comprehension and production of speech – and these areas were the principal concern of this book.

We introduced the topic of innateness by outlining the 'nature-nurture' controversy. Is language a 'natural' phenomenon such as walking or sexual activity? Or is it a skill which we learn, such as knitting? We saw that Skinner's attempts to explain language as purely learned behaviour turn out to be a dismal failure. The claim that the antics of rats can explain language is without foundation. Not only are animal experiments irrelevant to language acquisition, but language itself, on closer examination, is infinitely more complex than one might imagine. This, we saw, leaves us with a problem. If psychologists are unable to explain the acquisition of language by means of simple learning theories, how is it that humans become proficient at talking in such a relatively short period of time? One possible solution has been proposed by Chomsky: he suggests that a person's ability to speak is innate rather than learned – that the human species is 'pre-programmed' for language. This is the possibility that we examined in the next few chapters.

In Chapter 2 we looked at human language beside animal communication. We noted that, as far as we could tell, the human race is the only species which possesses language. Although a number of animal communication systems share some features of human language, no animal communication system possesses them all. And when we looked at the attempts made to teach a simplified language system to the chimps Washoe and Sarah, we saw that their achievements in this sphere do not seem particularly impressive compared with those of human children. The chimps seem capable of learning a language-like system, but they do not seem predisposed to learn it. In brief, the results of the animal experiments suggest (but do not prove) that language in humans is an innately programmed activity.

In Chapters 3 and 4 we examined the biological evidence. We noted that the brain, as well as the teeth, tongue and vocal cords, seem to have been adapted to the needs of speech. We also pointed out that talking requires the synchronization of so many different operations that it seems likely that humans are innately 'set' to cope with this task. We also noted that language has all the hallmarks of biologically triggered behaviour. It emerges when the individual reaches a certain level of maturation, then develops at its own natural pace, following a more or less standard sequence of 'milestones'. And direct teaching and intensive practice appear to have relatively little effect. We therefore came to the firm conclusion that there was biological evidence for innate language ability.

Our next step was to try and find out exactly what is innate. We started in Chapter 5 by outlining the suggestions of Noam

Chomsky, who proposes that every child is equipped with a Language Acquisition Device which has certain fairly specific properties. In Chapters 6 and 7 we looked at the acquisition of language in the light of Chomsky's proposals. We noted that children *do* instinctively realise that language is 'rule-governed' and they *do* seem innately predisposed to look for hierarchical structure and structure-dependent operations. However, Chomsky's suggestion that children are geared to looking for two levels of structure – a 'deep' level and a 'surface' one, was not borne out by the evidence. Instead, children appear to extract language from the jumble of speech they hear going on around them by following a set of inbuilt 'operating procedures'. In other words, they have relatively little advance knowledge about the actual *form* of language, but seem instead to have a remarkable ability for processing linguistic data.

We may summarize the contents of Chapters 1 to 7 by saying that we found strong evidence in favour of the suggestion that a human's ability to talk is innate. However, when it came to discovering exactly *what* is innate, we ran into difficulties. Chomsky's assertion that children are endowed with a highly structured acquisition device which incorporates a set of formal linguistic universals seems over-optimistic. His proposals are not borne out by the evidence. We preferred, instead, the suggestion that children have an inbuilt ability for *processing* linguistic data – though it is not clear whether this ability is specific to language or dependent on other general cognitive abilities.

In the rest of the book, we turned to the language of adults. Chapters 8 and 9 were devoted to our second main topic: how does Chomsky's transformational-generative grammar link up with the way a person *uses* his language? We first explained just why anyone would want to propose a transformational grammar. We then noted that such a grammar could not possibly be a direct model of the way a speaker actually understands and produces utterances. Instead, it is a hypothesis about a speaker's stored *knowledge* of his language. That is, a transformational grammar represents a 'linguistic archive' which is *available* for consultation by someone producing or comprehending a sentence, though the extent to which this archive is consulted varies from sentence to sentence. We could not say with any confidence that a transformational grammar had 'psychological reality'. At the moment it is merely the most coherent hypothesis put forward so far to account for the type of linguistic knowledge anyone who 'knows' a language must have internalized.

Having firmly concluded that a transformational grammar is no help in explaining how a person actually *uses* his language, we then turned to our final topic: what exactly *does* happen when someone comprehends or produces an utterance?

Chapter 10 dealt with the process of comprehension. We noted that, to a surprising extent, people hear what they expect to hear. They look for certain clues when they are decoding, and if they find them, they jump to conclusions about what the speaker is saying. In other words, people utilize perceptual strategies or short cuts in the comprehension of speech. Sentences are difficult to understand if the perceptual strategies do not work, or if they involve other, more general difficulties, such as backward processing.

In Chapter 11 we turned to speech production. This proved to be a highly complex process in which each clause is partially planned while the previous one is being uttered. Key words, outline syntax and intonation are possibly activated first, then the remaining words and endings are slotted into the correct place. The organization and integration of the various parts of the clause depend on a rhythmic principle. The tone group constitutes the unit of planning. Each tone group can be subdivided into feet, and each foot can be subdivided into syllables, which set up the basic rhythmic beat. There is also some evidence that the actual phonetic form of a word is not activated until some time after its 'idea' has been selected from storage.

Let us now outline our conclusions concerning the three topics we investigated.

We noted, firstly, that *something* connected with language is innate – though this something may well overlap with general cognitive abilities in a way as yet undefined.

Secondly, we realized that a transformational grammar is relatively little use in explaining *how* we comprehend and produce utterances. The link between language knowledge (as represented in a transformational grammar) and language use is extremely tenuous. We concluded that, at most, a transformational grammar had only 'weak' psychological reality, and even that weak claim is suspect.

Thirdly, we saw that people comprehend sentences by a series of short cuts or perceptual strategies which encapsulate what they expect to hear. When they produce speech, they follow a complex series of overlapping processes, whose correct ordering depends on a rhythmic principle.

Where do we go from here? This is the question we shall now consider.

Future Prospects

First of all, a basic task for the future is the integration of work that has been done separately by psychologists and linguists. Priority must be given to co-operation and co-ordination. However, this talk of integration is rather vague. We can, in addition, point out two major areas which seem likely to claim the attention of psycholinguists throughout the next decade:

1. *The relationship of language to general cognitive abilities.* We need to know how much of language is due to a specific language component within the mind, and how much is dependent on general cognitive abilities.

2. *The development of a psychologically real model of grammar.* It seems important to establish a closer link between a model of grammar and what is happening in the mind of someone who speaks and understands a language.

There are a number of ways of tackling the first problem. One promising avenue is further study of child language. We noted in Chapter 7 that children seem to be equipped with puzzle-solving mechanisms which enable them to extract language from the mass of speech they hear going on around them. Clearly, we need to know more about the operating procedures which a child uses when he performs this task. For this purpose, it is essential to gather information from a wider variety of languages. Psycholinguists are beginning to collect this data, though we still need to know much more about the acquisition of languages which differ structurally from English. Eventually, we should be able to add considerably to our list of operating principles, as well as finding out which are universal, and which differ from child to child. And of those that are universal, we hope to find out which are unique to language, and which are used in other types of problem-solving.

Of course, the study of a child's operating principles is not the only aspect of child language which can help us. We can undoubtedly obtain useful clues to the relationship between language and cognitive abilities if we pay closer attention to the child's total environment, especially the speech of the rest of the family and his development in other areas of mental activity – and there are signs that this integrated approach is gaining momentum. In this context we should perhaps mention briefly the 'functional-interactional' approach to language acquisition by scholars such as Michael Halliday (1975). Strictly speaking, Halliday is a sociolinguist rather than a psycholinguist, and he utilizes sociolinguistic techniques in his work. He has analysed the speech of his son Nigel from the point of view of the 'communicative functions' of language. For example, an utterance such as CAKE expresses an *instrumental* or 'I want' function, and HELLO expresses an *interactional* function. Although a number of psycholinguists regard this type of categorization as being too subjective to be reliable, there is no doubt that it is sometimes useful to approach child language from a totally different angle.

The second area that is likely to occupy the attention of psycholinguists in the coming decade – that of developing a psychologically real model of grammar – is perhaps rather more interesting, though also rather more tricky to deal with. Here we envisage a slightly different approach from that adopted in the past. In recent years it has been an implicit (and sometimes explicit) assumption that it is the task of linguists to produce models of grammar, and for psychologists to test them and explain how they work. The result of this artificial division of labour was that linguists proposed a transformational model of grammar which described language *knowledge*, but virtually ignored language *use*. As we have seen, we do not yet know whether a transformational grammar characterizes linguistic knowledge in a way that is psychologically real or not. However, the tenuousness of the link between such a grammar and language use may well be a sign that something is wrong. It seems likely that we shall have to abandon a model which proposes an abstract deep layer of syntax, and eventually replace it with one in which knowledge and use are more closely related.

The necessity of linking up language knowledge with language use has important implications for psycholinguistics: it is the task of psycholinguists to find out more about language use, in order that pure linguists may be more aware of the phenomena which their theories must explain.

How should we go about this? Clearly, we can continue work on encoding and decoding. As far as encoding is concerned, work on 'slips of the tongue' is relatively new, and much remains to be done, particularly on languages other than English. Until recently, tongue slips were considered to be the domain of phoneticians and a few neurolinguists. But, as we have seen, they can contribute valuable information as to what happens when we produce utterances. Similarly, work on the perceptual strategies which hearers use when they decode sentences is still in its infancy. In particular, we would like to find out which strategies are linked to a particular language and which are likely to be universal. Once again, this will involve studying the perceptual strategies used in languages unlike English.

However, clues as to the contents of a psychologically real model of grammar can be obtained not only from encoding and decoding, but from other aspects of language also. Two fringe areas of psycholinguistics which look promising are *language change* and *language variation* (though, as will become clear, these two are not totally separate).

Study of the factors which can cause language change may give us valuable insights into the mechanisms behind language. For example, it has recently been suggested that one possible cause of change is an imbalance between the needs of perception and memory capacity (Bever and Langendoen, 1972). That is, forms which are easy to remember are not necessarily easy to perceive, and this may lead to alterations in the grammar. This seems to have happened in Middle English. Somewhere between the eleventh and fifteenth centuries English noun endings were greatly simplified. This clearly eased the strain on the memory. However, this simplification caused problems in the recognition of relative clauses. Originally, if the same person or thing was both the object of the main clause, and the subject of the relative clause, it had to be included in the sentence twice: once as the object of the main clause, and once as the subject of the relative clause. However, when the subject and object endings came to be the same, the shared word only had to be inserted once:

e.g.   LETE FETCHE THE BEST HORS MAYE BE FOUNDE (Malory, fifteenth century)   (Fetch the best horse that can be found).

But this meant that it was not always easy to tell quickly which verb belonged to the main and which to the subordinate clause. This perceptual difficulty may have been the reason why the insertion of an introductory word such as WHO or THAT became obligatory in relative clauses of this type.

The kind of language change exemplified in the paragraph above can give us important clues as to the type of constraints we must set up within a psychologically real model of grammar. Equally important are the clues that we can obtain from a study of language variation. Here we are speaking about variation which involves a special type of linguistic 'rule', one that governs an *active* process. Syntactic rules of this type do exist, though it is perhaps simplest to give examples of phonological ones. For example, it is clear that most speakers have a pronunciation rule which says (among other things) 'Insert R at the end of a verb ending in -AW if it precedes the article A':

e.g.   I SAW [R] A HIPPOPOTAMUS
       PLEASE DRAW [R] A PICTURE.

Many people also have an unconscious rule which says, 'In fast speech you can omit the T at the end of words such as HOT, as in HO(T) WATER BOTTLE.'

When we add up these separate 'rules' we find that there are a considerable number of them in any one person's speech. We would like to find out how many active rules of this type a person is able to cope with. We are also interested in finding out how such rules interact with one another if two of them should clash. We need to know how the rules change, and how a change in the rules affects the stored lexical forms of words. One much quoted example will perhaps make this last point much clearer. At one time, the standard pronunciation of words such as WHAT, WHEN was [hwot], [hwen], with aspiration at the beginning – though in fast speech this tended to be omitted and the words were pronounced as [wot] and [wen]. In other words, speakers stored the lexical forms [hwot] and [hwen], and also had a subconscious rule which said, 'Delete H in fast speech'. Eventually, [wot] and [wen] came to be the normal form of the word, so at some point there must have been a change-over in the form in which the words were stored: [hwot] and [hwen] became [wot] and [wen].(According to one unsubstantiated theory, this change occurs between generations). Nowadays, there are still a few people who consciously insert the H in careful speech, and make a point of distinguishing between WHICH and WITCH. They have a rule which says, 'Insert H before W in careful speech'. So we have a strange phenomenon: what used to be a *deletion* rule has become an *insertion* rule. This example is clearly a very simple one. But more complex instances of this mechanism would help us to understand what type of psychologically real processes are going on in the mind of the speaker.

This survey has pin-pointed a number of areas which are likely to receive attention from psycholinguists in the next decade. On the one hand, psycholinguists are becoming increasingly interested in the relationship between language and other cognitive abilities. We can find out more about this problem by further work on child language acquisition – in particular by studying the operating procedures a child uses to extract rules from the multifarious utterances he hears going on around him, and by paying attention to the child's total environment. On the other hand, psycholinguists are likely to continue working on the psychological reality problem – isolation of the factors which need to be incorporated into a psychologically real model of grammar. For this task, a considerable amount of work still needs to be done on slips of the tongue and perceptual strategies. In addition, two further areas seem likely to yield promising results: language change and language variation. This state of affairs is represented on the diagram below:

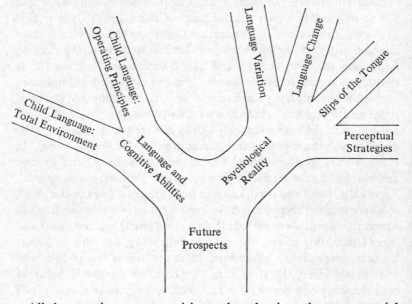

All these topics seem promising – though, given the controversial nature of the subject, I have been careful not to single out any branch as the main one. I have also left plenty of space for new branches to develop: psycholinguistics is a field of study likely to spring surprises on researchers. A seemingly dead and forgotten area may suddenly spring to life. A living and on-going subject 'is constantly sprouting new leaves on old wood, and sometimes quite suddenly the bush is ablaze with blossom of a novel shade' (A. L. Lloyd).

Notes and Suggestions for Further Reading

This section contains outline suggestions for further reading. I have kept these to a minimum, since the books recommended will give further references if these are needed. I have also drawn attention to certain over-simplifications or biases in the book which might mislead the beginning student.

Introduction

The distinction drawn here between psychological and linguistic psycholinguists is perhaps over-simplified. Psychological psycholinguists are sometimes divided into experimental psychologists and developmental psychologists. The latter often bridge the gap between psycologists and linguists, utilizing both natural data and the results of experiments – as in the work of Roger Brown and Dan Slobin.

For those who wish to acquaint themselves with linguistics there is an enormous number of elementary textbooks, and the one selected must depend on the needs of the reader. Most of the following (which are listed in alphabetical order of author) are orientated towards transformational-generative grammar (TGG), which is the type of linguistics discussed in this book, and the dominant approach at the current time:

AITCHISON, JEAN, *General Linguistics* (London: English Universities Press, Teach Yourself Books, 1972). A brief and general 'introduction to introductions' to linguistics.

AKMAJIAN, A., and F. HENY, *An Intoroduction to the Principles of Transformational Syntax* (Cambridge, Mass: MIT Press, 1975). A thorough and well-organized introductory textbook.

BACH, E., *Syntactic Theory* (New York: Holt, Rinehart and Winston, 1974). A useful, but compressed account of TGG syntax and the theoretical problems which arise from it.

GRINDER, J. T., and S. H. ELGIN, *A Guide to Transformational Grammar* (New York: Holt, Rinehart and Winston, 1973). Claims to be a 'crash-course' for beginners: TGG in one semester.

LANGACKER, R. W., *Language and its Structure* (New York: Harcourt, Brace and World, 1967). A fairly vague, but easy to read introduction to TGG.

LYONS, J., *Chomsky* (London: Fontana, 1970). A clear guide to Chomsky's *Syntactic Structures* (1957), the small book which 'revolutionized' linguistics.

SAMPSON, G., *The Form of Language* (London: Weidenfeld and Nicolson, 1975). A useful non-technical book which assesses the claims of Chomsky, and their relevance to the other social sciences.

Chapter 1

This chapter is based to a large extent on Chomsky's review of Skinner's book *Verbal Behavior*. This article, now a linguistic 'classic' is perhaps still the best starting point for understanding the direction taken by language acquisition studies in the 1960s:

CHOMSKY, N., Review of Skinner's *Verbal Behavior*, *Language* 35 (1959).

The review has also been reprinted in a number of places, for example in Jakobovits and Miron (1976).

In later writings Chomsky (wrongly) regards Skinner as typifying the mainstream of current psychological thought. For this reason he sometimes unjustifiably attacks psychology as a whole. Chomsky's fallacy is clearly pointed out by Sampson (1975).

Chapter 2

Animal communication is a vast and fast-expanding field of study. A useful anthology which gives some idea of the scope of the subject is:

SEBEOK, T. A., (ed.), *Animal Communication* (Bloomington: Indiana University Press, 1968).

Hockett's longest and clearest list of the 'design features' of language is perhaps:

HOCKETT, C. F., 'The problem of universals in language', in *Universals of Language*, edited by J. H. Greenberg (Cambridge, Mass: MIT Press, 1963).

However, this should be supplemented by a more recent article in which he points out some of the problems involved in the design feature approach, and suggests ways of overcoming them:

HOCKETT, C. F. and S. A. ALTMANN, 'A note on design features', in Sebeok 1968).

Note that in addition to the design features listed in this chapter, a number of people would consider it necessary to include 'Use of logical relations'. That is, human language makes use of the logical relationships of inclusion, incompatibility, and so on, whereas animal communication appears not to do so. However, since man's use of logical relationships is attributable to a general property of the mind, rather than language in particular, I have omitted this possible feature from the list (though the extent of the overlap between general cognitive abilities and language is a serious and controversial problem, as will become clear in later chapters).

The clearest information on the chimps Washoe and Sarah is in articles written by their trainers. The following are lucid and non-technical:

GARDNER, R. A. and B. T. GARDNER, 'Teaching sign language to a chimpanzee', *Science* (1965).

PREMACK, D., 'The education of Sarah', *Psychology Today* 4 (1970).

PREMACK, D., 'Teaching language to an ape', *Scientific American* (October 1972).

Rumours and advance reports of a number of other chimps are circulating, though as yet none of them has progressed significantly beyond the achievements of Sarah and Washoe. The Gardners, for example, are now training two infant chimpanzees together, and hope eventually to observe these two 'talking' together when humans are absent. This is not a unrealistic hope, since Washoe used to 'talk' to herself in the absence of humans.

Chapter 3

This chapter relies heavily on the early sections (Chapters 1–3) in Lenneberg's excellent book, which is highly recommended for further reading:

LENNEBERG, E. H., *Biological Foundations of Language* (New York: Wiley, 1967).

In the early chapters of Lenneberg's book there are two areas in particular in which his views are controversial. Firstly, he takes an extreme 'anti-localization' viewpoint over the location of speech mechanisms. That is, he is perhaps over-sceptical about the possibility of locating areas in the brain which control speech. Secondly, Lenneberg's claim that there is a 'biological beat' which underlies language and controls its rate of utterance to approximately six syllables a second is considered by some to be little more than speculation. However, in spite of the controversial nature of these claims, they could well prove to be right.

Chapter 4

Once again, the early part of this chapter relies heavily on sections in:
LENNEBERG, E. H., *Biological Foundations of Language* (New York: Wiley, 1967).
Lenneberg's Chapter 4, 'Language in the context of growth and maturation', is both lucid and stimulating – though his evidence in favour of a 'critical period' for language acquisition has been widely queried.

From page 79 onwards, much of the material in this chapter can be found in an expanded form in Brown's comprehensive and highly recommended survey of language acquisition:
BROWN, R., *A First Language* (London: Allen and Unwin, 1973).
This is mainly a summary of his own work with the 'Harvard children' Adam, Eve and Sarah, though he also compares and dicusses the results of other researchers.

Chapter 5

This chapter, for the most part, summarizes Chomsky's proposals for the 'innate schema' as put forward in:
CHOMSKY, N., *Aspects of the Theory of Syntax* (Cambridge: Mass. MIT Press, 1965).
Certain problems connected with deep structure have been glossed over in this chapter. For example, I have implied that active and passive sentences have the same deep structure. This is in fact a controversial issue, and many linguists (including Chomsky) take the opposite viewpoint.

Chapter 6

Most of the points raised in this chapter are discussed in more detail in:
BROWN, R., *A First Language* (London: Allen and Unwin, 1973).
Brown discusses the two-word utterance stage at length – concentrat-

ing in particular on the 'rich' versus 'lean' child grammar controversy. Should one attribute to the child's 'competence' far more than is apparent on the surface? Or not? Brown also discusses the fluctuation of endings in a fairly puzzled and agnostic way. In fact, the fluctuation of Sarah's -*ing* ending and similar phenomena have led a minority of psycholinguists to query whether child language really is rule-governed. However, this fluctuation ties in with the Piagetian notion of 'pre-structures'. Piaget claims that children go through a stage at which 'structures' are unstable prior to their firm acquisition. This notion has been examined more closely in connection with verb endings in Szagun (1975).

Chapter 7

A lucid account of the content-process controversy occurs in:
DERWING, B. L., *Transformational Grammar as a Theory of Language Acquisition* (Cambridge: Cambridge University Press, 1973).

The last part of this chapter relies heavily on Slobin's excellent description of the 'process' approach:
SLOBIN, D. I., 'Cognitive prerequisites for the development of grammar', in *Studies of Child Language Development* edited by C. A. Ferguson and D. I. Slobin (New York: Rinehart, Winston, 1973).

Chapter 8

As noted in the text, the reasons for rejecting a left-to-right (finite state) and a top-to-bottom (phrase structure) grammar, and for setting up a transformational model are given in Chomsky's 'pioneering' work:
CHOMSKY, N., *Syntactic Structures* (The Hague: Mouton, 1957).

Chapter 9

More detailed coverage of much of the material covered in this chapter can be found in:
FODOR, J. A., T. G. BEVER and M. F. GARRETT, *The Psychology of Language* (New York: McGraw Hill, 1974).
This book, while not being particularly easy to read, provides a comprehensive guide to the psycholinguistic literature surrounding transformational grammar. It is a first-hand account, since a number

of the crucial experiments were carried out by the authors themselves. It is perhaps helpful to balance their account against a useful, though turgidly written article which is often critical of their conclusions:

WATT, W. C., 'On two hypotheses concerning psycholinguistics', in *Cognition and the Development of Language* edited by J. R. Hayes (New York: Wiley, 1970).

Two points need to be made in connection with the experiments described on pp. 160–4. Firstly, the researchers were testing an early form of transformational grammar in which question and negative transformations were optional. In the later 'classic' version of transformational grammar, question and negative elements were included in the deep structure. Secondly, some psychologists mistakenly assumed that SAADs and underlying strings were identical. They therefore wrongly stated that SAADs involved no transformations.

Chapter 10

Much of the material in this chapter can, again, be found in more detail in:

FODOR, J. A., T. G. BEVER and M. F. GARRETT, *The Psychology of Language* (New York: McGraw Hill, 1974).

However, I have dealt with the material in a rather different order and form, and sometimes reached different conclusions (for example, concerning the 'versatile verb' hypothesis).

Chapter 11

Two useful collections of papers which deal with slips of the tongue and dysphasia are:

FROMKIN, V. A., *Speech Errors as Linguistic Evidence* (The Hague: Mouton, 1973).

GOODGLASS, H., and S. BLUMSTEIN, *Psycholinguistics and Aphasia* (Baltimore: John Hopkins University Press, 1973).

The examples in this chapter are taken mainly from my own collection of tongue slips, supplemented with examples from Fromkin (1971), Fromkin (1973) and Boomer and Laver (1968).

Chapter 12

I know of no straight 'prediction for the future' paper on psycholinguistics. The nearest is perhaps:

MACLAY, H., 'Linguistics and psycholinguistics', in *Issues in Linguistics* edited by B. J. Kachru *et al.* (Chicago: University of Illinois Press).

References

ABRAMS, K., and T. G. BEVER (1969), 'Syntactic structure modifies attention during speech perception and recognition', *Quarterly Journal of Experimental Psychology* 21, 280–90.

AITCHISON, J. (1972), 'Mini-malapropisms', *British Journal of Disorders of Communication* 7, 38–43.

AITCHISON, J. (1972a), *General Linguistics*, London: English Universities Press, Teach Yourself Books.

AKMAJIAN, A, and F. HENY (1975), *An Introduction to the Principles of Transformational Syntax*, Cambridge, Mass: MIT Press.

BACH, E. (1974), *Syntactic Theory*, New York: Holt, Rinehart and Winston.

BAR-ADON, A., and W. F. LEOPOLD (1971), *Child Language: A Book of Readings*, Englewood Cliffs, N.J.: Prentice-Hall.

BELLUGI, U. (1971), 'Simplification in children's language', in HUXLEY and INGRAM (1971).

BELLUGI, U., and R. BROWN (1964), *The Acquisition of Language*, Monograph of the Society for Research in Child Development 29.1.

BERKO, J. (1958), 'The child's learning of English morphology', *Word* 14, 150–177. Also in BAR-ADON and LEOPOLD (1971).

BERNSTEIN, B. (1972), 'Social class, language and socialisation', in *Language and Social Context* edited by P. P. Giglioli, Harmondsworth: Penguin.

BEVER, T. G. (1970), 'The cognitive basis for linguistic structures', in HAYES (1970).

BEVER, T. G. (1971), 'The nature of cerebral dominance in speech behaviour of the child and adult', in HUXLEY and INGRAM (1971).

BEVER, T. G., J. A. FODOR and W. WEKSEL (1965), 'Theoretical notes on the acquisition of syntax: a critique of "contextual generalisation"', *Psychological Review* 72, 467–82. Also in JAKOBOVITS and MIRON (1967).

BEVER, T. G., J. R. LACKNER and R. KIRK (1969), 'The underlying structures of sentences are the primary units of immediate speech processing', *Perception and Psychophysics* 5, 225–31.

BEVER, T. G. and D. T. LANGENDOEN (1972), 'The interaction of speech perception and grammatical structure in the evolution of language', in *Linguistic Change and Generative Theory* edited by

R. P. Stockwell and R. K. S. Macaulay, Bloomington: Indiana University Press.

BLOOM, L. (1970), *Language Development: Form and Function in Emerging Grammars*, Cambridge, Mass: MIT Press.

BLOOM, L. (1973). *One Word at a Time*, The Hague: Mouton.

BLOOM, L., P. LIGHTBOWN and L. HOOD (1975), *Structure and Variation in Child Language*, Monograph of the Society for Research in Child Development 40.2.

BLUMENTHAL, A. L. (1966), 'Observations with self-embedded sentences', *Psychonomic Science* 6, 453–4.

BLUMENTHAL, A. L. (1967), 'Prompted recall of sentences', *Journal of Verbal Learning and Verbal Behavior* 6, 203–6.

BOOMER, D. S. (1965), 'Hesitation and grammatical encoding,' *Language and Speech* 8, 148–58. Also in OLDFIELD and MARSHALL (1968).

BOOMER, D. S., and J. D. M. LAVER (1968), 'Slips of the tongue', *British Journal of Disorders of Communication* 3, 1–12. Also in FROMKIN (1973).

BOWERMAN, M. (1973), *Early Syntactic Development*, Cambridge: Cambridge University Press.

BRAINE, M. (1963), 'The ontogeny of English phrase structure: the first phrase', *Language* 39, 1–14. Also in BAR-ADON and LEOPOLD (1971), FERGUSON and SLOBIN (1973).

BRAINE, M. D. S. (1971), 'The acquisition of language in infant and child', in *The Learning of Language*, edited by C. E. Reed, New York: Appleton-Century-Crofts.

BROWN, R. (1958), *Words and Things*, New York: The Free Press.

BROWN, R. (1970), *Psycholinguistics: Selected Papers*, New York: The Free Press.

BROWN, R. (1973), *A First Language*, London: Allen and Unwin.

BROWN, R., and U. BELLUGI (1964), 'Three processes in the child's acquisition of syntax', in LENNEBERG (1964). Also in BROWN (1970).

BROWN, R., C. CAZDEN and U. BELLUGI (1968), 'The child's grammar from I to III', in *Minnesota Symposium on Child Psychology*, vol. II edited by J. P. Hill, Minneapolis: University of Minnesota Press. Also in BROWN (1970), FERGUSON and SLOBIN (1973).

BROWN, R., and C. FRASER (1964), 'The acquisition of syntax', in BELLUGI and BROWN (1964).

BROWN, R., and D. MCNEILL (1966), 'The "Tip of the Tongue" Phenomenon', *Journal of Verbal Learning and Verbal Behavior* 5, 325–37. Also in BROWN (1970).

CAREY, P. W., J. MEHLER and T. G. BEVER (1970), 'When do we compute all the interpretations of an ambiguous sentence?' in FLORES D'ARCAIS and LEVELT (1970).

CAZDEN, C. (1972), *Child Language and Education*, New York: Holt, Rinehart and Winston.

CHOMSKY, C. (1969), *The Acquisition of Syntax in Children from 5 to 10*, Cambridge, Mass: MIT Press.

CHOMSKY, N. (1957), *Syntactic Structures*, The Hague: Mouton.

CHOMSKY, N. (1959), Review of Skinner's *Verbal Behavior, Language* 35, 26–58. Also in JAKOBOVITS and MIRON (1967).

CHOMSKY, N. (1963), 'Formal properties of grammars', in LUCE, BUSH and GALANTER (1963).

CHOMSKY, N. (1965), *Aspects of the Theory of Syntax*, Cambridge, Mass: MIT Press.

CHOMSKY, N. (1967), 'The formal nature of language', in LENNEBERG (1967).

CHOMSKY, N. (1971), 'Recent contributions to the theory of innate ideas', in *The Philosophy of Language*, edited by J. R. Searle, Oxford: Oxford University Press.

CHOMSKY, N. (1972), *Problems of Knowledge and Freedom*, London: Fontana.

CHOMSKY, N. (1972a), *Language and Mind*, enlarged edition, New York: Harcourt Brace Jovanovich.

CLARK, H. H., and E. V. CLARK (1968), 'Semantic distinctions and memory for complex sentences', *Quarterly Journal of Experimental Psychology* 20, 129–38.

COHEN, A. (1966), 'Errors of speech and their implication for understanding the strategy of language users', in FROMKIN (1973).

CRITCHLEY, M. (1970), *Aphasiology*, London: Arnold.

CROMER, R. (1970), 'Children are nice to understand: surface structure clues for the recovery of a deep structure', *British Journal of Psychology* 61, 397–408.

CROMER, R. F. (1974), 'The development of language and cognition: the cognition hypothesis', in *New Perspectives in Child Development*, edited by B. Foss, Harmondsworth: Penguin.

CURTISS, S., V. FROMKIN, S. KRASHEN, D. RIGLER and M. RIGLER (1974), 'The Linguistic Development of Genie', *Language* 50, 528–54.

DE CECCO, J. P. (1967), *The Psychology of Thought, Language and Instruction*, New York: Holt, Rinehart and Winston.

DE REUCK, A. V. S., and M. O. O'CONNOR (1946), *Disorders of Language*, London: Churchill.

DERWING, B. L. (1973), *Transformational Grammar as a Theory of Language Acquisition*, Cambridge: Cambridge University Press.

DINGWALL, W. O. (1971), *A Survey of Linguistic Science*, Maryland: University of Maryland.

DRACHMANN, G. (1973), 'Some strategies in the acquisition of phonology', in *Issues in Phonological Theory*, edited by M. J. Kenstowicz and C. J. Kisseberth, The Hague: Mouton.

EIMAS, P., E. SIQUELAND, P. JUSCZYK and J. VIGORITO (1971), 'Speech perception in infants', *Science* 171, 303–6.

EPSTEIN, W. (1961), 'The influence of syntactical structure on learning', *American Journal of Psychology* 74, 80–5.

ERVIN, S. M. (1964), 'Imitation and structural change in children's language', in LENNEBERG (1964).

ERVIN-TRIPP, S. (1971), 'An overview of theories of grammatical development', in SLOBIN (1971).

EVANS, W. E., and J. BASTIAN (1969), 'Marine mammal communication: social and ecological factors', in *The Biology of Marine Mammals*, edited by H. T. Andersen, New York: Academic Press.

FERGUSON, C. A., and D. I. SLOBIN (1973), *Studies of Child Language Development*, New York: Holt, Rinehart and Winston.

FILLENBAUM, S. (1971), 'Psycholinguistics', *Annual Review of Psychology* 22, 251–308.

FILLENBAUM, S. (1973), *Syntactic Factors in Memory*, The Hague: Mouton.

FLORES D'ARCAIS, G. B., and W. J. M. LEVELT (1970), *Advances in Psycholinguistics*, Amsterdam: North-Holland.

FODOR, J. A. (1966), 'How to learn to talk: some simple ways', in SMITH and MILLER (1966).

FODOR, J. A., T. G. BEVER and M. F. GARRETT (1974), *The Psychology of Language*, New York: McGraw Hill.

FODOR, J. A., and M. GARRETT (1966), 'Some reflections on competence and performance', in LYONS and WALES (1966).

FODOR, J. A., and M. F. GARRETT (1967), 'Some syntactic determinants of sentential complexity', *Perception and Psychophysics* 2, 289–96.

FODOR, J. A., M. F. GARRETT and T. G. BEVER (1968), 'Some syntactic determinants of sentential complexity II: Verb structure', *Perception and Psychophysics* 3, 453–61.

Foss, D. (1970), 'Some effects of ambiguity upon sentence comprehension', *Journal of Verbal Learning and Verbal Behavior* 9, 699–706.

Fraser, C., U. Bellugi and R. Brown (1963), 'Control of grammar in imitation, comprehension and production', *Journal of Verbal Learning and Verbal Behavior* 2, 121–35. Also in Brown (1970), Ferguson and Slobin (1973), Oldfield and Marshall (1968).

Freud, S. (1901), 'Slips of the Tongue', in Fromkin (1973).

Fromkin, V. (1971), 'The non-anomalous nature of anomalous utterances', *Language* 47, 25–52. Also in Fromkin (1973).

Fromkin, V. A. (1973), *Speech Errors as Linguistic Evidence*, The Hague: Mouton.

Fry, D. B. (1970), 'Speech reception and perception', in Lyons (1970).

Gardner, B. T., and R. A. Allen (1971), 'Two-way communication with an infant chimpanzee', *Behavior of Nonhuman Primates* vol. IV, edited by A. Schrier and F. Stollnitz, New York: Academic Press.

Gardner, R. A., and B. T. Gardner (1969), 'Teaching sign language to a chimpanzee', *Science* 1965, 666–72.

Garrett, M. F. (1970), 'Does ambiguity complicate the perception of sentences?' In Flores D'Arcais and Levelt (1970).

Garrett, M. F., T. Bever and J. A. Fodor (1966), 'The active use of grammar in speech perception', *Perception and Psychophysics* 1, 30–2.

Gazzaniga, M. S. (1970), *The Bisected Brain*, New York: Appleton-Century-Crofts.

Geschwind, N. (1972), 'Language and the Brain', *Scientific American* April, 76–84.

Gleitman, L. R., H. Gleitman and E. F. Shipley (1972), 'The emergence of the child as grammarian', *Cognition* 1, 137–64.

Goldman-Eisler, F. (1964), 'Hesitation, information and levels of speech production', in de Reuck and O'Connor (1964).

Goodglass, H. (1968), 'Studies on the grammar of aphasics', in Rosenberg and Koplin (1968). Also in Goodglass and Blumstein (1973).

Goodglass, H., and S. Blumstein (1973), *Psycholinguistics and Aphasia*, Baltimore: John Hopkins University Press.

Gough, P. B. (1971), 'Experimental Psycholinguistics', in Dingwall (1971).

Grinder, J. T., and S. H. Elgin (1973), *A Guide to Transformational Grammar*, New York: Holt, Rinehart and Winston.

Grosu, A. (1974), 'On the complexity of center-embedding', Mimeo.

GRUBER, J. S. (1967), 'Topicalization in child language', *Foundations of Language* 3, 37–65.

HAKES, D. T. (1971), 'Does verb structure affect sentence comprehension?', *Perception and Psychophysics* 10, 229–32.

HALLIDAY, M. A. K. (1975), *Learning How to Mean*, London: Edward Arnold.

HAYES, C. (1951), *The Ape in our House*, New York: Harper.

HAYES, J. R. (1970), *Cognition and the Development of Language*, New York: Wiley.

HAYHURST, H. (1967), 'Some errors of young children in producing passive sentences', *Journal of Verbal Learning and Verbal Behavior* 6, 634–9.

HENDERSON, A., F. GOLDMAN-EISLER and A. SKARBEK (1965), 'The common value of pausing time in spontaneous speech', *Quarterly Journal of Experimental Psychology* 17, 343–5.

HOCKETT, C. F. (1963), 'The problem of universals in language', in *Universals of Language*, edited by J. H. Greenberg, Cambridge: Mass: MIT Press.

HOCKETT, C. F. and S. A. ALTMANN, 'A note on design features', in SEBEOK (1968).

HOTOPF, N. (1972), 'What light do slips of the tongue and of the pen throw on word production?' Mimeo.

HOUSEHOLDER, F. W. (1972), *Syntactic Theory 1: Structuralist*, Harmondsworth: Penguin.

HUXLEY, R., and E. INGRAM (1971), *Language Acquisition: Models and Methods*, New York: Academic Press.

JACKSON, H. J. (1932), *Selected writings*, vol. II, London: Hodder and Stoughton.

JAKOBOVITS, L. A., and M. S. MIRON (1967), *Readings in the Psychology of Language*, Englewood Cliffs, N.J.: Prentice-Hall.

JAKOBSON, R. (1962), 'Why "mama" and "papa"?', in BAR-ADON and LEOPOLD (1971).

JOHNSON-LAIRD, P. N. (1970), 'The perception and memory of sentences', in LYONS (1970),

JOHNSON-LAIRD, P. N. (1974), 'Experimental psycholinguistics', *Annual Review of Psychology* 25, 135–60.

JOHNSON-LAIRD, P. N., and R. STEVENSON (1970), 'Memory for syntax', *Nature* 227, 412.

JONES, L. V., and J. M. WEPMAN (1965). 'Language: a perspective from the study of aphasia', in *Directions in Psycholinguistics* edited by S. ROSENBERG, New York: Macmillan.

KACHRU, B. J., R. B. LEES, Y. MALKIEL, A. PIETRANGELI, S. SAPORTA (1973), *Issues in Linguistics*, Papers in honor of Henry and Renee Kahane, Chicago: University of Illinois Press.

KELLOGG, W. N., and L. A. KELLOGG (1933), *The Ape and the Child*, New York: McGraw Hill.

KIMBALL, J. (1973), 'Seven principles of surface structure parsing in natural language', *Cognition* 2, 15–47.

KIMURA, D. (1967), 'Functional asymmetry of the brain in dichotic listening', *Cortex* 3, 163–78.

KLIMA, E., and U. BELLUGI (1966), 'Syntactic regularities in the speech of children', in LYONS and WALES (1966). Revised version in BAR-ADON and LEOPOLD (1971).

LANGACKER, R. W. (1967), *Language and its Structure*, New York: Harcourt, Brace and World.

LASHLEY, K. S. (1951), 'The problem of serial order in behavior', in *Cerebral Mechanisms in Behavior*, edited by L. A. Jefress, New York: Wiley. Also in SAPORTA (1961).

LENNEBERG, E. H. (1964), *New Directions in the Study of Language*, Cambridge, Mass: MIT Press.

LENNEBERG, E. H. (1967), *Biological Foundations of Language*, New York: Wiley.

LIBERMAN, A. M., F. COOPER, D. P. SHANKWEILER and M. STUDDERT-KENNEDY (1967), 'Perception of the speech code', *Psychological Review* 74, 431–61.

LIBERMAN, A. M., K. S. HARRIS, H. S. HOFFMAN and B. C. GRIFFITH (1957), 'The discrimination of speech sounds within and across phoneme boundaries', *Journal of Experimental Psychology* 54, 358–68.

LIEBERMAN, P. (1972), *The Speech of Primates*, The Hague: Mouton.

LIVESLEY, B. (1972), 'The Alice in Wonderland Syndrome', *Teach In* 1, 770–4.

LUCE, R. D., R. R. BUSH and E. GALANTER (1963), *Handbook of Mathematical Psychology*, vol. II, New York: Wiley.

LYONS, J. (1970), *New Horizons in Linguistics*, Harmondsworth: Penguin.

LYONS, J. (1970a), *Chomsky*, London: Fontana.

LYONS, J., and R. J. WALES (1966), *Psycholinguistics Papers*, Edinburgh: Edinburgh University Press.

MACKAY, D. G., and T. G. BEVER (1967), 'In search of ambiguity', *Perception and Psychophysics* 2, 193–200.

MACLAY, H. (1973), 'Linguistics and Psycholinguistics', in KACHRU *et al.*, (1973).

MCNEILL, D. (1966), 'Developmental Psycholinguistics', in SMITH and MILLER (1966).

MCNEILL, D. (1970), *The Acquisition of Language*, New York: Harper and Row.

MARKS, L. and G. MILLER (1964), 'The role of semantic and syntactic constraints in the memorization of English sentences', *Journal of Verbal Learning and Verbal Behavior* 3, 1–5.

MARSHALL, J. C. (1970), 'The biology of communication in man and animals', in LYONS (1970).

MEHLER, J. (1963), 'Some effects of grammatical transformations on the recall of English sentences', *Journal of Verbal Learning and Verbal Behavior* 2, 346–51.

MEHLER, J., and P. CAREY (1968), 'The interaction of veracity and syntax in the processing of sentences', *Perception and Psychophysics* 3, 109–11.

MILLER, G. A. (1962), 'Some psychological studies of grammar', *American Psychologist* 17, 748–62. Also in JAKOBOVITS and MIRON (1967), DE CECCO (1967).

MILLER, G. A. and N. CHOMSKY (1963), 'Finitary models of language users', in LUCE, BUSH and GALANTER (1963).

MILLER, G. A., and K. MCKEAN (1964), 'A chronometric study of some relations between sentences', *Quarterly Journal of Experimental Psychology* 16, 297–308. Also in OLDFIELD and MARSHALL (1968).

MILLER, W., and S. ERVIN (1964), 'The development of grammar in child language', in BELLUGI and BROWN (1964).

MILNER, B., C. BRANCH, and T. RASMUSSEN (1964), 'Observations on cerebral dominance', in DE REUCK and O'CONNOR (1964). Also in OLDFIELD and MARSHALL (1968).

MORTON, J. (1971), 'What could possibly be innate?' in *Biological and Social Factors in Psycholinguistics*, edited by J. Morton, London: Logos Press.

NOOTEBOOM, S. G. (1969), 'The tongue slips into patterns', in *Nomen: Leyden Studies in Linguistics and phonetics*, edited by A. G. Sciarone *et al.*, The Hague: Mouton. Also in FROMKIN (1973).

OLDFIELD, R. C., and J. C. MARSHALL (1968), *Language: Selected Readings*, Harmondsworth: Penguin.

PENFIELD, W., and L. ROBERTS (1959), *Speech and brain mechanisms*, Princeton, N.J: Princeton University Press.

PINES, M. (1969), *Revolution in Learning*, Harmondsworth: Penguin.

POSTAL, P. M. (1964), 'Underlying and superficial linguistic structure'. *Harvard Educational Review* 34, 246–66. Also in OLDFIELD and MARSHALL (1968).

PREMACK, D. (1970), 'The Education of Sarah', *Psychology Today* 4, 55–8.

PREMACK, D. (1971), 'Language in Chimpanzee?' *Science* 172, 808–22.

PREMACK, D. (1972), 'Teaching Language to an Ape', *Scientific American*, 92–9

REICH, P. A. (1969), 'The finiteness of natural language', in HOUSEHOLDER (1972).

ROBINS, L. (1971), *General Linguistics: an Introductory Survey*, second edition, London: Longmans.

ROSENBERG, S., and J. H. KOPLIN (1968), *Developments in Applied Psycholinguistics Research*, New York: Macmillan.

SACHS, J. S. (1967), 'Recognition memory for syntactic and semantic aspects of connected discourse', *Perception and Psychophysics* 2, 437–42.

SAMPSON, G. (1975), *The Form of Language*, London: Weidenfeld and Nicolson.

SAPORTA, S. (1961), *Psycholinguistics: a Book of Readings*, New York: Holt, Reinhart and Winston.

SAVIN, H., and E. PERCHONOCK (1965), 'Grammatical structure and the immediate recall of English sentences', *Journal of Verbal Learning and Verbal Behavior* 4, 348–53.

SCHAERLAEKENS, A. M. (1973), *The Two-Word Sentence in Child Language Development*, The Hague: Mouton.

SCHLEŞINGER, I. M. (1967), 'A note on the relationship between psychological and linguistic theories', *Foundations of Language* 3, 397–402.

SCHLESINGER, I. M. (1971), 'Production of utterances and language acquisition', in SLOBIN (1971).

SCHLESINGER, I. M. (1971a), 'The grammar of sign language and the problems of language universals', in MORTON (1971).

SEBEOK, T. A. (1968), *Animal Communication*, Bloomington: Indiana University Press.

SINCLAIR-DE-ZWART, H. (1969), 'Developmental psycholinguistics', in *Studies in Cognitive Development*, edited by D. Elkind and J. Flavell, Oxford: Oxford University Press.

SKINNER, B. F. (1957), *Verbal Behavior*, New York: Appleton-Century-Crofts.

SLOBIN, D. I. (1966), 'The acquisition of Russian as a native language' in SMITH and MILLER (1966).

SLOBIN, D. I. (1966a), 'Grammatical transformations and sentence comprehension in childhood and adulthood', *Journal of Verbal Learning and Verbal Behavior* 5, 219–27.

SLOBIN, D. I. (1970), 'Universals of grammatical development in children', in FLORES D'ARCAIS and LEVELT (1970).

SLOBIN, D. I. (1971), *The Ontogenesis of Grammar*, New York: Academic Press.

SLOBIN, D. I. (1971a), 'On the learning of morphological rules', in SLOBIN (1971).

SLOBIN, D. I. (1971b), *Psycholinguistics*, Glenview, Illinois: Scott, Foresman.

SLOBIN, D. I. (1973), 'Cognitive prerequisites for the development of grammar', in FERGUSON and SLOBIN (1973).

SLOBIN, D. I., and C. A. WELSH (1967), 'Elicited imitation as a research tool in developmental psycholinguistics', in FERGUSON and SLOBIN (1973).

SMITH, C. S. (1967), 'An experimental approach to children's linguistic competence', in HAYES (1970). Also in FERGUSON and SLOBIN (1973).

SMITH, F., and G. A. MILLER (1966), *The Genesis of Language*, Cambridge, Mass: MIT Press.

SMITH, N. V. (1973), *The Acquisition of Phonology: A Case Study*, Cambridge: Cambridge University Press.

STRUHSAKER, T. T. (1967), 'Auditory Communication among vervet monkeys (Cercopithecus aethiops)', in *Social Communication among Primates*, edited by S. A. Altmann, Chicago: Chicago University Press.

SZAGUN, G. (1975), 'A cross-cultural study of the acquisition of tense forms and time concepts in young children', unpublished doctoral dissertation, University of London.

THORPE, W. H. (1961), *Bird Song: The Biology of Vocal Communication and Expression in Birds*, Cambridge: Cambridge University Press.

THORPE, W. H. (1963), *Learning and Instinct in Animals*, second edition, London: Methuen.

256 *References*

THORPE, W. H. (1972), 'Vocal communication in birds', in *Non-Verbal Communication*, edited by R. A. Hinde, Cambridge: Cambridge University Press.

VON FRISCH, K. (1950), *Bees: Their Vision, Chemical Sense and Language,* Ithaca: Cornell University Press.

VON FRISCH, K. (1954), *The Dancing Bees*, London: Methuen.

VON FRISCH, K. (1967), *The Dance and Orientation of Bees*, translated by L. E. Chadwick. Cambridge, Mass: Harvard University Press.

VYGOTSKY, L. S. (1962), *Thought and Language*, Cambridge, Mass: MIT Press.

WANNER, E. (1974), *On Remembering, Forgetting and Understanding Sentences: a Study of the Deep Structure Hypothesis*, The Hague: Mouton.

WASON, P. C. (1965), 'The contexts of plausible denial', *Journal of Verbal Learning and Verbal Behavior* 4, 7–11, Also in OLDFIELD and MARSHALL (1968).

WATT, W. C. (1970), 'On two hypotheses concerning psycholinguistics', in HAYES (1970).

WEIR, R. H. (1962), *Language in the Crib*, The Hague: Mouton.

WEIR, R. H. (1966), 'Some questions on the child's learning of phonology', in SMITH and MILLER (1966).

WELLS, G. (1974), 'Learning to code experience through language', *Journal of Child Language* 1, 243–69.

YNGVE, V. (1961), 'The depth hypothesis', in HOUSEHOLDER (1972).

ZANGWILL, O. L. (1964), 'Intelligence in aphasia', in DE REUCK and O'CONNOR (1964).

ZANGWILL, O. L. (1973), 'The neurology of language', in *Linguistics at Large*, edited by N. Minnis, St Albans: Paladin.

Acknowledgement

The extract from *Ending Up* by Kingsley Amis on pages 210–11 is reproduced by courtesy of Jonathan Cape Ltd.